AF265755

I Am
The Rise and Fall of the British Monarchy

The Secret of the Secret

Cynthia Gunn Lazuk

Library of Congress Control Number: 2008910571

ISBN 978-1-959071-70-9 (paperback)
ISBN 978-1-959071-78-5 (digital)

Printed in the United States of America

First Dedication

This work is dedicated to my twin flame, soul mate, my man, YUD CHET VAV. You are the key, I am the lock, Baby, I've been writing it all my life, inside me and it finally came out! You've said it best, "You ain't seen nothin' yet!" So you see my love, I've been paying attention, since that blessed day we played, in a MOTOWN swimming pool.

Forget You? Never! We need to be together again, to stop time and start FOREVERLAND, my friend. Golden Children, we are two, I'm your Baby, Love . . . MEM LAMED HEY, because you are the Sun, I am the Moon, while you are the word and I am the tune, playing. Love forever, The Lady, who is elegant, strong, honest and loving . . . Cynthia, Queen of Scots and America.

History

In silhouette you gaze past blinds, their handheld flames are burning. Liberty's likeness you bring to them, you're there the music's curling. Spotlight in view, my God it's You, behold you lights flare in view.

On Automaton arm to stretch you from yon, the Thames to Lausanne, Barcelona and the Champs elesee, et al Köln, to London anon, where upon you return, no crosses they burn. Oh, how I yearn! Airplanes return, your landing my concern.

Throngs gather . . . alas your face! You're here, the world embrace, they can't believe it's really You! Now waving, at babes, dog tag on blue. Must duck and cover, round cars they hover. To see your hand they'll hours stand.

Corral the sheep, who mourn and weep a flowers grasp and you are humbled. Photo op moments, with Mickey, you never grumbled. Geisha girls and boys arranged in Pyramid, their bated breaths, for you to be amid. Your script on their trust, they run to touch your hand, a finger, hoping you'll linger.

You did your part, my twin flame, soul mate, now let me do mine. The color red, the proper attire, your warrior dress regalia, they desire. Passing bobbies, backed by troops, you're ready now, flowing, glowing, gleaming, the voice, the melodies, the moves, the messages, all from You . . . streaming.

The explosions around you, the water pouring forth from your body, they all need to be near you, to hear you, to see you, to feel you, to see what is real You . . .

Oh my love, how you slay me . . . Oh, you beautiful man, the apple of my eye, of course I'll tell them why. They're crying and fainting, the light shines through you, a sea of souls, reaching, hoping, feeling, knowing, that you my beloved, are THE ONE. You're healing. With Liberty's stance, you propel upwards a yard off the floor, the cameras capture the launching. They see you at shore.

The Knight Templar wields his sword to the fiery face of the Dragon, destroying it in a blaze of glory, no rhyme. You emerge with the angels all around you. They're waving for Moon Walking, your love talking.

Soon, you appear from the light, the wind is blowing my love, the white sheets unfurling, they stop . . . they stare, they faint, they're flowing, over seas of arms, they wail and moan, they see the truth, away they go to healers, to see you they're feelers . . . still you continue on.

They bear the name on their foreheads, they're screaming in ecstasy's reigns, as in beds. You make your stand and wave your hand, the lights are white and glaring, there . . . they've seen the light, you take your stance, my God, my Love, they're praying!

Your hat goes on, they wear then you in awestruck wonder, they're crying to see you yonder. In the round you're dancing, they're flying, testifying, jumping, whirling, kneeling, you strike the pose, revealing. "Walking on the Moon . . . my feeling . . ."

Five beautiful boys on golden cover, ABC the number three, you look at me, like when we played together as children, so precious in your hat and fly cord coat, smiling, near the tree, the portrait in gold, I'm across the sea . . . the moat.

You tip your hat you're on your toes, time stands still, the lights expose, music with bows, going places, with other faces, the five come shining through in view. Switch to live, it's still the five, I see the eye, the cosmic swirl, a hurricane unfurled. The destiny at waters edge, like pearls. The distant lightning strikes on ledge, the eye again that sees . . . below the arrows tip, alas, WE know, the Pyramid is rising.

Look at you . . . you're OFF THE WALL . . . the mirrored sky is calling them all! You're beautiful, you reappear, this time it's me you're calling, we're falling. ROCK WITH YOU, the night away . . . we're hauling. Don't stop my love, crown is blazing, you strike the pose, cosmos explodes, now you're grazing, gazing, softly lying, amazing, the colors bold are raising, and yet . . . loves hold.

To "THRILL HER," now you're trying, she's flying, no denying. Your face appears, then danger nears, an outstretched leg is whining.

Rock with you? Look, there's Paul, white gook and clowns, amid the crying. It's dangerous and then you howl, with golden eyes and teeth, like Cowal, entwining. The claws come out and too the horns as spikes, the dead right now are staring.

They're reaching up to catch your lead, the blood-red suit you're wearing. Shining, you pulse, the toes, you're up again, black, white, amid their pining. You point and look, smiling in the Pharaoh's nook, spinning gold dust, amid spear points thrust; you're BAD in patent shining.

Street toughs gather at your command, you open their door to gently command, to gently hand, a snip, a sprite, dancing in the night, out on the street, snap, then dance, embrace that beat. Pose, the cover shows, full measure of your prose, you sing on toes, the plate then switches, stare down those witches, the ultimate question, in the looking glass fishes.

You're on the run, from crime that's done, smooth as the silk now running, with the pit bull, over golden loft concrete mountain tops. Looking out you see the night, ELECTRIC EYES in everywhere. You beam bright glow, from the depths of Nod, whoa! Until the face explodes, mouth with water, teeth gnashing, you step in time, too DANGEROUS with bones, Elephant man, ball and chain, to which they all will carry again.

You're first amid the Carnival, now above them all you're standing, blue light point down to toes, on tip of boots, with buckles dangling. Another taste of you, my love, you're wrangling, shaking hands with no glove, the touch, the pulse, your body's grinding. Dance and sing, give the look and point, then strike the poses, shades, no shades, up again, on toeses, you're MOSES, the hall of VANITY'S FAME FAIR climbing.

Relaxed, you look out, to find me rhyming. Your crest in view, defining. Me aligning, OBE ONE CANOBE . . . tour last you say it so be? The black storm soon arising, the Reich book bears your face true love . . . Oh, wait! Paris is chiding, them chiming, to you on book HITKRANT . . . what's this!!! Another country . . . calling? . . . Elephant?

In every language of the earth, yourself they are revering Gleaming white and glove shades, on skin, now look . . . you're peering. Skiing, climbing, pepper the salt of the Sergeants flock, with flavor still remaining . . . The eyes of us . . . the ones who know, the truth, my Elephant star, we're sailing.

The peacocks reign now DANGEROUS, the King and Queen we're raising, no flailing. BUBBLES and Angels, upon the wings, will give us flight from "SOUREGNAD'S," things. Earth's upside down, they've done it now, your watchful eyes are gazing. Again, through time, you pierce their veils, to see their wretched crumbling, climbing . . . whales . . . the monster machinery, of their fathers due dinosaurs, escape on ladder gleaning, stairway to Heaven? . . . We're careening. The warning again . . . the look, the window, blue ball shatters the silica sand panes, you're back my love, your eyes are trailing, like trains. Kick the orb blue, Jordan's friend at court, it's you who runs through the carpal tunnel . . . hotel in view. You rip your clothes, awash in blue, hue lights, shining like morning dew.

You take your stance and yet again, our romance, whilst blue angels you emit. Winging . . . whirling, winding, above the pit.

You've done your part, we're one true heart, our worlds collide, I do abide and you decide. Alas . . . to make the fix on BLANKETS, I will be bringing. I am young inside, so reach out for me, I'm clinging. Come hither my love, I'm singing, no song sung blue . . . so BRACE YOURSELF . . . REMEMBER THE TIME, my dove, we're from above, it's TRUE . . . we're still in love, forever your Golden Ewe, sharing THAT BEAT called love . . .

Cynthia

Black or White

Above the clouds you fly toward me, the Moon, I see you coming. You pause, trek down a city below, I focus on streets, you're floating. A house ahead, you turn . . . it's their approach, while parents fading, toward boy in room, air guitar in hand, giraffe and posters waiting, jumping, happily thumping, on floor, on ceiling too, now revealing, no feeling.

The pitch, the hit, he's ticked a bit, then sees four bobble heads nodding, equalizer throbbing. He's on the bed, jump, snap, kneel, Pop's face turns red, no sobbing instead . . . he's creaming, a boy gleaming, happily, playfully, teaming. Now up the stairs, Pop puts on airs, to teach the boy a lesson. Door opens, the lads chagrin, shown on the chin, to see the mad complaining. "What's wrong? It's fun never to hurt anyone?" Yet still, the Dad remaining . . . Lad pleads his case, yet still the face, the mean who hate song sailing. The threat . . . he's scared . . . door slams . . . breaks tears . . . ICON PICTURE, unfailing

Yes, Oh Yes! The shards fly loose, upon a floor, oh no . . . the image tumbles. He's crushed at first . . . the raise . . . the brow . . . the thinking . . . now . . . Unsnap the guitar case, huge speaker in room, slid like a BROOM, to JUMP in place, then poses with SCOOPER, UFOSES, Listen to MOSES, the truth coming.

Input, alignment, small space confinement, yet once the plug is lifted, into guitar, on red light afar, hearing not impaired, the dial turning far past the peg to, "ARE YOU NUTS?" Shades on the face, black glove in place, affixed. Oh . . . now she's looking . . . just long enough to see, he's tough, wipes mouth in rough, then stares to what is coming.

"EAT THIS!" he roars, and feeds their fears, the window panes exploding. Blue light, Dad's flight, into the night, through rooftop, he's raising . . . there where afore the Moon, who waits . . . come soon . . . Blue glowing, Indigoing, where's he going? The not knowing is showing.

Scene change to dusty mountain ridge, the down upon the grasses, lays the lioness and child of jungle's king, his tail contently wagging. "All's well," he roars, "we're safe, of course," from rampant tribesmen hunting she hears, he nods, who creeps nearby? . . . It's spears, to try and kill her Lion. They're creeping . . . still . . .

Chair lands, until he's stopped on Serengeti, to see you jump among the tribe; my God, you are proclaiming, "Let's do this dance, across the plain," to which I see my love, you're clapping. Now run to set, to girls who get, straight up in oriental fashion, the whirl, they kick, with you they stick, while through their fingers they . . . switch to me, little girl Cherokee, alas my love . . . we're dancing. The tribe all around us, to protect romancing, the HORSEMAN ride, we never break stride, you point the Sun is shining. You take my hand, my joy command, what's this . . . so now we're reading?

People are bleeding? She's right there with you, smokestacks in plain view, they drive machines to NOWHERE, we dance and whirl, I'm your girl, we have shown, we are not alone. Then, the snowflake angels flow . . . into Cossacks, dipping and spinning around you, you're winning, the message shows true and clear, you're in the round, they're bowing down, My God, in line now prancing, spinning, bowing, it's fine you're winning.

Blue orb with snow, you're winning, they're all inside, trying to hide, from my reach beginning I pick them up, our Toy, come into view, we both babes on planet sitting. You black, me white, it's day and night, at once, we two are playing. Just us, alone . . . upon the orb, made just for two hearts beating. That's what this gold smoke, when you reappear, now as a man, inflaming. The hell I wrought on us . . . can you forgive? My love . . . I killed, burned cross, it was myself and not the one called Caining.

You reappear to set me straight, I need your firm rebuking. For down through time, I did the crime of Abel's death by nuking.

I built machines, at serpents' behest, to kill those who came after; for I alone, brought tears to earth . . . it should have been just laughter.

Forgive me . . . forgive me, now switch to street, our children ghetto hanging, thank God you're there, he's got blonde hair . . . with shades now I am panging. He points to me, you all stand firm, you guide them past the money, gold Cadillac chain, red slapping five feet, dancing, you watch, they're telling. He circles face with bling on hand, you stand beside him kindly, they all look sad, that I was BAD, to bring them up so blindly.

Yet now I see, around the torch, you come to see me Honey . . . I take the blame, killed Liberty, my shame, you point, you move, I'm in the groove, I love to see you happy! Moving in time, ahead of this rhyme, you waited for me I'm coming, Big Ben, Eiffel, come into view, yet still your lamp light burning.

Across the sea, you came to me, like the torches we still carry . . . Oh Ancient of the old, Sphinx Temple I behold, and wait for you . . . to marry. Forever in love, we their faces now above, I see them morph through Babel, the Tower I built, to try and hide, that Cain did not kill Abel.

The time for truth, I give to youth, of every land and nation. I'll right my wrong, my love, I'm strong . . . I have the information. Hollywood, set to go, Black Panther, is in motion my love; you see . . . that God told me . . . they'll fall into the ocean.

Past Templar, Washington, you leave, the zone, now out on street, then staircase you strode on down to change around, erect now standing then place the hat upon your head, in Bo Jangles spotlight landing. You look at me, come face to face, I know what I have done, keep well my love, I have great news . . . the battles I have won!

You start to move, the pause and stance, to make sure I am looking . . . feet in the round, you're on the ground . . . Alas you're waiting. I jump out of the garbage can, the Leo cat noise making you turn, to look, I've caught your eye, blue haze to street, you go to prove your meaning.

Peel back, top shirt, expose winds truth, you're still, there's no betweening Wind stops, you stand, now right in direction, pointing you move with grace. Find the pool of water, that's been standing.

You kick your heels . . . splash, from the pain you've suffered, then make the signs across yourself.

You start toward the sidewalk, wet shoe you lift. They made you dance, to imitate Gene Kelley; I see it now, the inner pain deep inside your belly. You kicked their bottle, then throw the hat, to give what they've got coming . . . Detroit, their ills, which broke men's wills, with cars, you now are smashing. Crowbar lashing, they deserve the thrashing!

Triumphantly, you show them signs again of just what is coming, with hands on self . . . you reach for me . . . I'm waiting with intense yearning. Give me your seeds, I'm here . . . agreed? So throw their wheel for turning. Break down the door, you are the key, I am your lock, I'm waiting.

Show them again, we're one, it's done, and when you leap from metal, you grab the can to throw at sand glass door . . . the wind is blowing. Blue smoke through veils, of peaceful bliss, you start to feel my body, I'm here my dear, so come, draw near. Royal Arms Hotel for two? . . . Me and You, spinning in my water, you release a son, a daughter; so take me now, my love, I'm waiting. We'll wear no clothes and then expose, our loves to all the HATERS . . . You've won! They're done! Broken down by Gunn! Now 'round you blue angels reigning. Old Royals . . . will pass! You broke the glass, they're done, you did the slaying! They tumble down and fall on ground, you overcame their CANCER. They did their deeds but now they're done, move over . . . here comes the PANTHER!

So sit tight, my darlin', take pause on rub, whilst let ME entertain YOU . . . from ABOVE.

Love, Cynthia.

In Memorium

Of our first parents, so-called, Adam and Eve. You hold in your hand, see with your eyes and/or, hear with your ears . . . ALL THE INFORMATION NEEDED, Herein, book two and excerpts of books three, four, five and six, all of which, will help you, HELP US . . . as we continue, our Earthly experience, as HUMAN BEINGS, whilst we navigate, the stormy sea of consciousness, simply and directly, with regard to all that is, was and is yet to be . . . the TRUTH AND PROOF, directly from the CREATOR, to HIS CHOSEN SECRETARY of, "AUT PAX, AUT BELLUM."

Very soon, we will ALL BEHOLD, "THE HAND OF GOD," so BRACE YOURSELF, for that which is BAD, DANGEROUS AND SURELY COMING!!! So, "Be not afraid! Rise, Let us be on our way!" we are, "Crossing the threshold . . ." of faith, hope and LOVE . . .

Amore. Cynthia

P.S. Book seven, is vaulted and ready, for when the time, is just right . . . The back cover, of this work, has the information, of how to obtain Books: three, four, five and six . . . in their entirety.

Please be patient . . . Trust me . . . I can deliver! Again, I love you . . . Cynthia

Second Dedication

This work, is dedicated to my Grand Uncle, Father Walter Joseph Pilecki and moreso, to his friend, since 1964, in Krakow, Poland, behind the iron curtain, Karol Wojtyla, also known as, Pope John Paul II, in the hopes, that all may come, in to the LIGHT and the REVELATION, of all . . . that is SEEN and UNSEEN, may be FULFILLED.

Foreward

Book two, of trilogy, Cynthia. Dear Ones, please listen to me and understand, the first book and now the second, in the trilogy, as TRUTH. Not because I say so, not for monetary gain, or any other reason, but . . . because it is the; TRUTH OF THE CREATOR.

Webster's Dictionary defines slavery, as well . . . we all know, how horrible slavery is! First, most notable example, was the Pharaoh and the Jews and of course the Jewish, King, Prince, God SEER, was MOSES; and brought the message, foreward and then we had of course, Rabbi Yeshua, of Nazareth, and we've had other, holy, blessed, men and women, along the way.

Now, I Cynthia, Queen of Scots and America, do not claim to be blessed or Holy. I only claim to be, in touch, with the nine multiple intelligences, that . . . Doctor Howard Gardiner, spoke of.

Now, right now . . . I can only tell you, they are, nine intelligences and perhaps, after you read this book, the second in the trilogy, when I announce the third, in the trilogy and the foreward of the third, I shall describe, the nine multiple intelligences, as houses, so to say, of faith built . . . but, setting that aside . . . please, close your eyes . . . don't be mad, at anyone. Don't be mad at Mother, Father, Sister, Brother, Friend, Teacher, other Relatives, Employers, Local Governments, State or Civil Governments, no matter where you live. Municipalities, Powers that be, any Government, anywhere, any time, any amount of money; that they might charge, to do what they should be doing, because they should, be doing it; because . . . there is no such thing as MONEY!!!

But . . . we'll set that aside, for now. This foreward is only to . . . be a loop, between the first work, I AM WHY THEY KILLED

DIANA The Secret of the Red String . . . Cynthia Queen of Scots and America. The loop now, concedes and conforms to book two, which is called: I AM YOUR GOD MOTHER FORGIVE ME The Secret of the Secret . . . Cynthia Queen of Scots and America.

I did not ask for this task, nor the privilege, of loving you, one on one, one on one, mano ē mano, I speak to whoever, hears my voice, not because I am a follower, of a Rabbi Yeshua of Nazareth, or a follower of any Roman Church, or any Yogi, or any Mohammedite, or any Bahaiite, or any Buddhaite, I'm speaking to you, just as Cynthia . . . so, It's not for monetary gain, that I do, what I do. I do it, out of LOVE . . . and RESPECT, for EACH ONE of us, as HUMAN PERSONS, individuals, from the second . . . not moment . . . of CONCEPTION . . . but the SECOND OF CONCEPTION!!! Which well, if anyone, is up to the task, of studying the Tibetan Book of The Dead, then they will know, as I have learned, in the last two or so years, since I've been studying, all the religions of the world, after studying Roman Catholicism, for nearly forty nine years, and then, making it my life's work, to study all the religions, of the world . . . while, I'm still practicing, Roman Catholicism.

We all love our parents, we all love our siblings, those that we grew up with, we all love our Mother . . . our Father . . . and their mothers . . . and their fathers . . . and so on . . . and so forth, for better or for worse . . . and those vows, are not just taken, in a church, or a Cathedral, or in front of a Justice of a Peace, or by a Ships Captain.

Those types of vows, are made sanctrosanct, sacrosanct and we have two derivatives, of the word, which . . . I'll be adding another word, to Webster's Dictionary, or several over the course, of time.

Listen . . . if they can put FUCK, which is spelled F.U.C.K. into a dictionary??? Of Webster; Merriam Webster!?! And they can break it down, fuck, fucker, fucking, fucked up, whatever derivative . . . Now, I want to tell you now, that Cynthia knows, that FUCK is just . . . an anachronym and when, did I find, that out? Huh! When I was a young girl, in bonnie Scotland, living in the, our, "Onich," Toward by Dunoon. I came home one day, from Catholic School . . . of all places . . .

St. Mun's, of Dunoon, Scotland and as you'll see, in the first book, I AM WHY THEY KILLED DIANA The Secret of the Red

String . . . little, tiny, Once upon a time, Cynthia, had to grow up and live, under these conditions and one day, I came home and I said to my Mother, "Mummy . . . what's fuck?"

And my Mummy said, "Cindy, it's a bad word and we don't use it! Now, do you understand, what I said? Do I need to put Tabasco Sauce, on your tongue, or shall you never use it, again . . . until you see something, that's at least, equally as evil, as they've taken the term!" I said, "I don't know! Whatever! Who's gonna explain it to me?" She said, "Daddy will, when he comes home."

So, when my Daddy, William Thomas Phillip Gunn, the true KING OF SCOTLAND, came home that night . . . I said, "Daddy, I was in school today, at St. Mun's, with the Scottish children, from the orphanage . . . and they said, 'fuck you Cynthia!' I said what do you mean fuck you? And . . . they spelled it, for me, Daddy . . . it was F.U.C.K., fuck you, Cynthia!"

And so, I said to Daddy, that night, after I had already talked, to Mum about it, "What is FUCK?!?" So my father, William Thomas Phillip Gunn, the TRUE KING OF SCOTLAND . . . said, "It's! . . . DON'T use it! Or, I'll have to wash your mouth, out with SOAP!" I said, "Well, Mummy said, she's going to use Tabasco Sauce, on my tongue, if I ever use it again! When, I really don't NEED TO! Because it's, a horrible word and it shouldn't, be used, under the most, horrible conditions . . . ONLY! For it's an anachronym."

My father said, "Yes! Your mother was right, it's an anachronym and . . . ancient days, of Kings and Queens, etc. There were many charges, against many people in the court, but one of them was Adultery, Murder, Thievery, what have you . . . and the other one was capitol f., capitol u., capitol c., capitol k.!" And, my father had me write it out . . . on paper! Just as he had, me write my signature, all those times, before I even got, to bonnie Scotland, where I was now, asking him this question! And he said, "F.U.C.K. merely means fornication, under the court of the "King." And I said, "Well what does THAT mean?!?" And he said, "Listen, I'll tell you, down the road, what it means, but right now, it's just like . . . US NAVY . . . like, your Daddy, me . . . I'm in, US NAVY . . . just know, until the proper time comes, FUCK is just like US NAVY, it's an anachronym."

So putting that aside, Ladies and Gentlemen, boys and girls of the world, of all ages, the word is just an anachronym for . . . fornication under the court of the King and . . . I didn't ask for this, I love my parents, I love before them . . . the CREATOR! Whom I choose, to call GOD, Jehovah, Yahweh, Buddha . . . whatever you want to call, the ultimate BEING, that you think, CREATED ALL OF US!

Put whatever name, you want on it . . . it doesn't matter because, I Cynthia, not because I asked for it, but because it's so . . . have the information, that we all need, to get on the same page, on the same day, moving foreward and together, well . . . for now . . . please, do not leave me! Do not fail me, or forsake me, just stay with me . . .

I'm not looking for your money, I'm only looking, for you to understand, Cynthia and what, she's been through, what she may, or may not, have learned and where, she's coming from. So I say I Love You . . . and thank you for listening.

Cynthia

Chapter 1

Doomsday Clock. In the Bulletin of the Atomic Scientists, global WAKE UP CALL! STOP YOUR SNOOZING! "TIME'S RUNNING OUT!" said a Leon Letterman. It is 30 seconds, to midnight, in this, "NUCLEAR AGE" . . . Inside, ten minutes . . . is a serious concern, since 1947, of course. Seventeen times, they've moved the hand of the clock.

Roswell, then Israel, its weapons, then Japan, Nagasaki, from the Manhattan Project, the . . . "Genie out of the bottle, left up to; the likes of Simpson, Uri, Langshoff, Rabinowicz? To use . . . or not to use? That BOMB on JAPAN?

Well, as the Atomic Scientists noted, of Chicago, they published in December, of 1945 . . . "Never Again!" to harness, the Rabinowicz, Russian immigrant, brilliant, dedicated to positive science, force, in the WORLD!

There was a 16 page notation, in the journal, of the 1947, then magazine, by Schwartz, who was publisher . . . and that . . . Martyl . . . a Lady, named Martyl, was the concept artist . . . for THE CLOCK!

Now, the first clock face, appeared in June 1947, which of course, was the year . . . that Dad, William Thomas Phillip Gunn, TRUE KING OF SCOTLAND, graduated from the high school, in Decatur, Alabama . . . as mentioned, in the first, of the trilogy, I AM WHY THEY KILLED DIANA The Secret of the Red String . . . this is, the second, in the trilogy, the secret of the secret . . .

Back to that . . . when Dad graduated, high school and went to work, for Rickover and the Atomic Energy Commission, later in that year, Joseph Rike Gunn, my fathers father, the brothel owner, the alcoholic, the disappointment to Big Daddy . . . DIED DURING THAT TIME!

What was he doing . . . when he died? He was working, as a civil servant, for the Government, in Roswell, New Mexico, which I will, describe to you . . . LATER. But for now, we need to get back, to the doomsday clock and to, the fact, of . . . "AUT PAX, AUT BELLUM."

Now, it was Harry Truman, who really did not want to . . . take the office of President . . . He thought, for sure, that Roosevelt, would probably live, to finish, his forth term, but Harry Truman, not knowing anything, about the weaponry, the Atomic Bomb, which he would later, have to decide to use, was noticing, when he became President, that the Soviets, had the COLD WAR . . . already, underway and it was, only a matter of time . . . and they needed to be prepared, for the conditions, that were becoming and that, all started, of course, with the Manhattan Project, which back then, in 1945, was a point, of 2 BILLION! . . . With a, "B," Ladies and Gentlemen . . . DOLLARS!

Now, in 1949, the Soviets, detonated, their first, nuclear bomb and they discovered, how the hydrogen, could destroy . . . COUNTRIES . . . now, OVER the atomic, ATOM BOMB. We're going to set that, aside, regarding the COLD WAR. I will come back, to that and speak on that, in greater detail, shortly . . . but, let's now . . . go back, to Roswell.

July, the archives, of Roswell Daily Record, July the eighth, 1947, explain it all. then . . . at Kelso, B-25, there was a crash site, on 8/1/47 . . . that was a huge crash . . . and after, there was an intense fire, which spread quickly, there was no time, to stop it, there were 300 volunteers, that were called, to clear the debris.

The Calisonian Tribune, said . . . everything is under close guard, there are, "NO PICTURES," of the wreckage, as said . . . by the Calisonian Tribune. The field for the military? Well, they had people, like Barry Fisher, who was a grand helper, we had, Frank Brown, a crash victim, we had counter-espionage agents and all, of the items, were given, to Kenneth Arnold . . . the man, who saw the discs, over mount Ranier, prior to, Roswell.

And so, we need to, talk about, all of these things, which I'm going to, get into, greater detail and greater chronological order, on with you. So for now, let me just put, all this aside and tell you, that once again, not because of my personage, being Cynthia, but because, my father, the TRUE HIGH KING OF SCOTLAND, William Thomas Philip Gunn, instructed me, at the proper place and time, to divulge, all the TRUTH, which now, in the second dissertation, is called; The Secret of the Secret.

I, will be putting, all of the pieces, of the puzzle, together, for ALL OF US! Not just . . . for Cynthia! More so, for the Creator, the God, who loves us all . . . SO MUCH . . . you have no idea, what's waiting for us . . . But, with that, having been said, for now . . . let's just, set this aside, so that I can put everything, into proper order, so we will all, be interested, listen, pay attention, understand and make rational decisions, regarding our personal futures, the futures of our homes, towns, cities, states, 'Em . . . governments, nations, world, planet Earth.

So, for now, I bid you adue.

Love, Cynthia

Chapter 2

Fellow children, of the Earth, of all ages, the COMET RUP, which is spelt . . . R-U-P, the COMET RUP, is coming! You need to tell each other! It has been . . . DISPATCHED by the Creator, God. There isn't much TIME! Its 30 seconds to MIDNIGHT! And . . . the DOOMSDAY CLOCK . . . IS TICKING!

You FEEL IT NOW . . . because it's COMING! The World, will explode, in a, "BALL OF FIRE," if . . . the Comet Rup, makes impact! You ask me? . . . HOW I KNOW THIS? I'll tell you. I AM LUNA LEO THEO SOPHIA, sent here, to tell you, what WILL HAPPEN . . . UNLESS YOU AND I . . . DO EVERYTHING . . . the Creator, TELLS us, we need to do!

First, INRI, delivered the message! NOW, I, Cynthia . . . must speak to you, about the errors and ways, that NEED TO BE CORRECTED! . . . By, all of us!

You must watch EVERYTHING . . . I SAY and DO and FOLLOW ALL INSTRUCTIONS . . . in order to REACH The Creators, OBJECTIVE! You need to STOP the COMET RUP, from burning up, the planet! You CAN ask, any questions . . . Therefore, you must wait and reserve them, for later and ONLY LISTEN, FOR NOW and OBEY, ALL the Creator's INSTRUCTIONS.

I AM, the MESSENGER . . . He, is THE ONE . . . sending me! I am merely a DIVINE FEMININE ENTITY, nothing more, nothing less. I, Cynthia, will PROVE, that I AM, who I say, "I AM," down through time. You need to LET ME, show you, the PROOF, of the Creator's Mission. It starts, with me lineage and history I was born, Princess Moon, in The Age of Aquarius, descendant of an ancient, IRISH KING, named Gann. Among his children, were two boys, twins. They did, exactly as instructed, to them . . . and was told to them . . . and when to REVEAL IT! Because the conditions, in the climate, of bonnie Scotland, were so harsh, they HAD TO HELP EACH OTHER!

The sons and daughters of Gann and Sengann . . . and Genann, became the ancient clan, ANCIENT CLAN GUNN! And those, of the others, became . . . Hendersons. I AM THE SECRET OF THE SECRET . . . which, I cannot reveal, at this time. It has been passed down to me, by my father, William Thomas Phillip Gunn . . . and I, will show you EVERYTHING, that the Creator, wants YOU . . . TO SEE . . . and for ME TO SEE, Cynthia.

I am not alone, in this mission, there is, another! When children, we met at . . . I was eight and he was nine, swimming, in a Michigan swimming pool. We . . . HE and I, may VERY SOON, get together, because . . . TOGETHER, HE HAS THE REST of THE INFORMATION, which we BOTH . . . are GOLDEN CHILDREN! Sent down, through time, to attract YOUR ATTENTION TO OUR MISSION, to STOP The Comet Rup . . . from colliding, with our PLANET!

I have been instructed, to reveal ONLY the information, you need . . . WHEN YOU NEED IT! I, Cynthia, will be traveling, all over the planet. You must, WATCH ME and LISTEN. You MUST, see ALL I TELL YOU . . . as TRUTH, in order, to avoid, annihilation! You need to, "BRACE YOURSELF," for that which is . . . BAD, DANGEROUS and COMING!

It is essential; you LISTEN . . . because the OTHER MESSENGER has already SHOWED YOU . . . who's BAD! You just didn't understand HIM! Because, WE ARE GOLDEN CHILDREN and TWIN FLAMES, our ANCIENT NAMES are HIS; YUD CHET VAV and MINE: MEM LAMED HEY.

We will WORK TOGETHER, to STOP the COMET RUP, from BLOWING UP THE PLANET! 11:11 is all; you need to know, RIGHT NOW! To begin, to MAKE THE CHANGES, which are NECESSARY! TRUST ME! TRUST YUD CHET VAV! MJJ.

The RELIGIONS, of the WORLD and the EARTH are FLAWED! . . . and NOT IN proper ALIGNMENT! WE are HERE, to HELP AID, in their CORRECTION! They all, have only parts, of the information! Only HE, YUD CHET VAV and myself, MEM LAMED HEY . . . can REVEAL the SECRET OF THE SECRET . . . and ONLY at the Creator's APPOINTED TIME.

I am she, who holds, the LOCK and he . . . does hold, the KEY! So please, FOLLOW US, in order to SAVE OUR PLANET! We have AN ARMY! Our Creator has predestined. We will use it if we have to?!? Instead, we HOPE you'll LISTEN . . . the CHOICE is YOURS. It's up to you . . . and so, begins the mission, "AUT PAX, AUT BELLUM!" SCRIPTI, SCRIPTI, FOR WE ARE THE TEACHERS.

Now, I, Cynthia, MEM LAMED HEY, don't deserve to be here! For I have BROKEN one . . . and/or two . . . and/or, therefore, EVERY COMMANDMENT: And yet . . . the Creator, God, still LOVES ME . . . He wants YOU, ALL, to LISTEN, THIS IS NOT A STORY! These things ACTUALLY HAPPENED!

His BOOK, the BIBLE, has all the EVIDENCE, which . . . I will be CONFIRMING . . . yet, there are 72 LESSONS! Crossing the threshold, of HOPE! Which need, to COME TO LIGHT! Be not afraid! RISE, instead . . . Let us, be on our way!

IT STARTS HERE! At the First Knight Templar's Memorial, Washington, District of Columbus . . . Columbia . . . United States of America! PLEASE, BELIEVE what I am saying . . . I am, TELLING you THE TRUTH! PLEASE, make the CHANGES, NECESSARY to have BLISS! . . . And the FULLNESS, of the Creator, Gods, BLESSINGS!

It won't cost you a penny . . . there is, NO SUCH THING AS MONEY . . . the BAD ONE, "made it up," to CONTROL ALL OF YOUR FUTURES! You've been SLAVES of that BONDAGE! And . . . WE ARE HERE . . . to CHANGE THAT . . . if you, will only . . . LET US . . . HELP YOU!

We all NEED TEACHINGS; we will make it VERY SIMPLE, for you to LEARN. All YOU need to DO is LISTEN, UNDERSTAND and then . . . do EVERYTHING, the Creator, God, WILL BE ASKING! HE, the Creator, God, LOVES YOU! HE, the Creator, God, MADE YOU! HE, the Creator, God, IS SAD that YOU ARE HURTING!

We are here, to HELP YOU, STOP THE PAIN! The LESSONS, we will be helping you with . . . will be EASY! But, you will HAVE TO LEARN THEM! The Creator, God, WANTS NOTHING MORE, than for YOU TO LOVE HIM! And . . . SHARE IT, WITH EACH OTHER! EACH DAY FIRST . . . and then LISTEN . . .

BE NOT AFRAID OF ANYTHING! We will GUIDE YOU, EACH DAY and then . . . once, we have given you all, the information, TO YOU . . . at first, if you STILL . . . WILL NOT LISTEN! . . . Well, then, the God, the Creator, the God, has decided, that the Comet Rup, R- U-P, the JUDGEMENT, WILL COME!

So, we URGE YOU . . . to CHOOSE FAVORABLY, for then the Creator, will say, "ALL IS FORGIVEN!"

CHOOSE UNFAVORABLY, and MAY the Creator, GOD, have MERCY, on YOUR SOULS! So please, allow US, to be, the Lady and the Gentleman, who will be, ELEGANT, show that we are STRONG, know the TRUTH and also, HOW TO LOVE! TOGETHER . . . WE CAN . . . HEAL THE WORLD!!! I Love You, MJJ.

Love, Cynthia.

Chapter 3

Garabandal, Spain, Revisited . . . Scavenging occurs, household pets!!! Among us, dog eat dog! World, rats and mice appear, to take our scraps, raiding homes and storehouses, of remaining food! Then, they will eat all the papers, then turn wild, rodent predators, swarming!

Urban areas turn to wild areas. Coyotes, wild cats, will move in . . . To the field! Soon, THE BEARS WILL COME . . . to EAT US . . . AS FOOD! Plant life, will overgrow . . . creeping and destroying! Weeds, infiltrate everywhere, with moss and lichens, clover . . . pulling nitrogen from the air!

Domination, of HUMAN VULNERABILITY major structure damages . . . HOOVER DAM??? Will, shut down! . . . with the QUAKE! Mosul, from FAR AWAY . . . ATTACKING EVERYTHING! Rapidly MULTIPLYING . . . to BLOCK EVERYTHING!

SPREADING . . . LIKE CANCER! The seventeen generators, burn and SHUT DOWN! Las Vegas . . . at last . . . PLUNGED . . . into DARKNESS! Some rivers, RUN DRY, some dams COLLAPSE . . . when WATERS RECLAIM, SUPREMACY!

Wild FIRES . . . from lightening . . . PRIME FUEL IS EVERYWHERE! For the BURNING, of ALL CITIES! At first, ROME . . . BURNS AGAIN! Plants again, grow and thrive in the RUBBLE . . . ROADS . . . DISAPPEAR . . . all major buildings and CITIES . . . RECLAIMED . . . by NATURE!

Our MASTER is an ILLUSION . . . of subduing . . . the EARTH. Natures REVENGE, is COMETH! Fields become forests. Animals' predators increase. Great MONUMENTS . . .

SWALLOWED! Two hundred animals, escape confinement. Lions, Tigers and EVERY CREATURE, will need to EAT! Whatever . . . they can FIND!

Wormwood, Chernobyl, was the first to GO! It is the example, GHOST CITY . . . among, the decaying walls . . . Prypia, Ukraine, 20 years . . . ABANDONED! EVACUATED! Prypiat . . . GHOST TOWN . . . OVERNIGHT . . . DUST COVERED SCHOOLROOMS!

Children, RUN . . . from PLANTS . . . EAT BUILDINGS! No Carnival Park, in four days . . . to open, NOW! ROTTING, NO FUN . . . it's given . . . motionless . . . DECAY. Concrete JUNGLE, point . . . of NO RETURN!

NO CULTURE, NO FRIENDS . . . celebrations, music, dancing! WATER INFILTRATES and expands . . . weeds . . . grown like JACKS, pushing apart every MANMADE OBJECT! Absence of HUMANS brings INCREASE OF RED FOREST!

Vegetation dies . . . YET . . . then RESURGES, especially of WILD BOARS! In numbers . . . INCREASING . . . to DEVOUR, all ALL! THE NEED TO EAT! April, '86, Wormwood . . . children's former bedrooms . . . NOW EMPTY! No life . . . BIRDS OF PREY . . . perched . . . and VOMIT on their PILLOWS! Toys, strewn around, ANCIENT ARTIFACTS of A PLAN . . . GONE BY . . .

Public Arenas, now bear, the DEAFENING HOWLS . . . of NOTHINGNESS! What's BECOME? . . . of PEOPLE? Never, LIVING . . . HERE . . . AGAIN! Unless, life is RESILIENT . . . MEN . . . CAN CHANGE . . . GROW and THRIVE . . . to REBUILD . . . a LEGACY of LOVE and TRUTH!

Countrysides, ERASE . . . all EVIDENCE of MAN! Wild dogs, SEARCH . . . for next MEAL! Solid ground, great cities, turned to MUDDY WATERS . . . the GREAT LONDON . . . DEFENSELESS . . .

Amsterdam . . . SAME FATE. New York City . . . WINDOWS/ CHARDS are FALLING! Metals, expand/contract/stress . . . cause ALL, TO PLUMMET, DOWNWARD!

Winds create, SUCTION and CONVECTION . . . causing . . . GAPING HOLES!. on windswept DEBRIS . . . and STORMS . . .

MOVE . . . in LIGHTENING/STRIKING, turning all into RAGING INFERNOS! Gutted, CONCRETE JUNGLES . . . House PIGEONS . . . who STILL . . . SURVIVE!

Our ARTIFICIAL . . . cliff faces, UNSITTING . . . cockroach ARMIES . . . GORGE . . . on our SCRAPS . . . at the ROTTING matter . . . of EVERYTHING . . . that CAME from . . .

The TROPICS! To survive? Even the DINOSAURS . . . they will SURVIVE! and THRIVE! HIDING . . . under GROUND, UNTIL . . . the THAWS! Their GOLDEN AGE . . . of CONSUMPTION! The nescience ONLY . . . then COMES . . . the TERROR of the WOLVES! Who will . . . come . . . ONCE AGAIN! To Rome . . . roam To feed . . . on the FLESH SIXFOLD!

Each year . . . MILLIONS, on the wild, to FEED . . . in an AWFUL, AMAZING . . . COMEBACK? Humans . . . will no longer, keep them . . . AT BAY! They will OCCUPY . . . and RULE . . . their TERRITORY . . . in PACKS . . . of geographic . . . EXPANSION/ RECOLONIZING . . . EVERYWHERE . . . when deer, graze . . . on clover . . . WOLVES . . . are not . . . FAR BEHIND . . .

ALL WILD SPECIES will FREELY . . . NOW, roam . . . again . . . over the asphalt RIBBONS . . . we've MADE . . . to CONNECT the concrete JUNGLES . . . the grizzly BEAR . . . will RETURN and RETAKE . . . their habitats. To MAKE and MATE and RENEW, their DOMINANCE.

Using, OUR RIBBONS . . . of oil??? To OUR CITIES???

Neighborhoods . . . made of WOOL???

Have burned? Others? Now . . . in DECAY . . . termites, FEASTING on their building BLOCKS? DEVOURING . . . the SHELTERS? Rotting? In the . . . ELEMENTS? Microbes, methane, carbon dioxide . . . EMITTING . . . TERMITES!?! Trot . . . GIVE WAY boundaries, of INSIDE and OUT, forever ERASED!

NO SHELTER . . . CRUMBLING! Walls . . . no remnants NOW!

NATURE, SWALLOWS-UP our RUINES! Nature reclaims all structures.

Stone, Masonry, Above, Wood, YET . . . DISINTEGRATING! Melting . . . NOTHING WILL BE . . . LEFT . . . with NO ONE to

MAINTAIN . . . "themstone," WALLS! "Stonefalls," victim . . . to SALT CRYSTALS . . . as on PYRAMIDS, reign!

Bird droppings . . . "AIRCARRYING," the SALTS! The pores of THE STONES . . . pushing . . . them . . . APART! To DECAY, crumbling stone, TOTALLY . . . deteriorating in LESS THAN/3 WEEKS!

ORDER! DVD! . . . Only periods . . . can . . . PYRAMIDS! And periods . . . of PYRAMIDS . . . can survive due to HOT/ DRY/CLIMATES, no humans' interventions. COMPLETE . . . . CORROSION . . . of IRON'S and METAL'S bridges buildings, all MAD . . . MAN, MADE . . . TEMPLES!

San "Francisco," NO! Iron Workers? And Painters? To Upkeep? Cables? Snapbridge . . . COLLAPSES! 6 hundred MILLION cars . . . RUSTED? Remnants . . . of Henry Ford's Folly! "SALTAGAIN," erodes!

Paints, rumrubbers, 5 thousand of an inch . . . at the "TIME BECAME METALSKELETONS," of bygone . . . not, UNWITHSTANDING . . . cables . . . deckwarp and sway . . . FALLING/SPILLING . . . into the EAST . . . RIVER? Below ICON, of PASSAGE . . . NOW GONE!

The "crackedwires," FAILED! And SHREDDED, BREAKING when ALL FAILED . . . TWISTED . . . STEALS . . . CRASH BELOW?

As, "MYANUS?" and . . . SO-CALLED other . . . collapsed BRIDGE . . . Which you, "NOW-KNOWETH!"

In the DRINK . . . and the DRAIN . . . of CIVILIZATIONS ERRORS!

Our Hallowed, "HAULS," and vaults, of HISTORY . . . all control is LOST to ROTTING CONDITIONS . . . no paper or film, can SURVIVE!

The UNCONTROLLED . . . ENVIRONMENTAL NO, "POWERCLIMATE" . . . will DEVOUR . . . "ALLCELLULOSE," acetate bubbles, and wraps. "ALLHISTORY," large and small, will be ERASED . . . precious IMAGES . . . in DECAY! THEY ARE FINISHED!!!

Libraries, microscopic invaders, MOLDSPORES . . . lying dormant . . . STRIVE and STRIKE . . . in their, "OWNTIME!"

CONDITIONS . . . RIPE, they bloom . . . to DEVOUR, the printed pages . . . ONLY . . . dead-sea-scrolls, HIDDEN . . . properly . . . and the "ARKOFTHECOVENANT," will survive!

"THEHOLYGRAIL," TOO!!! . . .

Digital, "MEDIUM," DVD, CDS, BLUERAY . . . will DECAY not carved . . . in STONES . . . as the EGYPTIANS/DEGRADING/FORMATS!!!

Of greed's, money . . . MACHINERY . . . less real . . . than clay . . . tablets!?! And stonetools . . .

Subways . . . ENGULFED and COLLAPSE, their columns . . . can . . . no longer . . . hold THEM! Nor, the STREETS ABOVE! Sucked, into the UNDERWORLD . . . in sink HOLES!

Vines . . . covered SKY-SCRAPERS . . . as leeches . . . sucking . . . the MORTAR with, "NOFRUIT," or life to, Bear!!! Only INHABITANTS for predators . . . of INSECTS, rodents, CUTS, birds of prey, CATS . . . AGAIN!!!

Overtaking . . . our FORMER HOUSE?!? CATS HUNTING, in the open . . . the pickings . . . are EASY! High above . . . the CITY! Off, the GROUND . . . on once, "PENTHOUSES," of Donald Trump . . . and the LIKE!!!

As their, "MILLION DOLLAR VIEWS," they strangely . . . JUMP! And FLY! Like SQUIRRELS! On the out . . . now dogs, breed in PACKS! With WOLVES! Seeking . . .

PREY OF EVERY DESCRIPTION! From humans, and birds, to other animals . . . NOW ROAMING!

Oceans, flourish . . . TEAMING . . . with "SEACREATURES," as MEGA-CITIES . . . crumble! Welcome . . . THEIR DEMISE, since they were, once our PANTRY and SEWER . . . we NO LONGER LOOT . . . their RECOVERY . . . as WW2.

No FISHING, they all come back . . . STRONGER . . . when NOT fished . . . by our own, "IRON-WATER-SEAHORSES," . . . ships now . . . DECAYED! Once Again! Only, in the WATER . . . from where? Here? Made from, our "LIVESBLOOD," food and sustenance?!?

Seagulls . . . EXPLODED . . . while eating our, ONCE DUMPS . . . their FREE, LUNCH . . . ABOUNDING now! HUNGRY GULLS!

Teaming . . . remaining . . . RETURN, to OCEANS . . . And SCHOOLS . . . of FISH . . . forgetting our seedy DUMPS . . . of iron and STEEL ICONS . . . built in the SKIES . . . become steel jointed, LEVIATHANS! Corroded!

Falling PREY . . . to WINDS . . . Falling. OVER . . . piece bye piece . . . to crumble! NO MORE STANDING! In time, it ALL FAILS! Coming down . . . down . . . down to, MEET their DESTINED DEMISE!

IN 3 DAYS!!! The ERROR . . . of the GREAT COLLAPSE will OCCUR!!! Little more, than a strong BREEZE! Will be NEEDED . . . to BLOW all MANMADE structures . . . to NOTHING!

Vertical structures LEAN . . . as the Lower . . . the TOWER . . . at PISA. Toppling, collapsing, imploding . . . overtaking ALL, BELOW!

Sears Tower . . . FAILING . . . not by terrorist AIRPLANES . . . only . . . by TERROR, DECAY and DESTRUCTION!!! As ancient ROMANS . . . will stay . . . a BIT LOOSELY! Packed, AIRPOCKETS cracks, mesh BARS, inside . . . THEIR SKELETONS . . . Start . . . "REEBAR," corrosion . . . rust expanse, CONCRETE CRUMBLES.

Soon, any TRACE . . . of FALLEN . . . once, UNCIVILIZED . . . CIVILIZATION . . . Huh! Passes AWAY!!! No evidence of PEOPLE!!! Our CITIES!!! Our Cultures!!! 6.5 BILLION SOULS!!!

Half in cities, half elsewhere . . . NO LONGER . . . STANDING?!? No evidence, of the ACTIVITIES, of MAN!!! Look, . . . to the PAST and LEARN . . . from it to, SEE THE FOREST, FOR THE TREES . . . the flowing . . . RAINWATERS . . . of the SEAS, through STORMDRAINS . . . breaking apart, with VEGETATION . . . reestablishing itself . . . Such as when . . . Henry Hudson first EXPLORED . . . the GREAT NEW CITY! Buildings, downed trees . . . REGROW!!! NATURE . . . re-established ITSELF!!! To, the, "TRUEFORM, meaning . . . of the EARTH . . .

The CHANGE . . . TAKES PLACE!

Transformation, COMPLETE! Times Square . . . SILENCED! NATURE and NATURAL ORDER, returns!

The, "EXPLODING SHELL," of our altered ness, is . . . PAST!!!

Thewaves…SETI…SEARCH…for,"EXTRATERRESTRIAL INTELLIGENCE," our SIGNALS . . . FALLING . . . just PAST . . . our own SUN!

What trace of us . . . WILL REMAIN? After all . . . has . . . PASSED . . . AWAY?!? Wall of CHINA? Great Pyramid of GIZA? Hoover DAM? And then . . . the GREAT COLLAPSE . . . E.Q. Sandstorms, REIGN . . . Mount Rushmore REMAINS . . . as the FACIAL ICON . . . ONLY . . . to be SEEN.

Left, by OUR . . . REPLACEMENTS!?!

Chimpanzees, may make . . . "THE LEAP," to a clever-leveled . . . using TOOLS . . . to CONTEMPLATE . . . The SKY, the EARTH, a PLANET!

They CONTINUE, no talking . . . no thinking, no feeling . . . 24 hours, 10,000 years . . . FRACTION of a SECOND! Abandoned, VILLAGE . . . GLOBAL SCALE . . . LIFE . . . before HUMANS! LIFE . . . after HUMANS! Without FAIL!

SCRIPTI, SCRIPTI. FINI.

Love, Cynthia

Chapter 4

After, Garabandal, Spain. Which, would now, be called, perhaps . . . Chapter 4. Yes indeed! Hello Again, this is Cynthia, WE NEED TO GET REAL!!! With ourselves. Not just Cynthia, but . . . each one of us, as male, or female persons, on the planet EARTH, the ORB . . .

We need to, get real and the, only way to do that, in and amongst everything, that is happening, a crossed our planet, our globe, EARTH . . . RIGHT NOW! Is for us to realize, that, we are coming to, a CLIMATIC AGE, of a particular ERA . . . and also, ERROR! So here we stand, ALL OF US . . . including Cynthia, and You, my sister or my brother, young or old, mid-age or baby, in between, living or dead.

We stand here, at the CUSP . . . at the PRECIPICE, of an ERA and an ERROR. Which was propagated by, the first . . . female! . . . CREATION . . . HUMAN . . . LIKENESS . . . of the Creator, whom I, choose, to call, God. Some call Jehovah, Yahweh, Allah, Buddha . . . what have you. There's JUST ONE, Creator and the Creator, is a ONE TRINITY.

Now, I don't need to tell you, because you see the PROOF . . . of the PYRAMIDS . . . that, the Creator, is in fact, Ladies and Gentlemen, Boys and Girls, people of all ages, the GodHead, the Creator, the Godhead, is a TRIUNE God, as WE ALL, are TRIUNE. In nature . . . of divinity!

Now, if we so choose, to live a life, of divinity, we so choose to: KNOW, LOVE and SERVE . . . God! But, if we don't, we choose to either: NOT KNOW, NOT SERVE OR NOT LOVE . . . GOD!

Now, if we FAIL, in any of the 3 areas, of the TRIUNE GodHead; Knowing, loving and serving . . . the TRUE CREATOR

GOD . . . Then, we've failed, and yet, the Creator sent, ONE, amongst us, from of course, as He promised, to Abraham . . . ONE, would RISE UP, from the FRUIT of his loins, and so, Rabbi Yeshua, which the, Christian world and other worlds, call . . . JESUS Christ of Nazareth. But, getting to the TRUE ESSENCE, of THE SPIRIT, of the ESSENCE, of He who was SENT . . .

One of the; He's, She's, the Divine Entities, that were SENT . . . Rabbi Jeshua, being the HIGHEST, in the order . . . 'Em, second only, to the First Essence, of the GodHead, Rabbi Yeshua, called Jesus Christ of Nazareth, was the second, in the TRIUNE Essence, of the GodHead . . . and then, there is the third Essence, of the GodHead, the HOLY SPIRIT, which the Rabbi Yeshua, SENT DOWN, through and to . . . His Mother, Mary . . . Miriam . . . and they were, of direct lineage, of the House, of the great KING . . . DAVID, who was the Father, of son, Solomon, The Bathsheba . . . and we ALL KNOW, how Solomon, came into the WORLD, after LUST, after ADULTERY, NO . . . YES! After LUST, then ADULTERY, then MURDER, of the husband, of Bathsheba, before . . . DAVID took her, unto HIMSELF!

Well, all the things, and many things, through TIME, which, you know . . . WE don't NEED, or CANNOT HAVE . . . the ANSWER to, nor do I, have them, today, but . . . I will tell you, not because I'm Cynthia, Queen of Scots and America, do I proclaim, to know anything more, but . . . I proclaim, to be . . . heard, please? If you will . . . Please? By ALL POLITENESS, I ask you . . . to keep an OPEN; MIND, HEART, SOUL, WILL and DESTINY . . . to what I'm sharing, with You . . . 'Em, we've ALL seen RULERS . . . come and go, through the world, whether they were, so-called, Asians, Whites, Blacks, Am Eurasians, Hindis, what have you. EVERY HUMAN, WALK OF LIFE!

Now, where did the, Human Walk of Life, occur? It occurred, at Tower of Babel! And, as I mentioned to you, in the first book: I AM WHY THEY KILLED DIANA The Secret of The Red String . . . Well, Huh! QE2 herself, knows . . . because of her lineage to Anne Boleyn? The whore . . . Excuse me God . . . inasmuch, as I've sinned . . . the whore? Who took Henry VIII, away from his TRUE WIFE! Of Spain! But, we'll set that aside, for now.

And, eventually, QE1 ruled and down through TIME, of course, MY ANCESTOR, Mary Queen of Scots, as outlined, in the first book, first dissertation, of Cynthia Queen of Scots and America, I AM WHY THEY KILLED DIANA The Secret of The Red string . . . Mary Queen of Scots . . . had to ACQUIESCE!

I told you the reasons . . . why. 'Em, the only thing I can say, is to ultimately know, know, know and to LOVE the Creator, is to Love, Love, Love and to SERVE . . . Him! That comes, from Cynthia, through her own experience . . . But, getting back, to Mary Queen of Scots. Huh! She had to acquiesce to the Secret of the Red String . . . to the LIKES . . . of Anne Boleyn . . . Huh! As I said to you, was the, "French Tart," . . . and the daughter . . . of a tart!

And now, we have a HUGELY WATERED DOWN, version . . . so- to-say of a MONARCHY?!? Huh! NO! NO! A King is a king, like Bologna is bologna . . . no matter, HOW YOU SLICE IT!

And, a TRUE KING, Queen Elizabeth's Uncle, (in the event, he WERE!!!) A True King . . . Would NEVER, have ACQUIESCED, to his brother and then, NOW to QE2 . . . Elizabeth . . . who ORDERED, the ASSASINATION, of DIANA and she knows, that I know it and can, prove it . . .

Putting that ASIDE . . . Though! Madame, Queen Elizabeth the Second . . . and I don't need, Mr. Al-Fayed, which I would HOPE, Mr. Mohammed Al-Fayed, Dodi's father, would get on BOARD, with the CAUSE and say, "You know what, Cynthia, you've FINALLY, UNLOCKED, the MYSTERY . . . the PUZZLE PIECE . . . that was MISSING!"

Because, Diana, was, "Thought TO BE, the LUNAR DIETY, that would come to THE WORLD . . . and CHANGE . . . THE WORLD . . . She showed it! Through the LOVE SHE GAVE, to her children, through the LOVE, SHE TRIED TO GIVE, to the FALSE, BRITISH ROYAL FAMILY . . . and; HEAR ME NOW . . . ELIZABETH . . . the second and your, posterity . . . including the likes, of Charles and William and Beatrice, etc., etc., etc.

You know, that Cynthia Anne Marie Gunn of Scotland knows, how to delineate the lineage. Therefore . . . that having been said . . . I AM, WHO I SAY . . . I AM. I didn't ask for this, I was born to it, but . . . I'm HAPPY! To wear, the Coat of Arms, and the Cloak, the three, Ancient Celtic Cloaks, of me, "CANTANKEROUS," Family, "ECCENTRIC," Family . . . handed down, from the 12th Generation, of NOAH, who went into the ARK . . . and the people, of Noah's time . . . ALL THOUGHT . . . HE WAS NUTS!

But, as the Christ, Jesus, Rabbi Yeshua of Nazareth said, "and so . . . as it was, in the days of Noah, shall it be before, the COMING, of the SON, of MAN!"

I Love You . . . and . . . I wish, that each and every, one of you, male, female, black, white, no matter, what part of the Earth, no matter, where you are today . . . when you either, read, or see, or hear this, just know . . . without me telling you, that the END, of the ERA, of DECEPTION, of LUCIFER . . . the angel of Light, one of the Highest . . . of Michael, Raphael, Gabriel, Lucifer . . . shall I go on?!?

Lucifer himself, the angel of so-called, "Light," wanted, to take God's place, in the Heavenly Court . . . and you know what? "Deet Da Dee!" Like Carlos Mencia says . . . NOT HAPPENING!!! So he was, cast DOWN, as I told you, into the CORE, of the EARTH, that's the only PIT, on the, "GALAXUAL SCAGE," that he would, be relegated to . . . CONTROL. And, he CONTROLLED . . . the PIT, of the EARTH and all the, GROUND and partially UPWARDS, of the ground, to a CERTAIN LENGTH . . . in HEIGHT.

Now, whether we've flown, in helicopters, or jet planes, or 'Em . . . LUNAR MODULARS, or SHUTTLES . . . 'Em . . . then we know, that . . . there are DIFFERENT LEVELS, of REACHING the HIGHEST LEVEL, of God Consciousness.

I, Cynthia Anne Marie Gunn, I'm no-where near it, but, I have an inkling, I have a CLUE! And . . . I Love You All and I hope that you, will come with me, on the GREATEST JOURNEY, of a LIFETIME!!!

Love, Cynthia

Chapter 5

Well, Good Day, to you, Ladies and Gentleman, Boys and Girls, of the world! It's Cynthia, again and I'm, SO HAPPY and SO PLEASED and SO BLESSED, to be able to have the opportunity, to speak to you, again . . . I'm a little bit hoarse today, my throat is not, what it should be, but . . . then again, I have asthma, amongst other, health concerns. So, let's just set, that aside and let me just say, that 'Em . . . because of, asthma inhalers and other issues, this is why, I'm hoarse.

But that, being put aside, this chapter, is regarding . . . WELL . . . I'VE FOUND HIM!!! Ladies and Gentlemen, Boys and Girls . . . 'Em Princesses, Princes, Kings, Queens, Popes, Mullahs, 'Em . . . Dali Lama, I should, address you ALL IN PERSON . . . ONE DAY! When we ALL, SIT TOGETHER and get down, to the TRUTH, of the Secret of the Secret . . . but . . . putting that aside, for right now, I just want to speak, to the persons, like myself, the ORDINARY PERSON.

And, I just want you to know, that EVERYTHING . . . having been said, in the first dissertation, the first book and now, in the second dissertation, of Cynthia, the second book . . . PLEASE . . . come with me, on the GREATEST JOURNEY, OF A LIFETIME! And, as you may, or may not know, whether you BELIEVE in a GOD, or NOT . . . the Creator, has a BOOK, which has been edited, like most good books are, but . . . I TELL YOU . . . the book of Cynthia, the first, the second and the third . . . it's going to be called, The Book of Cynthia, which is The Book of the Moon, so now, I just renamed ALL THREE . . . "The Books of the Moon!" Book one: Secret of The Red String . . . Book two: (this one) The Secret of

The Secret . . . And Book three: Secret of . . . (which I shall hold for now . . . in reserve). Only, because, I don't have the right adjective to describe it . . . But, let me just tell you, Ladies and Gentlemen, children of the world, Boys and Girls, everywhere, of all ages . . . I'm no different than you!

In fact, as RIGHTEOUS . . . as I GREW UP . . . and as righteous, as I thought I WAS! (Up until the summer, of 2006) . . . I had a HUGE S PLIT, with the God, the Creator and went DOWN, a HUGE WIDE PATH, which LED . . . ALMOST . . . TO MY PERMANENT, TOTAL DESTRUCTION!!! But, by the grace of God and there's, many songs, that outline, the GRACE OF GOD! . . . He IS, THE CREATOR! I told you before, Yahweh, Jehovah, Allah, Buddha, whatever . . . you want . . . to call . . . THE GOD!

It's ALL THE ONE GOD! And, the God is a TRIUNE GodHead. It's a TRIUNE ENTITY. And, I can't speak, of it . . . right now . . . but, the Ancients, of the Old, as much as we think, we know, about what we're doing, RIGHT NOW . . . TODAY . . . and all the TECHNOLOGY and the, so-called, so-called, KNOWLEDGE . . . that we THINK WE HAVE . . . RIGHT NOW . . . Well, DAMN! Do we not see, on the television, this is June the 12th, right now, when I'm speaking to you, of the year, 2008???

'Em . . . Do we not SEE . . . DAMS, nearly being broken? Or the WATERS, flowing around, the sides of the dams? In what Wisconsin? The Cheese Place? Of the United States? Wisconsin, Michigan, what have you . . . Look . . . Huh! You don't need me, to tell you, OKAY!?! Whoever you are, wherever you are . . .

Even, in the most remote jungle, of the Amazon, or the Continent of Africa, or the Outback of Australia . . . wherever you are, if you're, the most primitive race . . . at some point, you will hear my voice. Not, because I'm Cynthia. I'm not Elisha, I'm not Elijah, I'm not Moses, I'm not Rabbi Yeshua, I'm NO ONE . . . but . . . Cynthia Queen of Scots and America.

And, I ONLY LOVE YOU, as a human, one to one, mano ē mano, myself to your self, whoever reads or hears this. OOPS! There's the PHONE . . . a nasty little snipe, which I do not need! Let me, interrupt the call, "Excuse me . . . I'm speaking . . . on the computer, I'll need to call you back, Goodbye . . ."

Well, Ladies and Gentlemen, please excuse me for that. That was my friend, Diane, who you read about, in the first book: I AM WHY THEY KILLED DIANA The Secret of The Red String . . . of course, that means, Diana Spencer-Windsor. If you've not read, the first book, well . . . then I'm glad, you're with me now!

All I can say, is that the first book lays the ground work, for the second and now, this book, the second, lays the ground work, for the third and just like GOD . . . Is a 3 FOLD, 3 SIDED, PRISM . . . a true TRIANGLE . . . a true TRIANGULATION of, the ESSENCE, of . . .

WE, HUMAN CREATURES! That He Created, in His Own Image and Likeness.

Which, I will NOT be ABLE to SPEAK to you, with GREAT CERTAINTY, until the NEXT BOOK, which is the third book . . . but . . . that, being set aside, let me just say, that 'Em . . .

I FOUND THE BEAST!!! Ladies and Gentlemen, Boys and Girls!

Ha! Ha! Ha! Ha! And you know WHAT?!?

OUR GOD . . . IS AN AWESOME GOD!!! Let me tell YOU!!! I don't remember, when I was first THERE, before . . . I CAME INTO this WORLD . . . through my PARENTS, whom I CHOSE . . . and, I'll describe that, more in-depth, LATER . . . how WE CHOOSE OUR PARENTS, when OUR SOUL, DECIDES to come to the EARTHLY EXPERIENCE . . . and, we SEE, ALL OF THE MEN and WOMEN, of the WORLD . . . "Making LOVE" . . . trying to conceptualize, trying to conceive a BABY, a SOUL, into their LIFE, into their LIKENESS, into their WORLD, into their HEART, into their HOME, into their FUTURE and . . . to be WITH THEM, up until, the end of this EARTHLY/PILGRIMAGE/JOURNEY, and then, LATER . . . to be REUNITED, AGAIN . . . FOREVER . . . in HEAVEN.

And that, Ladies and Gentlemen, Boys and Girls, all over the world, whatever, past, present, future, that is the ESSENCE, of WHY WE'RE HERE!!!

IT'S ALL ABOUT LOVE . . . its ONLY LOVE . . . doin' its thing! And, you know what . . . GOD IS LOVE! So, you know what . . . I don't give a care, if I have, a black face, a green left arm, a pink right arm, a purple torso, a grey polka-dotted right leg, and an orange and black striped left leg . . . I DON'T CARE!!!

I don't care, WHAT I LOOK LIKE, as a conglomeration, of a HUMAN . . . Huh! Doesn't MATTER! Because, the Creator, created us as the HIGHEST, because . . . we are TRULY the highest order, of HIS OWN LIKENESS . . . but, He gave us, all these other, creatures and companions to BEHOLD!

From the smallest . . . plankton, in the sea . . . and Ladies and Gentlemen, if the plankton dies . . . we ALL DIE! Because, who will feed . . . the GREAT WHALE? And who, will continue . . . You talk about the Whale? Well, Jonah and the whale.

Now, whether you believe, in the BIBLE . . . or not . . . doesn't matter . . . IT'S TRUE!!! But, it has been edited, which I spoke of, in the first book, perhaps earlier, in this book.

You know . . . PEOPLE 'Em . . . once they realized that there were "NEKED," . . . "NAKED," and then, they realized that they could "CONTROL," the: LIVES, HEARTS, SOULS, WILLS and DESTINYS . . . of OTHER PEOPLE . . . by creating, a FALSE, FALLACY . . . something called, "MONEY," something called . . . that which . . . if you don't use it, you're not gonna get, what you need . . . to go on . . . and go on . . . and go on . . . and go on!!!

And that's, when the message came to Adam and Eve, and I will speak more, on Adam and Eve, later . . . but, Eve was charged, to suffer, what she was charged to suffer! Our first God Mother! The one, that I understand . . . now, I don't condone, what she did! I merely, understand what she did and, I understand, the temptations, that she had, IN THE GARDEN . . . of EDEN . . . the PARADISE . . . When, the serpent, and I will describe that more, in detail . . . LATER!!! You know, the symbolism for the serpent, is the snake. But the snake . . . IS . . . COMES . . . in many different forms! And let's just, set that aside. But, she, having been tempted, and then . . . of course, she KNEW MORE! Than she would REVEAL . . . to Adam!!! So, she HELD certain things . . . BACK!!! And the fruit of her womb, held certain things back, that's why only certain things, are in the BIBLE, in the Torah! It's been edited. I shall, fill in the blanks.

There are certain things, in the New Testament, that were HELD BACK . . . by the children of EVE . . . edited. Because, she held back from Adam, from the FIRST!!! So you see, God warned her, do not be manipulated, by XYZ, (whatever you want to call it, ABC, 123,) Michael . . . . I love you, Cynthia . . .

But, putting that aside, once Eve was manipulated, then she, manipulated Adam, and so on and so forth, down through TIME . . . until, I'm speaking to you, right now, today. So let's just set THEM . . . and the first, great decision, toward all of our well . . . SUFFERING and ILL HEALTH and UNHAPPINESS and BROKEN HEARTS and DISAPPOINTMENTS, SETBACKS, CARES . . . and all the EVILS, we've ever ENDURED!!! Or, all the EVILS that we, SEE COMING! Through the media, through print, television, computers . . . all these WILD, vastly wild . . . and STRANGE . . . and OUTLANDISH, OUTRAGEOUS . . . FUCK! Fornication, under the Court, of the KING! And WHO is the King? The King is the King. And who is he, the King of? He's the LORD . . . and who is he, the LORD of? He's the Lord of Lords. King . . . of Kings and Lord . . . of Lords!!! That is who, we OFFEND, That is whose HEART . . . we BREAK . . . EVERYDAY!

And so, it reverberates back, onto us . . . and we are NEVER satisfied! Unless, or until, we get, on the same page, with . . . LOVE!

Cynthia

Chapter 6

LOVE . . . Now . . . Fellow Humans . . . of all ages, of all races, creeds, colors, religions, persuasions, etc., I, Cynthia Anne Marie Gunn, the Luna Leo Theo Sophia, not because, I asked for it, but because it is so, speak to you . . . out of LOVE, of God Mother. Please allow me, right now . . . today, if you can't do it . . . but in TIME . . . Please allow me, Cynthia, to perhaps take the stature, of God Mother for you? All I can say to you, right now, out of TRUE LOVE . . . and TRUE ESSENCE and TRUE TRUTH . . . is that, what I say to you, in the first dissertation, and this book, the second dissertation, THIS is NOT, a JOKE!!! This is REAL . . .

Wake Up!!! And smell the coffee, the matzo, the egg macmuffins, the munchkins, donuts, oatmeal, whatever it is . . . that you wake-up and smell, when you first wake up!!! But really, folks, Ladies and Gentlemen, women and children, boys and girls, of all ages, and all times . . . right now . . . on the Earth . . . of 2008 . . .

The God, wants to tell you, especially the children of Abraham . . . and now, just the children of Abraham, Isaac, Jacob, Moses, etc., etc., etc., down through time . . . through Rabbi Yeshua, until this very time. That true God is saying . . . I AM . . . and I gave you, EVERYTHING!!! And a piece, of land . . . and WHAT, did YOU do WITH IT!!! AHAH! AHAH! I will tell you . . .

That is what the Creator, has to say, to those that understand, what I just said. Now, I, Cynthia Anne Marie Gunn, am NOT going, to make EXCUSES . . . for the BAD that I . . . have DONE!!! As Rabbi Yeshua said, when you break, one commandment . . . you break, them ALL! And, I've broken them ALL! And, I've broken them, more than once! I've broken them, SEVERAL TIMES! And, as I'm speaking to you today . . . I hope, NOT to break one . . . or ALL, again!

But, this is part of the Human Condition. And that, having been said, the Creator, God, whom I, choose to call God, Yahweh, Buddha, Allah, 45 whatever . . . the God, needs to speak, to you again. Not by Cynthia. Not through Cynthia . . . just because SOMEONE . . . like Elijah, 'Em . . . John the Baptist, the cousin of, Rabbi Yeshua, who proclaimed, Rabbi Yeshua's COMING . . . in the desert . . . at the river Jordan, when he baptized, people in WATER . . .

And then he later, said . . . THE ONE, that comes after me, I'm not fit to tie, his sandal straps, or even, perhaps, look at his sandal, or his feet, for that matter . . . and then, didn't Rabbi Yeshua, SHOW UP! In the midst, of all that and Elijah said . . . NO! . . . I can't do this . . . I can't baptize YOU!!! . . . YOU need to baptize ME!!! And Rabbi Yeshua, said . . . NO . . . you, need to baptize me, so that All, down through TIME, will see, hear, know and believe, that I AM, who I say I AM. And . . . That's a quote, from Rabbi Yeshua, at the river Jordan. Way back when . . . about 2 thousand, or so, years ago.

I'm going only, by the Christian calendar, If I were going by the Hebrew calendar, It would be the year . . . 5 thousand . . . I don't know what. So, I do know, what I'm speaking of, and yet . . . you may not think so, but . . . today, I'm going to speak, directly to, the lineage of, Abraham, Isaac, Jacob, Moses, Joshua, etc., etc., down through Joseph . . . and, down to Rabbi Yeshua, his son. Now, the Christians say, that he was a foster son, of Joseph. Whatever, the case may be . . . and only the God, Yahweh, knows the truth . . . let's not question that any further, look where it's gotten us, SO FAR!

Let us just, go back, over the annals, quickly, of time, of what the Hebrews, have suffered . . . at the hands, of Pharaoh and then, 40 years . . . in the DESERT . . . With Moses . . . MOSES!!! And, Moses, himself, as wonderful and holy and blessed, as he was, only saw the Promised Land . . . from the highest peak! So be it. And then, the Promised Land became the Promised Land, but . . . all the other peoples of the earth, starting with the most closest, bands or sects, of people, the Arabs, perhaps . . . call them what you want today.

Call them: Iraqis, call them Iranians, call them Saudis, call them whatever you want to call them.

YOU NEED TO STOP . . . putting LABELS, on THEM! And they, NEED TO STOP putting LABELS, on YOU! To want to, DESTROY YOU!!! And after that, the REST of US, who branched out . . . from that region, can STOP . . . putting labels and demands . . . and etcetera, FREAKISH, WILD and STRANGE, demands . . . on one another, because as I said, to you before . . . I don't care . . . If I have . . . a green head, a pink right arm, a blue left arm, an orange and black striped right leg, or a grey polka dotted left leg!!!

WE ALL . . . have to STOP . . . the NONSENSE!!! Enough is ENOUGH!!! And if, you don't believe, what I've said to you . . . then JUST WAIT!!! WAIT!!! Not for Cynthia, or for the Pope, or for . . . I don't know . . . the highest of the HIGH!?! Dali Lama? The Highest of the high, of the FAITHS of ALL, the WORLD!!! All the highest . . . of the so-called Mohammedites, the so-called Islam.

"Em . . . and I, put this challenge out . . . TODAY! That, I will say to you, SIR, . . . and I will call you sir, because you're . . . you come from wealth . . . and you come from high education, but . . . I shall say to you, Sir, OSAMA . . . Bin Laden . . . who, is a Prince, of Saudi Arabia . . . and then, you studied in the UNITED STATES of AMERICA!!! Of all PLACES!!!

And then, you took your . . . money and you took, your ideals and your ideas . . . and I don't blame you . . . I can understand, where you're coming from . . . but, you know what?!? Osama Bin Laden . . . Cynthia Anne Marie Gunn, the Queen of Scots and America, will meet with you . . . Osama Bin Laden . . . son of Laden . . .

Anywhere, Anytime, Any place . . . to have, a mano e mano, one on one, discussion. Bring NO of your COHORTS . . . I'll bring NO of my COHORTS . . . and we'll just talk, amongst ourselves, in front of THE Creator. You call Him, Allah, and I, Cynthia, call Him, God.

Putting that aside, I'll not fight you, Osama Bin Laden. I merely, would LOVE to talk to you . . . because I think, I understand, what you're trying to say . . . to the world . . . and what, you're trying to do . . . and I, respect it and I, validate it and I understand, that it has merit, by everything you've grown up with.

And, believe and hold true and press, to your heart! Well, never fear, that Cynthia Anne Marie Gunn the Queen of Scots and America, has what she has, learned and came . . . to know . . . and come, to press close, to her heart and her mind and her soul.

So, I would say to you, Osama Bin Laden . . . Cynthia Anne Marie Gunn, would love to meet, with you, on COMMON GROUND! Who's neutral NOW?!? Is it Switzerland . . . is it still . . . Switzerland?

If not, 'Em, let us meet, in The Hague, Netherlands? Not you, as a war crime, not me as a Queen of a Country . . . whatever . . . but, as a man and a woman, who truly and firmly, believe . . . , in the cause, which we've been, charged and predestined, to follow through!

Now, Osama Bin Laden, Cynthia Queen of Scots and America . . . LOVES . . . YOU!!!

Just as much, as I love, every other . . . human being! Past, present, future . . . . Now, if the Russians, Heh! Heh! WE, we both know the Russians . . . we know, what they did or didn't do, in history, how they overthrew, their OWN MONARCHY!!! And how, they like . . . teamed up, with the United States and Great Britain, to slay HITLER . . . Adolph Hitler . . . ANOTHER CATHOLIC . . . BY THE WAY!!!

Listen . . . Osama, you know . . . I'm ready, to TALK! I'm not Barack Obama, I'm not John McCain . . . You're Osama . . . and I am Cynthia Anne Marie Gunn, so, therefore, I say to you . . . Osama supercedes Obama . . . and Gunn supercedes McCain. Now, if you can get with that . . . and you and I . . . can get together . . . I don't care!!! You, can bring me, to the deepest recesses, of the Mountains, of Afghanistan, where you MAY, or MAY NOT . . . be hiding.

If you, solemnly swear, to me, that . . . you and I, will have our own discussion . . . amongst ourselves, mano e mano and NO ONE, ELSE . . . will, EVER KNOW! . . . What we said to one another, by media or by any, other source . . . as long, as both of us, are living . . . if we, can come, to an understanding . . . of THIS PLANET . . . and the GEOPOLITICAL STRUCTURE, of what's REALLY, ACTUALLY . . . HAPPENING!!! Here! And don't think, for a minute, Osama, that Cynthia, does not know! Because, I KNOW! Because . . . well . . . it's on the back, of the, twenty . . .

dollar bill! And, they want to blame everything . . . on YOU?!? And your followers . . . Well, you know what???

Just meet me, Osama. Anywhere . . . I don't care! Istanbul? Gay Paris? 'Em . . . Greece? YOU NAME IT!!! NAME THE DATE!!! And Cynthia, will be there. And together, you and I, will discern, what's TRUE and what ISN'T! . . . Who's EVIL! . . . And, Who's GOOD! What's right and what's wrong . . . because, as YOU, Osama and I both KNOW, in the end times . . . WRONG, SHALL SEEM, RIGHT and RIGHT, SHALL SEEM, WRONG!!!

Now, I'm NOT a subscriber . . . to, Christopher Columbus . . . and all that came after him, because MY PEOPLE . . . THE GUNNS . . . were in America . . . FIRST! But, we did not claim it, because it was really, truly, not ours! We DID NOT overtake it!

But, only if you and I, Osama, sit down together . . . and have a lunch, and a . . . discussion and perhaps . . . I don't know, if it's in, your religion . . . to take a glass, of wine or two . . . or, if it's in, your religion to . . . 'Em, partake of perhaps, some type of, a relaxation method??? Osama Bin Laden, Cynthia Anne Marie Gunn, cordially invites you, to meet her, any day, any time, any where, or your choosing . . . and I know, that you won't kill me . . . and you know, that I won't kill you.

All we'll do, is we'll sit and we'll, talk and we'll, discuss and we'll decide, which is the GREATER, of the RIGHT . . . or the GREATER, of the WRONG . . . and support, either myself, you support, me and my future and my endeavors, or I, will get behind you, Osama and support you . . . and your future and your endeavors . . . and that's all, I can say to you.

And, I hope you're well, because . . . when I've seen you on TV, they say . . . OH! He's got kidney failure! He's got this . . . He's got that . . . I'm just, hoping and praying, that both of us . . . and I'm nearly, forty nine, Mister Osama . . . Master Osama. I only hope, that I'm well enough, to meet with you!

And, thank you, so much . . . for listening and PLEASE . . . let's set a time, to get together. Thank you . . . and . . . PEACE . . . PAX . . . the ROMAN word . . . PEACE, from . . . Cynthia Queen of Scots and America, to Osama . . . Bin Laden. Bye for now . . . OBL . . .

Chapter 7

Hello, Cynthia again . . . and thank you, for sticking with me. Today, friends . . . is Friday, 6/13/2008. Ugh! Ugh! MY GOD!!! As all the believers, of a superstition, Friday the thirteenth, subscribe to . . . and in the event, they're Christians and they, subscribe to the . . . falsehood! Ha! Ha! Of . . . Friday the thirteenth, being an . . . EVIL DAY . . . or a bad luck day?!? FORGET IT!!!

Now, I'm BACK!!! Osama Bin Laden. Now, Osama, Cynthia must say to you, out of love and respect . . . and common, human dignity . . . whether or not, you've decided, from my last . . . speaking to you . . . in the chapter before this . . . I'm going to speak, in LATIN NOW . . . and have your, Latin scholars, decipher, what I am, about to say . . . Not for Nothing! But . . . because, I am, Cynthia and I am, who I am and I, know what I know and I, understand and can feel, YOUR PAIN!!! I cannot describe, your pain, on this dissertation, only to you and me, in private and only, because I know that the Torah edited and left out, certain TRUISMS . . . not ALTRUISMS!!! But truisms, about who, did what, to whom!!!

Cain, Abel, Adam, Eve . . . I KNOW . . . THE TRUTH!!! Donney, donney . . . worrey . . . about it!!! And that's, from Cynthia Queen of Scots . . . but, Osama . . . PLEASE!!! Have your Latin People, check this message . . . which is now, called . . . Chapter 6/7 . . . book 2 . . . FANUM . . . and it's directed, to . . . . Benedict, XVI,

Fanum, flamen, missa, abavus, abbas abbatis, altor, amita, atavus, avus, compater, gigno (genuit), pater, paterna, paternus, patria, patria, patrius, patrizo, priores, proavus, sator, soccer, vitricus, cui, cuius, ego, hac, haec hec, hanc, hic, Hirenses Irenses, hoc, hoc, hoc,

hoc, Huic, huic, huic, huius, huius, hunc, l, lco, illae ille, illi, immo, inquam, Insula, Mei, moleste, quadraginta, quae, quam, quarum, Quibus, quibus, quibus, accendo, accumulo, accuso, adamans, adamo, adflicto aggligo, adsuesco assuesco, affamen, agna, agnellus, agonotheta, alea, aleator, alius, amaritudo, ambages, ambiguitas, ambiguos, ambio, ambitio ambitus, ambitus, ambivium ambulo, amens, amicabiliter, amicitia, amictus, amiculum, amicus, amissio, amita, amita, amitto, amitto, amnis, amo, amoena, amoenitas, amor, Luna, Lunatus, aboleo, adimpleo, caleo, compleo, compleo, condoleo, defleo, defleo, doleo, doleo, doleo, doleo, enucleo, expleo, expleo, expleo, fleo, fleo, impleo, impleo, impleo, Leo, palleo, panthera, pardus, polleo, polleo, praevaleo, repleo, sileo, soleo, soleo, suboleo, ualeo, valeo, valeo, aut:.aut, pax, pax pacis, pax pacis, artifex, auctor, auctorita, auctoritas, auctorizo, aut:. aut, autem, autumo, autus, bellus, caute, cautela, cautio, cautor, cautor, cautus, cautus, cautus, caveo, chirographum, comperte, décor, decoro, decorus, ditio, fautor, fautor, forma: forma, formose, formositas, formosus, formula, honestus, imperium, imculata, lautitia, lautumiae, lautus, licentia, licentio, nauta, potentia, potestas, praecautus, praecaveo, praecidentius, praeclarus, praevideo, professor, professorius, puchre, pulcher pulchra pulchrum, pulchritudo, regnum, sceptrum, scriptor, speciosus, venustas, vox, vox, bellum, bellum, labellum!!!

Amore, Cynthia Anne Marie Gunn Queen of Scots and America Amore . . . Luna Leo Theo Sophia, Et tu? Benedict XVI?

Love, Cynthia

Chapter 8

And, WE'RE BACK!!! Ladies and Gentlemen, Boys and Girls, of all ages, of the Earth, in the year 2008, in June, thirteenth . . . FRIDAY . . . the 13TH . . . 'Em, Huh! The last message, I just spoke of, was in TRUE LOVE, to Benedict XVI. Scripti, Scripti, FINI. Cynthia . . . Et tu? Benedict XVI?

Now, that having been said, "Em, now we're onto Chapter SEVEN??? Of book two and all, I can say . . . is, "Em, welcome back, to the English language! And, welcome back, to . . . REALITY . . . not Cynthia's reality, not the Popes reality, not the PRESIDENT OF THE UNITED STATES OF AMERICA . . . and . . . OH!!! Who's it gonna be, NEXT?!? Well, we now have, Barack Obama for the democrats . . . and we have, WHO?!? John McCain, for the republicans?!? Ha! Ha! Ha!

Ladies and Gentlemen, PLEASE . . . please . . . I BEG OF YOU!!! Not for Nothin' . . . but, not for Cynthia . . . but, not for any other, reason but, will you NOT . . . unless or until . . . the Comet Rup, makes impact with the Earth . . . BEFORE YOU DIE!!! A natural, or what have you, accidental, or unnatural death . . . will you NOT . . . get WITH, THE CREATOR???

The Islam calls Him, Allah. The Chinese, call Him Buddha. The Christians, call Him God . . . the Father of Rabbi Yeshua . . . and. whatever you want to name, the Superior Being . . . Entity . . . down through TIME!!! Now, if you've not read, Cynthia's first dissertation . . . and . . . WHO THE HELL AM I?!? Who the H E-double, hockey sticks . . . H E-double toothpicks . . . Who the HELL . . . is, Cynthia?!?

Well, she's NO better and, NO worse, than YOU!!! Man, Woman, Child (male or female). In the past, in the present, or in the future!!! I'm just like YOU . . . I'm an ordinary, Human Being. I'm NOT proclaiming, to be, anything BUT that!!! I'm NOT, proclaiming to be, A Savior, A Rabbi, A . . . any type, of . . . Seer, Psychic, what have you. I'm only proclaiming, to be, who I am . . . Cynthia Queen of Scots and America.

Now, how can I sit here, today . . . and make THAT CLAIM?!? Well, "Em, because . . . THE GUNNS, as I told you, in book one, I AM WHY THEY KILLED DIANA The Secret of The Red String . . . as I told you, in book one, The Gunns, in America, were successful, because they DIDN'T treat their . . . SO-CALLED SLAVES, as slaves . . . they treated them, as WORKERS!!!

Now, that being put aside, if Pharaoh . . . had treated his HEBREW WORKERS . . . as workers and cherished, them and understood, them and treated them, as TRUE workers . . . true BUILDERS and BUILDRESSES, in the female tense, of the word . . . of PYRAMIDS?!? Well, Ladies and Gentlemen . . . WHY??? After all these years . . . that we're here now, we're here, in the past, or in the future . . . why do THINK . . . the ancient Pyramids . . . of Giza, still stand?

Why? Because . . . they're four sided!!! Because, each side, one unto itself, let's just, take four sides. North, South . . . Let's just start from the beginning . . . North, East, West, South, North . . . "Em, you can start, from any vantage point, you want . . . but, if someone's compass, of the, Earth . . . Mercury, Venus, Earth, Mars, Jupiter, Saturn, Uranus, Neptune and . . . They've dropped the ninth planet . . . Pluto, but . . . you know what, forget it!!!

Because they, might have dropped, the ninth house, the ninth planet . . . but I, DID NOT!!! So, I don't care WHAT modern science SAYS!!! We have: Mercury, Venus, Earth, Mars, Jupiter, Saturn, Uranus, Neptune and Pluto!!! Now, that is VERY significant, Ladies and Gentlemen, Boys and Girls, of the world, of all ages, including Osama!!!

Ahah! Ahah! And, whoever's leading, the so-called, Promised Land??? Of . . . the world??? Listen Osama . . . I GET the WHOLE THING!!! Trust Me . . . when; I TELL YOU!!! I get the whole thing!

Now, what you need to do, Osama, is . . . you need to, prove to yourself, Osama Bin Laden . . . and the, REST of the WORLD!!! That you KNOW . . . and THINK . . . and think, YOU KNOW . . . and SAY, you know . . . and DO, what you think, you know . . . to be . . . TRUE!!!

And, IF you DO IT . . . and if, you SAY, it . . . and if, you KNOW IT . . . and if, IT'S SO . . . Well then!!! Sir, Osama Bin Laden . . . DON'T be, a HYPOCRITE!!! And you know, what . . . Mohammed . . . HIMSELF . . . in the Quran, would SAY!!! "Osama . . . Bin Laden, UNLESS or UNTIL . . . you're READY, WILLING and ABEL . . . and I pray, you're ABEL . . . because, I don't know your health, Sir . . .

Now, I only know mine, at nearly . . . forty nine. Unless or until . . . you're ABEL, to meet Cynthia Queen of Scots and America . . . and HER people, DID NOT CLIAM AMERICA!!! It didn't matter, they already had, what the God gave them . . . the British Isles, but we'll set aside, Scotland, Ireland, Wales and England . . . for now!!! Because Osama, Cynthia is; the TRUE MONARCH . . . of the FOUR, aforementioned, provinces. NOW!!!

The Hebrews . . . were given, a PLOT of LAND . . . by The Yahweh, the God . . . whether YOU like it, or NOT!!! Whether you think, it's TRUE or NOT!!! It's SO!!! Now, look over the whole world map. Look at every piece of LAND . . . not WATER!!! But . . . land and seven, tenths of the earth . . . IS water, so therefore three, tenths of the earth . . . RIGHT NOW exposed, is land!!! But . . . Osama, I say to you . . .

DO YOU LOVE YOUR CHILDREN??? I'm going to ask you the SAME QUESTION . . . that was asked, of the RUSSIANS . . . back in the nineteen eighties, by Ronald Reagan. Ronald Wilson Reagan . . . who MANY thought, was the six, six, six . . . well you know what . . . Osama . . . it wasn't Ronald Wilson Reagan . . . IT'S NOT, Osama Bin Laden . . . it's NOT Cynthia Anne Marie Gunn Queen of Scots and America . . . Osama, I Cynthia, and I'm sure, YOU, KNOW IT Sir and I acquiesce to your intelligence . . . I'm gonna sit down, with you, at lunch, as I asked you, in the last chapter.

I'm going to WAIT!!! Unless or until, YOU can tell ME, where you, THINK and KNOW . . . that the ANTI-GOD . . . the ANTI-

ALLAH . . . don't even call IT . . . the, ANIT-RABBI YESHUA, Jesus Christ, of Nazareth!!! JESUS CHRIST, of Nazareth . . . Rabbi Yeshua; does NOT CARE . . . whether you believe IN HIM . . . or NOT!!! But, the MESSAGE . . . of the Creator . . . who SENT HIM . . . who sent all of us . . . and we, CHOSE our PARENTS . . . as I outlined, in the chapter, before this . . .

Unless or until, we ALL, get ON . . . the SAME PAGE, with a person, who happened to be, a descendent of Abraham, Isaac, Jacob, Moses, Joshua, the House of David . . . King Solomon, down through TIME . . . to the House of Joseph, his so-called, foster father??? And Mary, Miriam . . . . his Mother . . . Rabbi Yeshua's Mother!!! OKAY!!! So, you know what, Osama . . . you're EITHER, a MAN . . . OR YOU'RE NOT!!!

So . . . MAN UP!!! Osama Bin Laden . . . DON'T play GAMES . . . with Cynthia, or anyone ELSE, or the world!!! MAN UP!!! Because, you know what . . . Osama . . . Bin Laden . . . IF YOU DON'T KNOW, that I UNDERSTAND . . . YOU and I LOVE YOU . . . and I GET YOUR PAIN!!! But . . . YOU DON'T GET MINE!!! And YOU won't LISTEN, to ME . . . YET!!! And YOU, won't understand me and you, WON'T GET . . . with MY PAIN!!!

So you know what . . . UNLESS or UNTIL, we get TOGETHER . . . Huh! Well . . . STOP THE INSANITY!!! SHALL I??? WILL you STOP the INSANITY?!? I ACQUIESCE!!! Cynthia Anne Marie Gunn Queen of Scots and TRULY of AMERICA!!! Which, I DID NOT claim . . . BUT . . . I CAN PROVE . . . I was, HERE FIRST!!! It's not important!!! DON'T be CLAIMING . . . ANYHTHING!!!

Don't be claiming, the LAND . . . that the Creator . . . Allah, God, Yahweh, Jehovah . . . DON'T . . . DON'T!!! Don't. I don't CARE who YOU ARE . . . don't sit there and say that you THINK . . . you OWN . . . that LAND!!! BECAUSE you don't!!! And, it's not, for Cynthia, to say!!! But . . . in the FINAL ANALYSIS . . . The Creator, Allah, Yahweh, Jehovah, GOD . . . Buddha, OF COURSE . . . WILL RIEGN SUPREME!!!

Now, if you don't know . . . that YET . . . then . . . I don't know, what the HELL, YOU think you're DOING!!! Excuse me Sir, for saying, H E-double toothpicks, H E-double hockey sticks . . . I don't know what, you and YOUR FOLLOWERS, "THINK?!?" You're doing??? BUT . . . IF YOU HONESTLY, "THINK . . ." that you can circumvent . . . the true Creator?!? Then, you don't know nothin' as SMART, as you THINK, you ARE?!?

And, as smart, as you think, that the HEBREWS, thought . . . THEY WERE?!? And, as smart, as you think that the REST of US . . . The GENTILES!!! NOT the JEWS!!! NOT the ARABS!!! But . . . EVERYONE . . . that came after that . . . from the TOWER of BABEL!!! TO this DAY!!! If you . . . don't THINK . . . the rest of us . . . KNOW . . . that we're justified, by FAITH and NOT by SIGHT!!! YOU PEOPLE . . . you Jews and you Arabs, have ALWAYS . . . been in close proximity, to the SIGHT!!! Of, the LAND . . . that God . . . Promised to the HEBREWS . . . the JEWS!!!

Who you . . . HATE!!! And, you want, to TAKE, off the FACE, of the EARTH!!! Well, you know what . . . Deet Da Dee!!! And, I don't need, Carlos Mencia . . . to back me up, ON THIS!!!

If YOU think, for a COTTON PICKIN' MOMENT . . . that the likes, of Cynthia Anne Marie Gunn of SCOTLAND . . . and her, ANCESTORS . . . who did NOT . . . overtake . . . the United States of America . . . from the Native Americans, who were here . . .

Whom, I Cynthia, am one sixteenth . . . Oklahoma CHEROKEE!!! Which I can PROVE . . . and I am, so-called, in the TRIBE . . . setting that all aside . . . do you not think, Osama Bin Laden . . . that for, one cotton pickin' moment . . . do you, REALLY and TRULY, HONESTLY think . . . you're gonna DEFEAT . . . Cynthia Queen of Scots and America . . . and HER FAMILY . . . and HER TROOPS . . .

I DON'T, need COHORTS!!! You can bring, cohorts, from wherever you want. Cynthia has a family . . . and we have TROOPS . . . and we all LOVE ONE ANOTHER!!! And, we all understand, the DIFFERENCE!!! Between, the TRUTH and a LIE!!! So, you know what . . . Osama . . . I am, willing to meet you, READY WILLING and ABEL!!! Only on common ground. Because, Ha! Ha! Ha! Ha! Ha!

Well, FORGET David . . . and GOLIATH!!! You Sir, Osama Bin Laden . . . son of Laden . . . and Cynthia Anne Marie Gunn of

Scotland . . . I would love . . . to challenge you . . . to a . . . KNIFE FIGHT!!!

You choose your knife! It may not be, longer, the blade . . . than, four to six inches . . . and I Cynthia Anne Marie Gunn of Scotland . . . AND America . . . CHALLENGE YOU!! To a knife fight . . . and we'll SEE . . . if DAVID . . . can again, "SLEW" . . . Goliath!!!

You know what?!? Let's just . . . PUT our KNIVES . . . down . . . Osama. Look, WE'RE STILL HUMAN . . . I don't care . . . if I have, a black face, a white face, a black right arm, a left-right arm, a black left arm, white left arm, a black torso, a white torso, a black right leg, a white right leg, a black left leg, a black-white leg . . . Osama Bin Laden, son of Laden.

DO NOT . . . challenge me . . . to a DUEL . . . because, in the event, you DO?!? Then . . . Da-Dink!!! There's the great satan . . . through the computer . . . BUT . . . I won't, get into THAT . . . RIGHT NOW!!! Osama. But, I challenge you, FIRST . . . to MEET . . . and SPEAK . . . as one Human female, entity . . . to another, male, Human entity . . . and if, We cannot, agree on something . . . in that meeting . . . then, Let's DUEL EACH OTHER!!! D-U-E-L . . . to the, DEATH!!!

And if, you Osama, kill me . . . then . . . by the God, Allah, as you call Him . . . it was meant to be . . . and so be it . . . BUT . . . in the EVENT . . . little old, Cynthia . . . of little old, Scotland . . . that's all we want . . . is our, little old, bonnie Scotland, we don't ask . . . for ANYTHING MORE or LESS . . . we don't claim, anything, more or less . . . but, we acquiesce, to the Creator . . . of ALL OF US!!! Allah, as you, call Him . . . and God.

Now, in the event, I Cynthia and you, Osama, can't reach am agreement . . . then . . . let us, AGREE to DISAGREE!!! And let us, agree to a, knife fight!!! In front of CNN, in front of, the cable news network, of the Americans . . . whom you, CAME HERE . . . to STUDY . . . you HYPOCRITE!!! And who, YOU HATE!!!

Let, Osama Bin Laden . . . and Cynthia Anne Marie Gunn . . . IF you so say, Sir, after our so-called, preferential, non-preferential meeting, mano e mano . . . one on one . . . where, I swear, I don't KILL YOU . . . and you swear, you don't KILL ME!!!

Then . . . let us, challenge each other, to a duel . . . for the world!!! For Allah, God, as you call Him, or for God, Jehovah, Yahweh, Rabbi Yeshua . . . the, TRIUNE GODHEAD . . . as I call Him . . . So let's, just do that . . . Osama. You know, in the event you don't want, to meet with me, I think . . . It's gonna come, down to that, in THE END . . . Osama.

That you and I, shall fight each other . . . in a knife fight . . . WINNER, TAKE ALL!!! For better, or for worse, for richer, for poorer, in sickness . . . and in health . . . be the world, come to a THOUSAND YEARS PEACE . . . or come, TO AN END!!!

So Be It!!! By the God!!! AMEN. ALLELUHIA!!!

Love, to ALL, most especially . . . Creator . . .

Love Cynthia

Chapter 9

Well, we're back! Ladies and Gentlemen, Boys and girls . . . the world over . . . thank you, for staying with me, through all of this . . . through the first dissertation, the first book and now, this the second. I do have, all the information, that we need . . . I am working very diligently, this is now, the Fathers Day, of June 2008 . . . and it's Sunday and this, is chapter nine, of the second book.

I first need . . . to again, speak to the children, of Abraham, Isaac, Jacob, Moses, Joshua, down through time . . . to King David, King Solomon, down through time . . . again, to the house of Joseph, from which, Rabbi Yeshua . . . is the FRUIT . . . of the WOMB . . . of Mary, Miriam . . . who was betrothed, to Joseph, of the house . . . of David. That is why, the LAMB . . . so-to-say, of God . . . Rabbi Yeshua, is from the house, of David . . . and I need to . . . speak to you, because, SO FAR . . . LISTEN!

GOD LOVES ALL OF US!!! Gentiles, Hebrews, Arabs, all the scattered, earthly, remains and our fruits, of our loins . . . from the Tower of Babel . . . to this time! HE LOVES US ALL!!! Equally! Equidistant!

But, He DID . . . and it's a matter of FACT . . . and as I, spoke to, Osama Bin Laden . . . before . . . you're NOT going to TAKE, that piece of LAND . . . away from . . . WHO YOU HATE!!!

You only hate THEM . . . because you're JEALOUS . . . of THEM . . . and THAT is the TRUTH!!!

We Gentiles, are NOT jealous . . . of the Hebrews, as YOU ARE!!! Because . . . WHY?!? Because we follow, ONE AMONGST THEM!!! We FOLLOW . . . Rabbi Yeshua!!! Who COMES . . . FROM, the Hebrews and WE . . . will NO LONGER, LET you

THINK, or let you think that . . . we think, that the Hebrews, killed Rabbi Yeshua!!! Jesus Christ of Nazareth!!!

THEY DID NOT!!! They, merely ordered, the release, of Barrabbas . . . and so, Jesus and the, two others, were crucified. Rabbi Yeshua . . . and the two, others and they, said . . . take Him . . . away with . . . away with Him . . . Crucify Him. They merely, chose Barrabbas . . . and said, well what, do you do, with this one. Well, of course, it's . . . we're talking . . . about a day, of crucifixion.

So, off . . . He had, to go . . . and even . . . I'm speaking NOW, to the children, WHO follow Mohammed . . . the Muslims . . . the Islam! You recognize, Rabbi Yeshua, Mary, Miriam . . . His Mother . . . you recognize THEM!!! As TRUE; God ENTITIES!!! In your, Quran . . . your Holy Quran . . . and I've read it . . . and I, understand it and I, GET IT!!! And, Mohammed . . . certainly was, a BLESSED, HOLY, PROPHET!!!

But . . . he was NOT, a SAVIOR!!! Now, once again, I need to speak, directly to the children, of Abraham, Isaac, Jacob, Moses and down . . . the line. YOU NEED to FORGET . . . that, it's gonna be ANOTHER . . . one or two, THOUSAND YEARS . . . UNTIL, YOUR SAVIOUR . . . COMES!!! Your Savior . . . has ALREADY, BEEN HERE!!!

He's OUR Savior!!! Of the WHOLE WORLD!!! And, the SOONER . . . you get, that INFORMATION . . . through, your HEAD!!! The BETTER OFF . . . we're ALL gonna BE!!! Because why???

Listen, EVERYBODY . . . in the, United States of America, there's a HUGE THING . . . going on now, which . . . people don't UNDERSTAND!!! Anyone, who knows Cynthia, myself, KNOWS . . . that I PREDICTED a, "RACEWAR" . . . in the, United States, in the, nineteen nineties!!! The LATE, nineteen nineties!!!

Well, I'm OFF, by about TEN YEARS!!! But, that's OKAY! Because, in the Creators . . . TIME . . . a YEAR is like, a DAY . . . a day is like, a THOUSAND YEARS . . . a thousand years, is like, a DAY!!! There is . . . NO SUCH THING . . . There IS . . . no such thing . . . as the, TIME and the . . . CALENDAR . . . that WE, understand. Because we're OUT OF, a STATE . . . of GRACE!!!

We're in a, STATE OF DEATH!!! We're in a CULTURE . . . of death, NOT LIFE!!! ETERNAL!!!

Not LIFE . . . EVERLASTING!!! We need to get, BACK to the FRUIT, of the TREE, of THE GOOD!!! Not the fruit, of the tree, of the Serpent . . . the so-called, serpent . . . and that was SYMBOLISM . . .

I could speak more, on Adam and Eve, after this . . . but I need to talk to, ALL of THEIR POSTERITY!!! Which includes . . . EVERYONE down; UNTIL . . . the Deluge, the FLOOD . . . of Noah . . . and everyone . . . AFTER, that . . . and, I as I've told you before, I can direct my lineage, BACK to, NOAH . . . and we ALL CAN!!! We don't need to do it.

TRUST ME, when I tell you!!! We are ALL, DECENDENTS . . . of those, who survived, the Deluge . . . of the Ark!!!

Because, Cessair and Fintan, DID NOT!!! They were AGAINST, Cessair's Grandfather . . . NOAH!!! So, Noah and the chosen . . . animals, creatures, etc., and the, humans . . . that DIDN'T think, Noah . . . was NUTS!!! And, you people, my brothers and sisters, of the world . . . you must think . . . I'm NUTS . . . RIGHT NOW!!!

You know what?!? I'M AS NUTS . . . AS NOAH and/or MOSES . . . for that matter . . . That's gonna be, the TITLE, of my THIRD book . . . I AM AS NUTS AS NOAH AND MOSES . . . don't we ALL KNOW . . . in the final analysis, that THEY WERE, the WISEST, most; God LOVING, most God FEARING . . . MEN . . . on the EARTH at THEIR TIMES!!!

Now, we find ourselves, as the, Holy Bible SAYS . . . we're LIVING . . . LIKE we DID . . . in the DAYS of NOAH!!!

When all these, INSANE . . . and HIDEOUS . . . and HORRIBLE THINGS . . . will be, GOING ON . . . ACROSS the FACE . . . of the EARTH!!! Inside of, FAMILIES . . . inside of, MARRIAGES . . . the EARTH . . . Mother Earth . . . Earth . . . is my Mother . . . NO OTHER . . . MY SANCTUARY . . . Earth . . . is a PRISON, a GRAVE and a, MORTUARY . . . but, putting that, ASIDE . . . so we can, RISE UP and let us . . . be ON OUR WAY . . . as "Em, my Uncle's good friend, Karol Wojtyla said, on one of HIS books!!!

We're GOING, to DO THAT!!! And, Karol Wojtyla, has gone . . . AHEAD OF US!!! And, he's working . . . SO HARD . . . on his MESSAGES . . . be NOT, AFRAID!!! RISE . . . let us, be on our, WAY . . . we're, crossing the threshold . . . of HOPE!!! And he did it!!!

Did anyone SEE HIM?!? In the; Millennium . . . 2000?!? When, he ushered in, the so-called MILLENNIUM!!! Well, the man, he was a man, was a Christian, was a priest, a Bishop, Cardinal, Pope!!! John Paul the second!!! And, a VERY DEAR . . . friend, of our family, through my Uncle . . . Father Walter Joseph Pilecki, who sought him out, BEHIND the IRON CURTAIN . . . in 1964!

But . . . that's outlined, in the first book, a bit . . . and I will give you, the photographic evidence, in this book . . . two . . . of the CONNECTION, Of the F-B-I . . . and, I'm not talking . . . Federal Bureau of Investigation, HERE!!! I'm talking, Fathers Bureau of Investigation . . . and what kind, of fathers?!? The Fathers of, the CHURCH, upon the ROCK, of PETER!!!

Now, I DIDN'T, say IT . . . YOU didn't, SAY it . . . but . . . Rabbi Yeshua . . . HIMSELF SAID . . . you are SIMON . . . now, your NAME is PETER . . . AND upon, YOU, MY ROCK . . . I BUILD MY CHURCH!!!

So . . . ALL the religions . . . of THE WORLD . . . as I've told you before . . . have SOME, of the INFORMATION . . . and have, SOME of it . . . RIGHT!!! NONE . . . of the religions . . . of the world . . . have ALL the information . . . and have it right.

NOT EVEN . . . the so-called, ROCK . . . the Catholic Church!!! The Roman Catholic Church!!! They . . . don't HAVE IT, all RIGHT!!! ANYMORE!!! They HAD, it RIGHT . . . in the BEGINNING . . . there's been, all kinds, of dissenters and ANTI-RABBI YESHUAS . . . Anti- Christs, Anti-Popes, Anti-WHATEVER!!! Down, through TIME!!! And, there's been, SUCH CORRUPTION!!!

You know . . . corruption, is corruption, like bologna, is bologna . . . NO MATTER . . . how, you SLICE IT!!! And, there's corruption, EVERYWHERE!!! So Let's, GET with the TREE of LIFE!!! And, I will, speak to you, MORE . . . on this . . . because; the Tree of Life . . . BEARS the FRIUIT . . . of FORGIVENESS . . .

And that is the piece of fruit . . . that the . . . Tree of Life . . . GIVES!!! And, if you, take a piece, of fruit, of FORGIVENESS . . . off the, Tree of Life and if, you just partake, OF forgiveness . . . if we ALL, partake of, the fruit of forgiveness . . . ON A CERTAIN DAY . . . at a CERTAIN TIME . . . Whether, it's a REAL, ACTUAL, piece of FRUIT . . . doesn't need to be!!! I just, NEEDS TO BE . . . a community . . . EARTH COMMUNITY! A ONENESS!!! An INTENTION!!! On the, SAME DAY . . . at the SAME TIME . . . for the, SAME THING!!! To say, ENOUGH is ENOUNG!!!

Eve . . . Well, thanks a lot Eve!!! You know . . . and I'll get into THAT . . . a little bit LATER. But, what EVE, WANTS TO SAY, TO ALL OF US . . . IS . . . I AM YOUR GOD MOTHER!!! FORGIVE ME!!!

She . . . realized . . . even before, she tempted Adam, that it was the WRONG THING TO DO!!! BUT . . . HER EYES, has already been, OPENED!!! And, she kept it, from him. Therefore, she said, "HAVE IT!!! HAVE THE FRUIT!!!" And, he listened, to her . . . and . . . I'll NOT, get into the DYNAMIC . . . right now!!! But, we have to FORGET . . . about ALL THAT . . .

We SHOULD, have STARTED OVER . . . from fresh, "SCRATCH!!!" If you will, after the FLOOD!!! But, WE DID NOT!!! And, BECAUSE of THAT . . . Rabbi Yeshua, had to . . . TAKE the FORM, of a HUMAN . . . and the, SPIRIT ESSENCE . . . the . . . ONE OF . . . the . . . ANGLES, on the TRIANGULATION . . . of the, SUPERIOR GodHead . . . HAD TO COME DOWN!!! To the EARTH!!! And, ACTUALLY, as part of, the GREAT-grand EXPERIMENT . . . Which was . . . FROM the BEGINNING . . . OUR CREATOR is not only . . . a SCIENTIST!!! Ha! Ha! A TRUE SCIENTIST!!! Of, EXPERIMENTATION . . . and LOVE . . . and CARING . . . and CONCERN . . . BUT!!! . . . EVERYTHING is VERY MYSTERIOUS!!! With, our Creator . . . Now, I've not had, any of the ANSWERS . . . or all of, the ANSWERS . . . and I still, DON'T!!!

BUT!!! . . . I have SOME OF THEM!!! And, I merely am here, to ENHANCE . . . the INFORMATION . . . we ALREADY HAVE!!! So . . . that . . . on a particular day, at a particular time, we can ALL . . . DECIDE . . . what WE NEED TO DECIDE!!!

And, THE QUESTION WILL BE . . . "Will you KNOW, will you LOVE and will you SERVE . . . THE CREATOR?!?"

Now, let us NOT . . . be LIKE LUCIFER . . . the angel of light . . . WHO REFUSED!!! And, we SEE . . . his WORKS . . . and EVERYTHING, that's HAPPENED . . . to our HUMAN CONDITION!!!

Because of the, FALL of Adam and Eve . . . and ALL the REST, of the EVIL!!!

Listen, Ladies and Gentlemen, I predicted . . . and people will tell you, it's the God TRUTH!!! THAT . . . as SOON . . . as Karol Wojtyla Would DIE . . . that the, GATES OF HELL . . . would be COMPLETELY OPENED!!! And, I want you to KNOW . . . THEY'RE OPEN!!!

And all the DEMONS . . . have . . . LEFT HELL!!!

The Hell, the GEHENNAH . . . is . . . TORMENT . . . for all, the SOULS, that . . . LIE THERE . . . NOW!!! And all, the souls, that WILL BE, lying THERE . . . for FOREVER!!! At the . . . JUDGEMENT!!!

Which, IS . . . COMING!!! Sure as I'm, sittin' here. I CAN'T WAIT!!! I HOPE, to be ALIVE . . . but, if not, I WILL serve and I WILL know and I WILL love . . . The Creator!!! And, I WILL . . . I acquiesce . . . if He needs to take me, beforehand . . . I'm doing my part . . . right now, TODAY!!!

And if, I were to PASS . . . RIGHT NOW . . . it doesn't matter. Because, SOMEONE . . . will take UP, the Reigns . . . take up the, MANTLE . . . and GO FOREWARD!!!

THIS CAN'T BE STOPPED NOW!!! This MOVEMENT . . . cannot BE . . . stopped!!! And that is ALL . . . I'm gonna say, to you . . . at the moment. I'm going to, bid you . . . adue . . . and have, a bit of dinner, and then . . . I will, come back and I, NEED to, speak to you, a little bit more . . . about, "Em . . . Some of, the MYSTERIES . . . that we DON'T, know . . . and SOME, of what's COMING!!!

And I say this . . . to ALL . . . PEOPLE, OF THE EARTH!!! EVERYWHERE!!! BUT . . . MOST . . . ESPECIALLY . . . to the, CHILDREN OF, Abraham, Isaac, Jacob, MOSES!!!

Because, if you DO NOT . . . PAY ATTENTION . . . to the, God . . . THIS TIME . . . and to, His MESSAGES . . . THIS TIME . . .

Well, it'll BE TOO LATE!!! Huh! And that's, ALL I CAN SAY . . . But, I LOVE YOU ALL . . . and BE NOT, AFRAID!!!

There's NOTHING . . . to FEAR!!! For THOSE, who have . . . even a, MUSTARD SEED . . . of LOVE, IN THEIR HEART!!! For . . . the . . . THEMSELVES!!! Even IF, YOU just, love YOURSELF!!! PERHAPS . . . you CAN love ANOTHER . . . human CORRECTLY . . . But, MORESO . . . LOVE GOD FIRST!!!

And then, SELF and then, NEIGHBOR, other people . . . AS SELF . . . for the LOVE of God!!! BUT . . . we're going, to set, all that aside . . . for now, because . . . I don't, want to get, too preachy, because I'll LOSE people . . . if I get, too preachy!!!

PEOPLE FEAR . . . WHAT THEY, DO . . . NOT UNDERSTAND!!!

It's TIME; to STOP FEARING . . . what you don't, understand!!! I have, the REST . . . of, the PIECES of, the PUZZLE . . . So, let me . . . GIVE THEM, to you . . . and then, you'll DECIDE!!! IF . . . I've been, TELLING you the . . . TRUTH?!? Or . . . I've been lying . . . BUT . . . I tell you, I haven't BEEN LYING!!!

So, please . . . COME WITH ME . . . on the GREATEST ADVENTURE . . . of . . . an EXHISTANCE!!! OF . . . a FOREVER!!!

And, Thank you . . . for LISTENING . . .

Love, Cynthia

Chapter 10

Dinosaurs! Well, Ladies and Gentlemen, it's Cynthia again . . . And hello! I hope that . . . you're doing well, after the last, recordings . . . By, paper or, by audio, that you're . . . might be partaking of. Please excuse me, if I got too preachy . . . or UP on a HIGH Horse!!! Of a Celtic . . . Queen!!!

But, more so . . . you know!!! I don't even, claim to be anything near . . . or, LIKE . . . Joan of Arc. I could NEVER, aspire . . . to be as, HOLY . . . as Saint Joan of Arc . . . or, as TRUE, whatever . . . she WAS!!! And, I've NOT, studied her . . . at great length. At GREAT LENGTH!!! But, listen . . . she did, what she did, for a LOVE . . . of, her COUNTRY . . . for love of, FRANCE . . . I do, what I do, FIRST . . . as she did, and . . . I need to correct it . . . she did it . . . for the LOVE of, GOD and country.

And, I do, what I do . . . for the love of, God and WORLD!!! NOT JUST COUNTRY!!! Not JUST America!!! Because, you know what . . . Ladies and Gentlemen . . . I . . . Cynthia Anne Marie Gunn, the TRUE Queen of Scotland and America . . . and . . . as I've told you, there's a CLIFF . . . in a New England State . . . which is, a the TESTAMENT . . .

And, It can be, CARBON-DATED . . . whatever you want . . . which PROVES . . . that, THE GUNNS were here, approximately . . . a HUNDRED YEARS . . . BEFORE Christopher COLUMBUS!!! But . . . we did not TAKE . . . America, because we did NOT, believe . . . in TAKING ANTHING . . . THAT WASN'T . . . OURS!!!

All we cared for, wanted, needed, or could HOPE, to love and remain . . . would be, little, old, little, bonnie Scotland!!! But . . . we would go out . . . on EXPEDITIONS . . . I'm NOT, going to LIE to you . . . Ha! Ha! As my Grandmother, on my Father's side, Ruth Lewis Gunn, Dad's Mum . . . was a direct descendent, of Cousin . . . Meriwether Lewis, of the Lewis and Clark Expedition . . .

We LOVED expeditions!!! And so, when we went fishing . . . and we went exploring . . . WE FOUND . . . The United States of America!!! About a hundred years . . . BEFORE COLUMBUS!!!

And, you know; it's not ours . . . we wouldn't take it . . . and yes, later on . . . once it was populated, BY THE ENGLISH!!! And 'Em . . . you know, I could get into, that whole THING . . . right now, Listen, all I can tell you, is if . . . Mary Queen of Scots, did NOT have to ACQUIESCE, to the likes of . . . Elizabeth the first . . . HERSELF!!!

The fruit, of the loins, of Henry VIII and Anne Boelyn . . . the French TART!!! I don't care, if she was French . . . or if she was . . . Martian or, Plutonian or, Saturnian whatever Planet or, whatever you want . . . to call it!!! Henry VIII . . . did a HUGE, HUGE, HUGE . . . for the third time . . . INJUSTICE . . . to the people, of ENGLAND!!! Ha! Ha! Ha!

And, you SUFFER it . . . TODAY!!! And, you're living with, a FALSE MONARCH!!! Elizabeth the second!!! OOH! And now, isn't THAT interesting!!! THAT . . . RIGHT NOW!!! In this true AGE . . . of the TRUTH . . . and, the TRUE INFORMATION . . . coming FOREWARD . . . Elizabeth, the second . . . QE2 . . .

You know what . . . ELIZABETH . . . you know . . .

When I was young . . . I'd pick my nose . . . and, I think we all, picked our noses, when we were young . . . and when, we'd pick our nose, HOPEFULLY . . . we DIDN'T . . . EAT IT!!! The boogie . . . now, children have been AFRAID, of boogiemen, boogiewomen, the boogieman . . . what have you!!!

BUT . . . I'll NOT pick MY nose, at nearly . . . 49 years of age . . . and FLICK 'YA . . . as the BOOGIE . . . that YOU . . . TRULY ARE!!!

Because, if it weren't for Henry, BREAKING TIES . . . with the ROCK!!! WELL! WE WOULDN'T . . . be WHERE . . . we ARE TODAY!!! And then, the people, who, who, could no longer

STAND, the King at, THAT TIME!!! Was it George?!? I don't know . . . and I don't, care.

Because, you're ALL FALSE!!! You're AFTER . . . Henry VIII . . . you're all false!!! Because, Henry VIII . . . was EVIL!!! And, did all the WRONG things!!! And I've, done all the wrong . . . things . . . and I've BROKEN . . . all the COMMANDMENTS . . . but, there's a DIFFERENCE!!!

I'm SORRY!!! And, I make AMENDS!!! And, I TRY, EVERY DAY . . . to live, a BETTER LIFE!!! And I, don't . . . TAKE PEOPLE . . . down the, TURLET . . . with me!!! I don't FLUSH . . . ENTIRE COUNTRIES!!! With me . . . AS he . . . flushed, ALL his SUBJECTS . . . because of LUST!!!

Now THAT . . . IS your LINEAGE!!! From QE1, right down . . . to YOU!!! And look at your UNCLE!!! Look what HE did!!! He ACQUIESCED . . . for a WALLIS SIMPSON?!? PLEASE!!!

Listen . . . I'm speaking, DIRECTLY . . . to William and Harry, NOW!!! IF your MOTHER, was HERE . . . DIANA . . . Spencer-Windsor . . . the TRUE, Spencer . . . Mother of, you children . . . a BEAUTIFUL WOMAN!!! Who was MURDERED!!!

And, as I've TOLD you . . . before . . . by HENRI PAUL . . . at the BEHEST . . . and the BEHOOVEMENT, of your father's-mother . . . your so-called grandmother . . . and shame on her, for keepin' you both . . . away from a truly-good-woman, your Mum's, Mum Frances Shand-Kidd!!! Elizabeth, QE2 . . . you did it . . . and . . . I can PROVE IT!!! And, YOU KNOW, THAT I CAN . . . Elizabeth . . . so DON'T, play with me, don't trifle with me . . .

You're going to NEED, to just . . . STEP OFF . . . Elizabeth!!! You're going to need, to step AWAY!!! Because, on a certain DAY . . . at a certain TIME . . . in a certain PLACE . . . I, shall challenge . . . YOU . . . to a DUEL . . . I've challenged, Osama Bin Laden . . . to a duel . . . for THE WORLD!!! Because he . . . DOESN'T GET IT . . . YET!!! He's a PSEUDO-CHRISTIAN . . . a Mohammedite . . . who CLAIMS . . . to UNDERSTAND . . . Rabbi Yeshua and His Mother Mary . . . and yet, they're SO, JEALOUS of the Hebrews . . . from day . . . GOD KNOWS . . . only when?!?

And then . . . the REST of US . . . the Gentiles?!?

Look, if you don't understand, the GEOPOLITICAL RAMIFICATIONS . . . of what I'm saying, to you . . . NEVER MIND . . . the INTERPLANETARY RAMIFICATIONS!!! . . . Of what, I'm saying to you . . . then, Elizabeth . . . you're a STUPID, stupid, woman!!! And I think you ARE, stupid!!! And I KNOW . . . that you're stupid!!!

But . . . Charles . . . the little snipe . . . who DID your BIDDING!!! Just enough time . . . to bring forth . . . William and Harry!!! And then, treated a GOOD, woman . . . a good, PURE-BLOODED . . . English GIRL!!! A COUNTRY VIRGIN!!! A Daughter, of Blue Blood . . . and NOBILITY!!! "HIGHER . . . than YOU!!!" Elizabeth . . . from the, GIT GO!!!

Diana's blood is . . . TRUE BLUER . . . than YOURS!!! And your . . . half-whatever . . . husband!!! Half this, half that, you know . . . YOUR monarchy . . . is so, WATERED-DOWN . . . Cynthia knows!!!

So . . . I challenge you, Elizabeth, to a duel . . . but, our duel . . . won't be, with WEAPONS!!! Our DUEL . . . will be . . . at the place . . . or your choosing . . . on a particular day, at a particular time. I, Cynthia challenge Elizabeth . . . QE2 . . . to a duel!!! And I . . . shall PROVE, to the WORLD . . .

On CNN, I don't care. 'Em . . . British television . . . what did they call it, when I lived, in the bonnie Scotland? BBC?!? International?!? What have you . . . I shall, prove to the world, that I am . . . who I say, I am . . . and I can DO . . . what I say, I CAN do . . . and . . . I KNOW WHAT I KNOW!!! And you . . . miss . . . know NOTHING!!!

YOU are NOTHING!!!

The ONLY thing that, I will say, that you did GOOD, Elizabeth . . . and I will GIVE, you this . . . and I'll give you NOTHING, beyond it!!! Is, you were probably . . . a very good daughter and you, WERE a good princess, during WW2. And that's IT!!! After that, FORGET IT!!! You CANNY rest, on your LAURELS . . . 'Cuz your SINS . . . are RECORDED . . . in the Book of LIFE!!!

YOUR sins . . . YOU need . . . to come CLEAN!!! To the WORLD!!!

And, ADMIT . . . that YOU ORDERED . . . the MURDER . . . of DIANA!!! My . . . Diana!!! And, I'll NOT, tell you HOW . . . I know her and I'll NOT, tell you HOW . . . SHE revealed . . . the SECRET, of your plot, to ME!!! And, I'll NOT tell you how two weeks, before she died, she said . . . "Don't be surprised if I die in a car accident!" Doesn't take a psychic, or a . . . ROCKET SCIENTIST . . . to unravel, YOUR WEB of DECEPTION . . . Queen Elizabeth the second . . . herself!!!

SHAME ON YOU!!! Capital: S-H-A-M-E . . . SHAME ON YOU, Elizabeth!!! Shame, for Shame!!! May GOD forgive YOU, for what you've done. But first . . . you need to CONFESS IT . . . and BE SORRY!!! And make, an AMENDS!!! And do, the RIGHT THING!!! You know darned well, that you're NOT . . . the Monarch!!! Nor is your son, Charles . . . nor are any, of your children, nor Charles' . . . nor all . . . your other children's, children!!! It's Cynthia Anne Marie Gunn of Scotland.

So . . . QUIT, playing GAMES!!! Alright?!? WOMAN UP!!! They say, in America now . . . when men are, acting like . . . pansies . . . they say, man up! So . . . I say, to you . . . Elizabeth, Ha! Ha! Ha! Ha! Ha! Ha! I don't think . . . you have it in you . . . Woman UP!!! And Let's do this dance . . . in front of the God . . .

And we'll see, at the end, of the dance . . . who's STANDIN' and . . . who's NOT!!! Who will be . . . STRUCK DOWN . . . and who won't!!! Who can look . . . DIRECTLY at GOD . . . and say, THIS is the TRUTH!!! And who, CANNOT . . . LOOK . . . directly at God . . . and say, this is the truth.

So, with that . . . I bid everyone, who's reading or hearing this . . . adue . . . and we have so MUCH MORE to COVER . . . but, NEVER . . . LET IT . . . be SAID . . . that the Gunns . . . TOOK, America . . . AWAY, from the Native Americans. NEVER!!!

It was the ENGLISH!!! Who couldn't STAND . . . the PHONY KING!!! At that time . . . who CAME over HERE . . . and DID the DEED!!! And aren't we ALL . . . livin' NOW . . . with the FRUIT, of their EVILS!!! And THEN . . . they're going like, "Okay, wait a minute, we've been ALL OVER the WORLD . . . WHERE are the STRONGEST . . . most INTELLIGENT . . . most ABLE-BODIED, PEOPLE . . . we've EVER met?!?"

So WE can TURN THEM . . . into OUR SLAVES!!! Just like the Pharaoh, did to the . . . Hebrews!!! And you DID IT!!! You English!!! And DAMN YOU, for DOING IT!!! And Cynthia, the Queen of Scots and America . . . DAMNS you to HELL!!! For WHAT you've DONE!!! To the AFRICANS!!! "Cuz, you WENT THERE . . . and I don't need, Alex Haley's ROOTS MOVIE . . . to TELL ME . . . although, it did depict it, QUITE WATERED DOWNLY . . . I must SAY!!!

It was QUITE . . . WASHED UP!!! And quite, CLEANED UP . . . for CONSUMPTION of the PUBLIC!!! I know, through my Father . . . and me lineage . . . EXACTLY . . . how you, WENT into the jungles . . . and how, you RIPPED FAMILIES APART!!! And ruined, TRIBES!!! And took, MEN and WOMEN and CHILDREN . . . and you, "PICKED" . . . the PICKS of the LITTER!!! And how, DARE YOU . . . EVER . . . COMPARE another HUMAN BEING . . .

I don't care if they have a green face, a pink arm, an orange one leg . . . a green torso, I don't care!!! YOU'RE so EVIL!!! The children, that came . . . from Anne Boleyn and Henry . . . WERE SO EVIL!!! That, THEY . . . once they, through the Spanish . . . who they . . . THREW Catherine OUT!!! For Anne Boleyn . . . etc., etc., etc.,

Then they USED, the Spanish . . . Isabella and Ferdinand . . . and used THEIR MONEY?!? To entice, an ITALIAN!!! Christopher COLUMBUS!!! To go FIND . . . this PLACE . . . that the SCOTS . . . had ALREADY FOUND!!! And TAKE IT!!!

Look, if you don't think, I know WHAT HAPPENED . . . and WHO DID what to WHOM!!! This is how, EVIL . . . you ARE!!! YOU don't KNOW NOTHIN'!!!

And I'm just . . . about, to EXPOSE YOU ALL . . . for the CHARLETONS and the LIARS . . . and the EVILDOERS . . . that you ARE!!! OKAY?!? Don't . . . just sit there . . . and say . . . the Pharaoh, treated the Hebrews . . . as slaves!!!

ENGLISH . . . the descendents, of Henry and Anne Boleyn . . . DOWN to QE2 herself!!! Someone, should go over there, RIGHT NOW and GIVE, that woman . . . a GOOD TALKIN" TO!!! And it . . . will be, myself.

But she's not the true Monarch, she's the fruit of MORE EVIL!!! And, watered down, watered down, watered down, watered down . . . lineage!!!

Now, my lineage . . . is PURE!!! Because . . . I'm Scottish, Irish, Cherokee and Polish . . . I'm of Polish, descent . . . half polish . . . and that's the part . . . that justifies me . . . and one, of the greatest, ROCKS of our time. Karol Wojtyla

But, putting that aside . . . right now . . . LOOKIT' . . . I don't want, ANYBODY out there, ANYBODY . . . I don't care . . . how old you are, how young you are. I don't care . . . what color you are, what your health is like, where you live, how much money you have, who you think you know, who you think knows you, who you think you love, who you think . . . DON'T THINK, of ANY of THOSE PEOPLE!!!

You just think about Cynthia!!! And I'm, HERE FOR YOU!!! And I LOVE YOU!!! And I, will do EVERYTHING . . . in my power . . . 'til I draw my LAST BREATH!!! To ASPIRE . . . to the likes . . . of Joan of Arc!!! Who loved GOD and COUNTRY!!! And Cynthia's God, is the God Creator . . . and Rabbi Yeshua . . . Jesus of Nazareth . . . and the HOLY GHOST . . . the HOLY SPIRIT!!!

Now, don't ANYONE . . . say ANYTHING . . . AGAINST the Holy Spirit . . . or the Holy Ghost . . . "Cuz for then . . . you're SURE . . . DAMNED . . . to HELL . . . from MOMENT ONE!!! From EVEN . . . if you THINK it!!! If you think, ONE BAD THING . . . about the, HOLY SPIRIT . . . who's speaking . . . even THROUGH me . . . right now!!! "Cuz I'm JUSTIFIED, by FAITH . . . and NOT . . . by SIGHT!!!

Because, I've been BAPTIZED . . . and CONFIRMED!!! And I'm a SOLDIER!!! And I PUT the ARMOR ON!!! And the, Pope Benedict XVI, knows EXACTLY . . . what I'm saying!!!

I can say all these things . . . with SURETY!!! Even though, I've broke . . . ONE COMMANDMENT, TWO, THREE . . . I've broken them ALL!!! And I'm, FORGIVEN!!! And I, HOPE . . . I don't break them again!!!

But . . . you know what?!? Just GET WITH LOVE!!! OKAY?!? Let's ALL . . . get with . . . the TREE, of the FRUIT, of LIFE!!! And . . . on that tree . . . is FORGIVENESS!!!

Now, Elizabeth . . . if you come CLEAN . . . the God will say . . . ALL IS FORGIVEN!!! Not Cynthia. But . . . YOU need to, COME CLEAN!!! Elizabeth . . . QE2 . . . you need to come clean . . . because . . . if you EVER CARED . . . for ANYONE . . . you need to do it.

I LOVE YOU ALL!!! Thank you for listening . . . AUT PAX AUT BELLUM . . . QE2 . . . Cynthia Queen of Scots and America

Chapter 11

Hello Again! This is Chapter 11 . . . and please excuse me, for giving such a strong REBUKE . . . to Queen Elizabeth the second . . . herself . . . QE2. But, you know . . . there's a PROVERB . . . of King David, that says . . . BETTER and open REBUKE . . . than a LOVE, that lies HIDDEN!!! Now, it was either written by David, or by his son . . . Solomon. I'm not sure, but . . . it's in there.

So Elizabeth, don't think for a moment . . . that Cynthia doesn't, love and respect you, for the good, that you've done! But, you really need to, come clean . . . and you really need, to acquiesce NOW . . . to Cynthia!!!

Because, Mary Queen of Scots . . . acquiesced, at the RIGHT time, for the RIGHT reason . . . to QE1. So now, QE2 . . . needs to ACQUIESCE . . . at the right TIME, for the right REASON . . . to Cynthia Queen of Scots and America!!!

I'll NOT take, what's MINE . . . by FORCE!!!

It will, either be restored to me, FULLY . . . by the GOD . . . or it won't!!! But . . . that's not the most pertinent issue . . . whether, or not, I'm ever restored, as Monarch . . . of the four Celtic provinces!!! Being, Scotland, Ireland, Wales and England. That's NOT important.

I know who I am. I'm not insecure. And it, doesn't bother me. I'm moreso, sister . . . QE2 . . . because you do, have SOME Celtic blood in your veins . . . no much . . . no much . . . but 'Em, just . . . for the Celtic blood . . . you DO have, coursing in your veins . . . I give you love and respect, after I've given you, 'Em . . . the truthful . . . 'Em . . . rebuke, that you needed and I HOPE . . . you come clean . . . because your SINS, will BEFALL . . . WELL, look at Charles ALREADY!!!

And look, at your other kids . . . already . . . look at ALL, the SINS of the parents . . . BECOME the sins, of the children . . . LOOK, at how your POSTERITY is PAYING!!! All the way DOWN, from Henry and Anne Boleyn!!! Well let's, set ALL that aside . . . and EVEN, the great husband, of yours . . . and the . . . the . . . so-called, uncle . . . Mountbatten?!? Whatever?!?

That Charles has been, missing . . . and grievin' for, for so long . . . I can get with that, Charles . . . but you know what . . . there's such a thing, as a CURSE!!! And . . . do you REALLY want, to continue . . . to live . . . YOUR LIVES . . . under a CURSED LIFE?!? I don't! And I hope, you'll WISE UP, WISE UP, WISE UP . . . Elizabeth!!! And her, BROOD, of so-called . . . VIPERS!!!

But, I'll cut you a BREAK . . . 'cuz I LOVE YA'. AND . . . I'm your TRUE MONARCH!

But, listen. There's something, I want to talk . . . to people about, on a LIGHTER note . . . 'Em . . .

OUR GOD . . . the Creator . . . is an AWESOME God!!! You know?!? There are so many, MYSTERIES . . . that, AHAH . . . until NOW, 'Em . . . not because, I say so . . . but because, I have . . . VERY DISTINCT . . . and IMPORTANT, parts of the INFORMATION . . . handed down, through me lineage . . . by my Father and by, my STUDIES . . . I may NOT, have a DEGREE . . . I may not have a, bachelors, a masters, a doctorate, a what have you . . . for, there's an old saying . . . my Father subscribed to . . . EVEN though, he was HIGHLY degreed . . . and highly EDUCATED, to work with . . . Admiral Rickover and the, NUCLEAR NAVY and having, BUILT THREE MILE ISLAND!!! My Father was, Senior Project Engineer, Site Project Manager . . . HANDPICKED, by Rickover . . . and the ATOMIC ENERGY COMMISSION, but . . . we're setting THAT aside . . . RIGHT NOW!!!

And I'm, just going to talk to you, now . . . about some FUN FACTS! 'Em . . . Ladies and Gentlemen, Boys and Girls, of the world . . . have you ever heard . . . of SUCH a THING . . . as the LOCH . . . LOCH which means lake, in Scottish . . . LOCH NESS, Lake NESS? In bonnie old, wee old, bonnie Scotland. In Loch Ness, Heh! There truly IS . . . a UNIT . . . which is a pre-historic, unit. Now, shall I Tell ya' what it is . . . and WHY it's THERE . . . and how, it sustains it's LIFE . . . and how, it's the ONLY DINOSAUR . . . livin' . . . RIGHT NOW!!! But, because of . . . that ONE, lowly little Nessy . . . and Nessy's offspring . . . down through time . . . that ALL other dinosaurs, WAIT . . . in the COLDEST . . . DEEPEST recesses . . . of the EARTH!!! And WILL, THAW OUT!!! And will COME BACK . . . to LIFE!!!

It's NOT, just . . . about, HOLLYWOOD!!! Anymore. You know, I love Hollywood . . . it's a like a, LOVE/HATE relationship . . . I have going, with Hollywood. 'Em . . . SIMPLY, because they've SOLD US . . . so many bills of goods!!!

I ask you . . . I'm not gonna mention, names . . . but, just LOOK at some, of the PEOPLE . . . on the NEWS at night!!! Let's just look at the, CELEBRITY NEWS!!! 'Em . . . if so-called actress, XYZ . . . married to, actor XYZ . . . and having, two . . . a child . . . on the way, a . . . TWINS and then a BABY BEFORE . . . named Silo??? Some kind of, a place that keeps grain??? I don't know!!!

Would you EVER . . . have CARED . . . about THAT woman . . . and her MAN . . . whom she's, NOT MARRIED TO!!! Whom she STOLE, from his Greek . . . little Greek wife, Jennifer . . . and Jennifer, was a FRIEND!!! She was ONE, of the friends!!!

So, you know . . . we just have to get, with that whole SCENE!!! Now EVERYBODY . . . needs to CUT THE BOLOGNA!!! CUT the MULLARKY!!! STOP LOOKING UP to . . . OTHER HUMANS . . . as being, ABOVE 'ya!!! Because, they're NOT!!!

And that's ALL . . . my good friend . . . John LENNON . . . was trying to say!!! When, the parents, of the United States of America . . . the BIBLE BELT parents, said . . . BRING ALL your BEATLES RECORDS, in and we're gonna BURN them . . . in EFFAGY and we're, gonna destroy it!!! WHY?!?

Because, John Lennon . . . a VERY GOOD, TRIED and TRUE . . . ENGLISHMAN!!! And Paul McCartney . . . ANOTHER, very good, tried and true . . . Englishman!!! And George Harrison . . . tried and true, good Englishman!!! And Ringo Starr . . . Richard Starkey . . . another tried and true, good Englishman!!!

'Cuz THOSE Englishmen, set forth . . . on . . . set sail on . . . a sea of MUSIC and WENT . . . and DID, the whole . . . BERLIN SCENE!!!

You people, don't EVEN know . . . about the Berlin Scene. But, we'll set that aside, for now.

In know what went on THERE!!! Sir, Paul McCartney . . . NOW . . . isn't it, HYPOCRITICAL . . . HUH!!! You DO, deserve it SIR Paul McCartney . . . because of the good, that you and John and Ringo and George . . . did DO!!! But, isn't QE2 . . . herself . . . a HYPOCRITE!!!

"Cuz, they could have, CARED LESS . . . about you . . . until it was, CHIC . . . to care MORE, about you!!! WHY??? Because, they were in TROUBLE!!! House of Windsor . . . was in trouble, because of all the DIVORCES . . . of her children!!! And all, the SCANDALS!!! Of what Charles, was DOING . . . with, Camilla!!! And oy!!!

JESUS!!! Oh my GOD!!! In HEAVEN!!!

And that's, NOT BLASPHEMY!!! Jesus God in Heaven . . . are YOU taking NOTES??? PLEASE!!! Rabbi Yeshua!!! Please!!! But, anyway . . . people wanted to KILL, my good English buddy . . . John Lennon . . . and the, LIKES of John Lennon . . . AND they FINALLY, did KILL HIM!!! Ladies and Gentlemen. BUT, I'll touch on that . . . LATER!!!

Alright?!? They wanted to KILL HIM!!! They were so, TIcKED OFF!!! And, T-P-O'D . . . when he said, WOW I can't BELIEVE THIS!!! We're MORE POPULAR . . . than JESUS CHRIST!!!

He didn't SAY it . . . because he THOUGHT it!!! He said it, because . . . he OBSERVED it!!! And, he thought . . . it was ABSURD!!! And, he thought . . . it was INSANITY!!! Because, he was . . . a GOOD person!

And Cynthia . . . and Julian . . . NEVER think . . . he didn't LOVE YOU!!! But, when YOKO came along . . . and all, she had SUFFERED . . . and THEY met, on a whole . . . DIFFERENT WAVELENGTH!!! The ARTISTIC wavelength!!! So, you know what . . . GET . . . CUT, Yoko Ono and HER son . . . SEAN LENNON . . . A BREAK!!!

FORGIVE!!! Forgive!!! Forgive!!! Take the Tree, of the fruit of LIFE!!! Take a PIECE, off of . . . that tree!!! I want to SEE . . . Cynthia Lennon and Julian Lennon . . . and Yoko Ono and Sean Lennon. I want to SEE . . . if you can, MAN UP and WOMAN UP!!!

And show, QE2 . . . Queen Elizabeth the second, herself . . . that she needs to, WOMAN UP!!! And, her SON . . . needs to MAN UP!!! And take the tree, off the fruit of Life!!! WHICH is . . . FORGIVENESS!!!

Because, you know what . . . isn't . . . in the final ANALYSIS . . . isn't it NICE . . . to have, EXTRA PIECES . . . of JOHN . . . Lennon?!? A true Godly, man . . . even though, he was HUMAN!!! And, he had his WEAKNESSES!!! I told you . . . I've broken one commandment . . . I've broke tow or three, I've broken them all.

If you, whoever you are . . . across the world . . . I don't care, what persuasion, or faith, or color, or ethnicity, or sexual . . . I don't care!!! I don't care, if you're . . . lesbian, gay, bestial . . . I don't care!!! You're still a HUMAN!!! And, you need . . . to get, on the same page . . . and we ALL, need to pick, the fruit, off the Tree of life!!! And, THAT fruit . . . is the fruit . . . of forgiveness.

And, IF you DON'T . . . I'm just, going to TELL YOU . . . that, although they FAKED, a PICTURE of NESSY . . . of Loch Ness . . . Now, I'm gonna get . . . CELTIC AGAIN, on you!!! Cynthia Anne Marie Gunn Queen of Scots and America . . . I'll tell 'ya . . .

That . . . the God . . . HIMSELF . . . has left us, at LEAST . . . one Dinosaur!!! And, it's a Plesiosaurus . . . Akh Eye!!! Akh Eye!!! It's one of, the Plesiosaurus' who . . . SWIMS the DEEP and COLD waters . . . of Loch Ness!!! But, it's not JUST that . . . Ladies and Gentlemen . . . because, there's a CREVASS . . . there's a deep, DARK, cold, crevass . . . where the LAVA, of the EARTH . . . does NOT TOUCH!!! Where ALL, of Nessy's LIKE . . . and all the DRAGONS . . . of the Earth, that were here . . . BEFORE it . . . all the GIANTS!!! Of the Earth . . . as mentioned, in the Old Testament . . . they, were just called . . . GIANTS!!! And it wasn't, just GOLIATH!!! There were OTHER giants!!! And that, is the MYSTERY!!! Those are the things, that the . . . Hollywood!!!

The GREAT children, of Abraham, Isaac, Jacob, ALL of those . . . beautiful Hebrew people, who . . . CAME to THIS country . . . AFTER the ENGLISH!!! And went, WEST . . . young man, young woman, young this . . . and ESTABLISHED HOLLYWOOD!!! Huh! They DID it, on the FURTHEST . . . PLOT of LAND!!!

AWAY, from the King, of England . . . and the furthest, what they THOUGHT . . . plot of land, AWAY from the, ARABS!!! Then they, ESTABLISHED all, of Hollywood . . . and then, they BEGAN . . . to GIVE US . . . BITS and PIECES!!! Little TINY pieces!!! Of the PUZZLE!!! Down . . . through time!!!

And in, the nineteen thirties, forties, whatever . . . DIDN'T they make something . . . called BUCK ROGERS . . . in the 21st Century?!? And didn't, Buck Rogers . . . go LIKE, in a SPACESHIP . . . to the MOON . . . and things, like THAT?!? Listen, Ladies and Gentlemen . . . the Hebrews, that came, to this country, and established, Hollywood . . . to TRY and CONTROL our . . . HEARTS, MINDS, SOULS, WILLS and DESTINIES!!!

By, CREATING WHAT?!? STARS!!! Are they NUTS!!! Are you CRAZY?!?

The God, of ABRAHAM SAID . . . that YOU descendents . . . you BLESSED Hebrews . . . would be, MORE NUMEROUS!!! Than the stars, in the SKY!!!

And what, did YOU DO?!? For MONEY!!! For MACHAYENNA!!! For MONEY!!! You didn't CARE, that God gave you a PIECE of LAND . . . over THERE!!! A Promised Land.

YOU, have FLOWN . . . in the FACE of GOD . . . and HIS Promised Land . . . for FAR too LONG!!! And I'll, NOT quote . . . Steely Dan . . . BUT . . . they've PREDICTED . . . HOW you'll FALL OFF . . . and DRIFT OFF . . . into the SEA!!!

San Andréa's Fault . . . I don't care!!! And I'll, NOT be BUYING . . . property, NEXT TO . . . the San Andréa's Fault . . . because I don't WANT or NEED . . . OCEAN PROPERTY . . . because, I am Cynthia of Scotland and America!!!

Now, that having been said . . . I could care less, about . . . MONEY. I could care less, about LAND. I could care less, about MONARCHYS, TITLES, AGENDAS . . . I don't care! "Cuz I, SERVE the Creator . . . and The Gunns, serve the Creator! And, as I told you . . . my Father's Father . . .

SAW THE DISC at ROSWELL!!! And saw, WHAT was LEFT from IT!!!

And then, DIED . . . MYSTERIOUSLY!!! We'll set that, aside . . . and then, OOH!!! In 1947, when . . . Admiral Hyman G.

Rickover, PUT my Father . . . William Thomas Phillip Gunn . . . ON BOARD!!! For the NUCLEAR REACTOR!!! The FIRST ONE!!!

FOR the . . . PEACE?!? For the so-called . . . they KNEW, that the RUSSIANS, were ALREADY . . . starting, the COLD WAR?!? So they go . . . OOPS!!! WE gotta' HURRY UP . . . and BUILD a REACTOR . . . WE can USE, to like do what, we . . . WHATEVER!!! WHATEVER!!!

There was, a HUGH SCIENTIST . . . by the name of, GUNN . . . who already had, a FOOTHOLD . . . with OPPENHEIMER, RICKOVER and the BOYS!!! And, when MY FATHER . . . came along . . . they were WAITING!!! For HIM to come along!!!

Now, this is all predestined, by GOD! And I can't, speak to it anymore . . . right now. Because, it's too INTENSE and it . . . BRINGS UP, too MANY MEMORIES!!!

But . . . PLEASE!!! Ladies and Gentlemen . . . Boys and Girls, of the world . . .

DON'T BELIEVE . . . the bill of goods, that the ENGLISH . . . have SOLD YOU!!! DONE!!!

DON'T BELIEVE . . . the bill of goods, that the HOLLYWOOD . . . has SOLD YOU!!! DONE!!!

And, DON'T BELIEVE . . . for a cotton pickin' moment, the bill of goods, that the CHOSEN PEOPLE . . . of GOD . . . the descendents of, Abraham . . . as numerous as, supposedly . . . the STARS IN THE SKY . . . ACCORDING to GOD . . . WHO they FLY, in His FACE!!!

By making . . . STARS?!? Out of . . . a HUMAN?!? In a . . . WHAT?!?

HOLLYWOOD?!? Give me a BREAK!!! GIVE me a break!!!

In HEAVEN . . . there are different, streets. And in Heaven, there's a street, of GOLD!!! And ANYONE . . . who is WORTHY!!! Their name, is CARVED . . . on a street of gold . . . in Heaven.

Now, FORGET the FALSE STREETS . . . of HOLLYWOOD!!! With their, OH . . . walk of FAME . . . and FOOTPRINTS and HANDPRINTS!!!

FORGET . . . ALL . . . THAT!!!

Unless or UNTIL, you want . . . to SEE EVERYTHING . . . except for the Hoover Dam, the Pyramids and the . . . Great Wall, STILL STANDING!!! Let's . . . you only want . . . and MAYBE, Mount Rushmore!!! As an indication, that we were . . . EVEN HERE!!!

UNLESS or until, you UNDERSTAND . . . that I'm about to, TELL YOU . . . in the next chapter . . . and chapters, and then . . . in the third book, which will come . . . very SOON and RAPID succession . . .

Unless or until, you understand . . . this is a, FIRM REBUKE!!! Not FROM Cynthia . . . but, it's GIVEN . . . by the Creator . . . GOD!!! And, I'll be speaking on HIM . . . and the second POINT, of the TRIUNE GODHEAD . . . the Rabbi Yeshua, Jesus of Nazareth . . . And DON'T, think its NOT SO!!! Sons and Daughters, of ABRAHAM!!! Because you've got . . . a RUDE AWAKENING!!! And may GOD, have MERCY on . . . your SOULS!!! If you DON'T BELIEVE it . . . THIS TIME!!!

And then, of course . . . MAY NO ONE!!! EVER!!! BLASPHEME!!! Or NOT, think . . . that Rabbi Yeshua, Jesus of Nazareth . . . DID give US . . . HIS SPIRIT!!!

The third, POINT . . . of LIGHT!!! ON the Triune, GODHEAD!!! The SUSPREME . . . LIGHT!!!

Now, as I TOLD you . . . in the, FIRST book . . . I got HALF-WAY, to the LIGHT!!! I don't need, an NDE . . . I don't need, ANYTHING . . . to TELL me . . . what I already know.

I merely want . . . to share it with YOU!!!

And, I get up . . . so much . . . on a, a, a, a, PILLAR of PROCLAMATION!!! Because, TRUST ME . . . if I could go, into OUTER SPACE . . . and stand there . . . with a, HUGE MEGAPHONE . . . and say, PLEASE, LISTEN TO ME . . . I KNOW, WHAT I'M TALKING ABOUT . . . I CARE . . . I KNOW WHERE, I THINK THE GOD . . . HAS DESIGNED, A PLACE . . . FOR ME, TO BE . . . WHERE HE GOES . . . I, ALSO FOLLOW!!!

Do not think . . . for a MOMENT . . . that . . . DO YOU . . . how many, of you know . . . a PERSON . . . OVER a hundred, or a hundred and five or ten!!! EVERYONE . . . who, came BEFORE

US . . . is DEAD!!! And, they've all been JUDGED!!! Along the WAY!!!

And, the FINAL JUDGEMENT . . . will COME to us ALL . . . FOREVER and EVER and EVER!!! Now, unless or until . . . YOU know SOMEBODY . . . that's a hundred and fifty, or OLDER!!! You Don't know NOTHIN'!!!

I don't care, if you're Hebrews, Christians, Martians . . . I DON'T CARE!!! Plutonians, Saturnians . . . I DON'T CARE!!!

Unless or until . . . you, UNDERSTAND that . . . the TRUTH is the TRUTH . . . like bologna is bologna . . . NO MATTER . . . HOW YOU, SLICE IT!!!

Well, I'll tell you, in the NEXT chapter . . . what you need to BRACE YOURSELF for . . . that, which is . . . DANGEROUS and BAD!!! Which is . . . COMING!!! But . . . I am not AFRAID!!! And I, will HELP you to understand . . . how NOT to be, AFRAID!!! But . . . you have to, FOLLOW . . . the Creators MESSAGES, to the LETTER . . . of the LAW!!! NOT, Cynthia's law.

But . . . He's HAD ENOUGH!!! Don't you SEE it?!? Across the world . . .

. . . YOU FEEL it . . . NOW, because . . . you KNOW, He's JUST about READY . . . to SEPARATE, the WEEDS . . . from the WHEAT!!! So, I would LIKE . . . to be AMONG the WHEAT! NOT the WEEDS!!! SO, I'm working, TOWARD . . . that GOAL! Of, LOVING the Creator . . . and becoming, wheat . . . for His GOOD HARVEST! NOT weeds . . . that he will cut, DOWN . . . and THROW, into the UNQUENCHABLE FIRE of GEAHENNAH . . . to be BURNED!!!

And, that's ALL I can say to you. So, please . . . don't be AFRAID, again!!! Just listen to me. I have, QUITE a BIT . . . of the information!!! Which will, HELP us . . . in the COMING, days, weeks, months and . . . FEW YEARS, that are LEFT!!!

And, I DON'T, know the . . . DAY or the HOUR!!! But, I KNOW!!! That WE don't, have MUCH TIME . . . YET!!! Because, the DOOMSDAY CLOCK . . . is SET . . . thirty seconds to MIDNIGHT!!!

And that's from, the CREATOR Himself!!! Through Rabbi Yeshua . . . and trickling down . . . through, the Holy Spirit . . . so DON'T blaspheme, ANY of the TRIUNE GODHEAD!!!

I'm trying to HELP you! AS He HAS . . . from the BEGINNING!!! So, Let's JUST . . . show EACH other . . . LOVE!!! And, FORGIVENESS!!!

And, CONCERN!!! And, CARE . . . and, and, and, and . . . LET US, just LOVE one ANOTHER . . . as God has LOVED US . . . For the LOVE of GOD!!!

And, that's all I can say. And, I love you. And I bid you . . . adue. And don't be, FRIGHTENED!!! There's NOTHIN' to be frightened of . . . FEAR LUCIFER!!! FEAR SATAN!!! Don't fear anything else.

I Love You, Cynthia

Chapter 12

I would like to speak, to you now . . . regarding some of the things, that we've all, either experienced personally . . . or read about, in historical reference . . . and some, or my own . . . 'Em . . . revelations and ideas, about . . . some of the things, that caused PROBLEMS . . . for US, in the 20th century.

As you know, there was the, first WORLD WAR!!! And, it was BRUTAL!!! And, it was HOPED, that there would . . . NEVER BE, ANOTHER!!! But . . . that was NOT, to be . . . because, there were POWERS, such as the German . . . Third Reich, and the Japanese, Emperor . . . who wanted, to TAKE OVER . . . different PARTS of the WORLD!!! Other than, their OWN countries . . . and of course, Ah . . . you had, the Italian . . . Mussolini, coming IN ON . . . the coattails, with Hitler . . . and Ah . . . the Emperor of Japan!!!

Well, Ladies and Gentlemen, I would like to share, a TIDBIT . . . of information with you . . . that I think is, HIGHLY . . . HIGHLY . . . HIGHLY, to BLAME . . . for a LOT, of the . . . DOWNWARD SPIRAL, that society took . . . AFTER BOTH, of those World Wars!!! World War 1 and World War 2.

Most especially, with the onslaught . . . of GREATER, TECHNOLOGIES . . . for World War 2!!! And foreward . . . to time, 'til I'm speaking, to you NOW . . . and this is, June the 24th, of 2008. And, this is chapter 12 . . . of book 2. And the title, of this book is: I AM YOUR GOD MOTHER FORGIVE ME The Secret of the Secret . . . which, I will speak more, to you about, toward the LAST chapter . . . of the book. I will divulge, what I CAN, DIVULGE . . . regarding, THAT SECRET . . . when I get, to the last chapter. So, PLEASE . . . stick with me!

I want to THANK YOU, so much, for sticking with me and my Celtic, brogue . . . which comes and goes, from time to time . . . and 'Em . . . we're going to discuss, Ladies and Gentlemen, you know . . . when World War 2, came about . . . ESPECIALLY, for the Americans . . . There was, a HUGE . . . EFFORT . . . a huge WAR effort . . . here on the United States Home front!!!

And, something . . . VERY DREADFUL, HAPPENED!!! To the HOMES . . . the Men, the WOMEN . . . HUSBANDS, WIVES, etc., what have you. This is, MY OWN THEORY!!! But . . . it's backed up, in FACT . . . and I do feel, that the Creator God . . . I choose to call Him, God and I've OUTLINED . . . ALL the OTHER, NAMES . . . that other people choose, to CALL the, SUPREME/CREATOR/BEING . . . the Triune Godhead . . .

We don't need, to get into that, again . . . but . . .

What happened then, Ladies and Gentlemen . . . WAS, men of every AGE and DESCRIPTION . . . and RACE . . . and CREED . . . and ETHNICITY . . . etc., PERSUASION . . . were SENT, to World War 2!!! Drafted, joined, what have you!!!

So that, left the Home front . . . of the United States, with MANY HOMES . . . where the men, were AWAY . . . in the war effort!!! So, what needed to be DONE . . . when the men LEFT their JOBS . . . and we needed, factories . . . to crank out things . . . the WEAPONS, of WAR!!! The Machinery of WAR . . . and just, the OVERALL . . . SUPPORT, in the . . . industrialized COUNTRY, of America . . . DURING, this World War 2 . . . TIME!!!

What happened??? Well, MANY of, the WOMEN . . . had to LEAVE the NEST . . . so-to say, they had to leave, the HOME!!! And, go OUT . . . and TAKE the JOBS . . . that the MEN . . . who went AWAY to WAR, were DOING!!! So, women . . . became Rosie the Riveter, Wendy the Welder, what have you!!!

Women went into, the FACTORIES . . . and ASSUMED the POSITIONS and the, JOBS . . . of the MEN!!! And so, there was a HUGE SHIFT . . . at that TIME . . . in the ROLES, or men and women . . . and a man, WENT away . . . and LEARNED, oh . . . I don't know . . . how MANY . . . a HUNDRED?!? . . . different WAYS . . . to KILL SOMEONE . . . with a GUN, with a KNIFE, whatever . . .

How to SURVIVE . . . how to KILL, hand to hand COMBAT . . . just the, CULTURE of DEATH!!! . . . that CAME . . . from the World Wars!!! And, I'm only speaking, right now . . . of World War 2!!!

So, the men . . . WENT AWAY . . . and became, TRAINED KILLERS!!! DESENSITIZED!!! To, the FACT . . . of TAKING another,

HUMAN LIFE!!! For God and Country!!! It was DEEMED NECESSARY!!!

Then, you had MANY . . . of the women, who LEFT the HOMES . . . left the NURTURING ENVIRONMENT . . . of the HOME!!! And had, to go do . . . those MANLY TASKS . . . in the factories!!! WELL!!! So now, the women . . . were STARTING, to . . . Ah . . . WEAR THE PANTS . . . so-to-say!!! They were, TAKING . . . the ROLE of . . . men AND women . . . in the HOUSE!!!

In the HOUSEHOLD!!! When the men, were OFF . . . at WAR and KILLING!!! And, the women . . . were WORKING!!! To TAKE CARE of the Home front . . . in the WAR effort . . . AND the CHILDREN!!! So, you see, Ladies and Gentlemen . . . THAT was a HUGE, DESPICABLE, WAR!!! That did, SO MUCH more . . . DAMAGE . . . than God FORBID!!!

Hiroshima!!! Nagasaki!!! Blew the LIVIN' daylights . . . out of MOST . . . of EUROPE!!! Turned . . . LOTS of PLACES, in Europe . . . to RUBBLE!!! Had to be, REBUILT . . . and JAPAN!!! But, the LIVES . . . of the American PEOPLE . . . I'm ONLY speaking, of the American people . . . right NOW!!! I DO HAVE a HEART . . . for ALL, the others . . . ACROSS the world . . . that SUFFERED!!!

The HOLOCAUST VICTIMS!!! The VICTIMS of the NUCLEAR BOMBS . . . in Japan!!! The VICTIMS of, 'Em . . . the regular AIR, sorties and COMBAT . . . and hand to hand FIGHTING . . . and SNIPER fighting in EUROPE!!!

Now, WE were . . . SO FORTUNATE . . . that the, war . . . was NOT WAGED, HERE on this SOIL . . .

BUT . . . it's NOT gonna be LONG . . . Ladies and Gentlemen, before . . . we're GOING to SEE, MORE . . . ATTACKS . . .

HERE in the United States of America!!! 9.11.01 was JUST, the BEGINNING!!! Ah . . . they've thwarted a COUPLE of OTHER, times . . . and I'm SURE, they're thwarting them . . . DAY by DAY!!!

But . . . It's GOING TO, happen AGAIN . . . and I, can't speak to that right now. Just KNOW . . . and BRACE YOURSELF, for that, which is . . . DANGEROUS . . . and COMING . . . and VERY SOON, toward the end, of this book . . . you'll find out, EXACTLY . . . who's BAD!!! And, who's CAUSING ALL THIS!!! But, setting all that aside . . . So, the women . . . became AS men, working!!! While . . . the men were AT the war!!! LEARNING . . . how to KILL, fifty ways . . . to Sunday!!! Then, the men come . . . HOME from the war, AH!!! Ahah!! Ahah!!

Now, they're TOTALLY CHANGED . . . FOREVER!!! Post Traumatic Stress Disorders . . . Separation Disorders . . . of, not having BEEN with the FAMILY!!! Disorders, of having to KILL . . . other HUMANS!!! Across the GLOBE!!! And, just an OVERALL . . . sense of DESENSATIZATION!!! That TOOK PLACE . . . IN those men . . . and so, the culture, of DEATH . . . got its TRUE FOOTHOLD, beginning in the World War 2!!! HUGELY!!!

Another arm, on that HORRIBLE . . . tentacleized, octopus . . . of a culture of DEATH . . . that had begun, during the World War 2 . . . was that the women . . . you know, were DOING, jobs OF men!!! And so, they started wearing pants . . . in their family . . . and they started to, THINK for THEMSELVES . . . and make their, OWN MONEY . . . and want to, be LIKE men!!!

And, that's all cool . . . that's all well and good, but . . . they asked FOR and DEMANDED, something ELSE . . . over the next, say ten to fifteen years!!! They demanded . . . that they BE in CONTROL . . . of their REPRODUCTION!!!

Of, PROCREATION!!! Of, CHILDREN!!! A LOT of them, had a TASTE . . . of a MANS WORLD . . . and didn't, WANT to JUST be . . . an . . . AT HOME . . . and be a, MUMMY and have, HUGE FAMILIES!!! What have you!!!

So, you had 2 DIAMETRICALLY OPPOSED . . . FORCES!!! You had men . . . that were, HUNTERS and GATHERERS . . . but, came BACK so DESENSATIZED, to the TRUE ESSENCE, of a hunter gatherer!!! It was more like, a hunter KILLER!!! And the, you had the women . . . who were . . . supposed to be, NATURE and NURTURE . . . doing things, that were OUT . . . of THEIR, NATURE!!!

Working in the man's world!!! And, I'm not AGAINST . . . womens liberation and I'm not . . . FOR IT!!! I merely, SEE the FOREST . . . for the TREES!!! I see the ERROR, that came AFTERWARDS!!!

And so, there was always . . . ABORTION!!! Let's NOT say, that there WASN'T!!! Because, there WAS!!! But, the women, wanted more control . . . OVER their BODIES . . . and over their LIVES . . . and over their WALLETS . . . and over their FAMILIES . . . and DECIDE, whether or NOT . . . to CONTINUE, to STAY married . . . to THESE men!!!

The FIRST husband . . . the SECOND!!! What have you!!! You know, Hollywood . . . ONCE AGAIN!!! You know, the people . . . OUT THERE!!! Who EVERYBODY, was IMITATING . . . and EMULATING!!! Because . . . the Hollywood, SOLD US . . . a FALSE . . . BILL of GOODS!!!

And God love, a certain . . . BEAUTIFUL . . . lavender eyed ACTRESS . . . that was born, in the year . . . 1932!!! Same year, as my Mother . . . God rest HER soul!!! Little English girl . . . VERY POPULAR . . . very FAMOUS woman . . . I'm NOT even, going to NAME her . . . it's not NECESSARY!!!

BUT . . . she went down a ROAD, of seven or eight, HUSBANDS! And, you know . . . that was CHIC!!! For HOLLYWOOD!!! And, now . . . the REST of SOCIETY, ONCE AGAIN . . . desensitized, by World War 2 . . . by the PILL . . . by ROE v. WADE!!! And, the ABORTION!!!

'Em, is just emulating . . . all of these, DISGUSTING, TRENDS . . . that the Hollywood, PEOPLE . . . 'Em, SOLD!!! As a false bill of, GOODS!!!

And, you know, the sons and daughters . . . of Abraham, the Hebrew people, as I mentioned . . . BEFORE . . . that came to THIS country . . . and FORMED Hollywood . . . and are STILL, forming MANY . . . of our THINGS . . . that CONTROL, our LIVES, HEARTS, SOULS, WILLS and DESTINIES!!!

'Em, NOT . . . Anti-Semitic . . . just, MATTER of FACT!!!

Many of the Hebrews, came to THIS country . . . and CHANGED, their NAMES to . . . MORE ENGLISH-SOUNDING NAMES!!! Now, I can't say . . . for SURE, WHO they ARE!!! I could . . . I could GUESS, at SOME of, the HUGE . . . FAMILY NAMES!!! That were, PROBABLY . . . ORIGINALLY . . . the CHOSEN!!! Of, ABRAHAM!!!

But, they came HERE . . . and they became CORRUPT!!! They FORGOT . . . ABOUT, ABRAHAM . . . and the STARS in the SKY!!!

And, they FORGOT . . . about, the PROMISED LAND . . . and that they . . . REALLY NEEDED, to CONCENTRATE . . . their EFFORTS . . . on THAT BLESSED PARCEL, which God GAVE THEM!!!

Which NO ONE!!! Will EVER take AWAY!!! And, I've spoken EARLIER, in this dissertation . . . to Osama . . . I've spoken to QE2 . . . on the ERRORS of, THEIR WAYS!!! I'm speaking NOW, to the HOLLYWOOD!!! Also, in this book . . . on the ERROR, of THEIR ways!!! And now, I want to . . . speak to, the GENERAL PUBLIC . . . On the ERROR . . . of, THEIR ways!!!

The men and the women, UNFORTUNATELY . . . did NOT, come away from, World War 2 . . . a BETTER class . . . of PEOPLE!!! In mind, heart, soul, will and DESTINY!!!

They came away, DEPLETED!!! A PART of them . . . FOREVER GONE!!! JADED!!! If, you will!!! And so, we HAVE this CULTURE . . . of DEATH!!! Heh! The culture of death, STARTED . . . with EVE!!!

Now, I HAVE information . . . because, of me lineage . . . as DIRECT descendent, of Noah's son, Japhet . . . which, I've PROVED . . . in the first book . . . and my, STUDIES . . . with my FATHER!!! On the, SECRETS . . . that, were ONLY, handed down . . . JUST to myself . . . and the LAST, was given . . . to me, on the last VISIT, PRIOR to, WHEN HE DIED!!!

I RECEIVED the LAST, secret. 'Em, which will BE . . . in the THIRD book . . . from my Father, in December of 2004. And, I NEVER, laid EYES on HIM . . . AGAIN!!!

But, he GAVE it, to me . . . in PERSON!!! And then, he passed away . . . in April, of 2005. So, he DID . . . FINISH . . . his TASK at HAND!!! And . . . I DO have ALL, the information . . . I don't want anyone, to think . . . that I don't. Because, I DO! And, I'm merely HERE . . . as long I'm here, as we all are . . . to CARE, and SHARE . . . and I WILL be, sharing the information . . . with you, that is SO IMPORTANT . . . But, for right now, I just wanted to . . . touch QUICKLY . . . on the SAD STATE, of AFFAIRS . . . of the WORLD . . . ESPECIALLY, the people, that SUFFERED . . . in World War 2 and the, FAMILIES . . . in the United States, who were . . . NEVER EVER, the same . . . AGAIN!!!

The women, were NEVER the same . . . the men, were NEVER the same . . . they became desensitized, by THAT WAR!!! And hence, MORE KILLING . . . culture of, death . . . Ah . . . BIRTH CONTROL . . . culture of, non-procreation . . . ie: DEATH!!! Culture of, ABORTION . . . they call it, CHOICE!!!

I call it . . . MURDER!!! And, I THINK . . . I KNOW . . . what the Creator, CALLS it!!! MURDER!!! It's NOT . . . a CHOICE!!! The ONLY choice . . . is whether . . . to DO IT . . . OR NOT!!! Not . . . WHAT to CALL it!!! 'Em, and the people, that are FOR abortions . . . are NOT going to LIKE, what I'm GOING, to SAY . . . with this!!!

And I, RESPECT you . . . for your OPINION . . . but, you NEED to STOP and THINK . . . about the other, FLIP SIDE . . . of the, TRAVESTY . . . and the, TRAGEDY . . . of the, MILLIONS and MILLIONS and MILLIONS . . . of . . . LITTLE SOULS!!!

That, CHOSE . . . to COME, to the EARTH . . . CHOSE their PARENTS . . . and THEN, the parents . . . chose NOT, to ALLOW them . . . to come, to this EARTHLY JOURNEY!!! And, THAT'S a TRAVESTY!!!

So, as much as, we could ALL, get DOWN, on EVE . . . and say . . . THANKS A LOT . . . EVE!!! You know . . . NONE of US, deserved all THIS!!! But . . . NO ONE'S . . . holding a GUN . . . to our HEAD!!! We DO have, FREE WILL!!! And, we DO have, a SET of, GUIDELINES!!! Called . . . The 10 COMMANDMENTS!!! OF . . . GOD!!!

And then, we have the BE-ATTITUDES . . . of the, Rabbi Yeshua . . . that's . . . Jesus Christ . . . of Nazareth!!! THE . . . SON . . .

OF . . . THE . . . CREATOR!!! The Second POINT of LIGHT . . . on the . . . TRIUNE GODHEAD!!!

AND THEN . . . of course . . . let . . . NO ONE!!! NO ONE!!! EVER think, that there is NOT . . . the GOD FATHER . . . SON . . . and HOLY SPIRIT . . . SPIRIT!!! The Holy Ghost . . . (once called) . . . THE HOLY SPIRIT!!! Do NOT . . . THINK, for a MOMENT . . . that the. HOLY SPIRIT . . . is NOT ALIVE . . . AND WELL!!! ON the PLANET!!!

That's the, ONLY THING!!! That's KEEPING . . . us at BAY . . . right now!!! Before ALL . . . HAS to HAPPEN!!! To BRING us, to the POINT . . . and we're NEARLY THERE!!!

As I said, the DOOMSDAY CLOCK . . . is set ABOUT . . . thirty seconds, to . . . MIDNIGHT!!! It's probably, MORE LIKE . . . TWENTY by now!!! But 'Em . . . setting that aside . . .

The Holy Spirit, is HERE!!! Ladies and Gentlemen!!! The Holy Spirit, is ALIVE and WELL!!! From the day . . . of, PENTECOST . . . in the UPPER ROOM!!! And, the TIME . . . of, The Holy Spirit . . . IS NOW!!! The Holy Spirit . . . IN ACTION!!!

The Holy Spirit . . . is GOING, to MOVE . . . in such, STRANGE, MYSTERIOUS, NEW, EXCITING, INVIGORATING, EVANGELIZING, and just . . . LOVING, GODLY, WAYS!!! Because, the TIME . . . for The Holy Spirit . . . to MAKE, the PRESENCE KNOWN . . . is UPON US!!!

So, I WELCOME, that time.

And I, will do EVERYTHING . . . in my power, to LIVE UP . . . to the . . . EXPECTATIONS . . . of, The Holy Spirit . . . the Son and the FATHER!!! To BE, a GOOD Christian . . . SOLDIER!!! Who put ON, the ARMOR . . . of, the ARMY . . . of, God . . . when I was, BAPTIZED . . . and then, CONFIRMED!!!

So, don't ever FEEL . . . ABANDONED!!! By the, Creator!!! He STILL . . . LOVES US!!! He's NOT, given UP . . . on US . . . YET!!! There IS . . . a LAST . . . HOPE . . . for DELIVERANCE!!! For ALL of US!!! Rabbi Yeshua, DID His BEST!!! And, HE did an, EXCELLENT, EXCELLENT . . . JOB!!! Of, FULFILLING . . . I will, KNOW . . . I will LOVE . . . and . . . I will SERVE!!! The GodHead . . . WHILE he WAS here!!!

Now, The Holy Spirits . . . STEPPIN" UP . . . to the PLATE!!! Ladies and Gentlemen . . . and SAYING . . . I will KNOW . . . I will LOVE . . . and . . . . I will SERVE!!!

Despite, EVERYTHING . . . that's EVER happened, BAD . . . from EVE . . . OUR first . . . GOD MOTHER!!!

WHO . . . is GOING, to GIVE us . . . a TOTAL, EXPLANATION!!! Of, EXACTLY . . . WHAT HAPPENED!!! IN the GARDEN . . . of EDEN!!!

AND, EXACTLY . . . what HAPPENED . . . TO her SON . . . ABEL!!! Because . . . CAIN . . . did NOT!!! . . . KILL ABEL!!! . . . and THAT, my friends, IS the SECRET, of . . . the SECRET!!! And, I HAVE IT!!! And, its been GIVEN . . . to ME!!! HANDED DOWN!!! From . . . the NOAH . . . people . . . MY people . . . THROUGH, the CELTS!!! Down, to me. To . . . I'm speaking, to you.

So, PLEASE . . . stick with me! Please BELIEVE, what I am telling you . . . is a, THOUSAND PERCENT TRUE . . . times, God's OWN . . . SECRET NUMBER!!!

And so, let us . . . just . . . TOGETHER . . . PREPARE, OURSELVES!!! For . . . NOT, the WORST . . . of TIMES!!! But, the BEST . . . of TIMES!!! It's NOT OVER . . . YET!!!

There's ONLY, a FEW things . . . that HAVE, to be DONE!!! To get US . . . to the POINT . . . where, WE can MAKE . . . a RATIONAL, LOVING, STRONG, KIND . . . and BEAUTIFUL!!! . . . DECISION!!!

To . . . KNOW, LOVE and SERVE . . . the Creator. That's ALL . . . He WANTS!!! . . . FROM us!!!

And, ALL . . . WILL . . . BE . . . FORGIVEN. So, TRUST me.

I'm gonna . . . GET 'YA . . . to the . . . TREE . . . of, the FRUIT of LIFE!!!

The Tree . . . of FORGIVENESS!!!

I'm gonna get 'ya there.

I'm gonna show you, how to get there. It's gonna be, SO EASY!!!

You're gonna say, WOW!!! It's SO . . . GOOD . . . that you're, DOING this! And that, the GOD . . . has spoken, to your . . . heart and your . . . mind and your . . . soul and asked you, to please . . . step up . . . to the plate. Woman up! And, get with us . . . all.

I'd like to think, that I could aspire, to be . . . as . . . PARTLY . . . as great as, Saint Joan of Arc . . . who did, what SHE did . . . for love of, GOD and COUNTRY!!!

I want to do, the work . . . that I NEED . . . to do . . . that I'm, CHARGED . . . to do . . . by the Creator, for first . . . love of, GOD and WORLD!!!

And, that means . . . EVERY single ONE of YOU . . . out there!!! You're JUST like ME!!! Doesn't MATTER . . . if you're, a man . . . or . . . a woman . . . doesn't matter, what color . . . you are . . . what kind of, hair you have . . . if you're healthy, or you're not . . . if you're young, or you're old . . . If you're weak, or you're strong . . . DOESN'T MATTER!!!

You . . . God . . . DOESN'T MAKE JUNK!!!

You're NOT . . . NOTHIN'!!! You're SOMETHING!!! In God's EYES!!!

And, we're GOING . . . to CORRECT . . . the WRONGS!!! The wrong, FALSE bills, of GOODS . . . that the world . . . HOLLYWOOD . . . MONEY!!!

We're GOING to, ADDRESS all, THOSE ISSUES!!! . . . and RESTORE . . . NATURAL ORDER . . . on this, PLANET!!! If, it's the LAST THING . . . I DO!!! Before I leave . . . and if, I don't SUCCEED . . . there'll be SOMEONE . . . to TAKE UP . . . my work!!! When, I'm gone.

Because, LISTEN folks . . .

DO YOU . . . love your children . . . DO YOU . . . love your family . . .

You've GOT, to get on the . . . on the PAGE . . . of LOVE and FORGIVENESS!!!

It CAN . . . be DONE.

TRUST me . . . I'm going to, explain it further . . . as we go along. But, just for now . . . PLEASE . . . if you've NEVER, given ANYONE . . . a SHOT . . . at PROVING . . . to you, that there . . . IS A GOD?!?

Please, give Cynthia, the PRIVILEGE!!! Of . . . the OPPORTUNITY!!! To PROVE, to YOU . . . that there, IS a CREATOR!!!

And, He still . . . LOVES US!!! And, He still . . . WANTS US!!! To be . . . HAPPY . . . with HIM . . . FOREVER . . . in HEAVEN!!! He's WAITING!!! Not LONG . . . but, He's STILL waiting.

And, with that . . . I bid you adue . . . for now . . . PAX . . . which means . . . PEACE . . . and LOVE . . .

Cynthia

Chapter 13

It is TIME, to truly EXPLAIN, the MISUSED word, "NIGGER!!!" And, it's not a BAD, explanation . . . RATHER, the word, "NIGGARDLY," Is EVIL . . . IT explains, the TRUE EVILS . . . that men did, in their, indolence, sloth and inclination . . . to LAZINESS!!!

I put THAT word, DIRECTLY . . . on the BACKS . . . of the TRUE white, ENGLISH!!! And, the SONS . . . of ABRAHAM . . . who took, English sounding NAMES!!! To HIDE, their Hebrew IDENTITIES!!!

HOW DARE THEY!!!

And the, white English . . . PROPOGATE, a LIE!!!

And, place SLAVERY . . . which is TRULY, DRUDGERY, TOIL, SUBMISSION . . . to DOMINATING INFLUENCES . . . over a PERSON, who is a CHATTEL, to another!!!

The practice, of SLAVEHOLDING . . . the Chattel, being an ITEM!!! Of, PROPERTY!!! MOVEABLE!!! Except for, REAL ESTATE!!!

Onto, the LIVES and the, HEARTS and the, SOULS and the, MINDS and the, WILLS and the, DESTINIES . . . of BEAUTIFUL, African . . . Men, Women and Children!!!

As I've told you before, my family . . . the Gunns . . . the TRUE MONARCHS . . . of the British Isles . . . LED an EXPEDITION . . . With the Sinclairs . . . WE, were the two Clans . . . of CAITHNESS!!! And, we LANDED . . . in a, New England State . . . as I've mentioned, before . . . approximately, a hundred years . . . BEFORE, Christopher Columbus!!! Of, Italy.

We, did NOT take it . . . for it was NOT, our land. WE LEFT, our MARK . . . and our, Coat of Arms . . . and the YEAR . . . ETCHED, on a cliff, in that, New England state. Now THAT, friends . . . is FACT!!! Not fiction.

As I, Cynthia . . . have said before . . . WHAT did the English DO?!? They HYPOCRITICALLY, sent that . . . Christopher Columbus . . . to GET the SHIPS . . . and the MONEY . . . to the SPANISH MONARCHY!!! Ferdinand and Isabella.

The English, USED . . . the Spanish, to FINANCE . . . the ENDEAVOR!!! Another, SLAP in the FACE!!! To the Spanish!!! They had ALREADY GIVEN, a HUGE . . . slap in the face, to Catherine . . . of Spain!!!

Once . . . the first and TRULY . . . OWN WIFE, of King Henry VIII, himself!!! But, Henry . . . OH! What an EVIL, man!!! To BED . . . his French ADULTRESS . . . Anne Boleyn?!?

He LEFT . . . the ROCK . . . OF ROME!!!

Which, Rabbi Yeshua . . . had established!!! And, formed . . . a WATERED DOWN, givin' HIMSELF . . . ABSOLUTION . . . and SUPREMECY OVER . . . a FALSE and PHONY . . . PROTESTANT CHURCH!!!

What does that MEAN?!? A Christian-based church . . . in THOUGHT . . . yet . . . PROTESTING and DENYING . . . the UNIVERSAL AUTHORITY . . . of the DESCENDENTS . . . of Simon PETER!!!

POPE Peter, the first . . . WHOM, Rabbi Yeshua . . . himself, CHOSE . . . with the TWELVE . . . to CARRY, The Holy Spirit . . . OF the TRIUNE GODHEAD . . . Down through TIME!!!

UNTIL, Rabbi Yeshua's FEET!!! DESCEND . . . Ha! Ha! From HEAVEN . . . and will TOUCH down . . . on the MOUNT of OLIVES!!! AGAIN!!!

A FACT . . . Ladies and Gentlemen . . . It WILL HAPPEN!!! Boys and Girls . . . So, let all who have, EYES . . . SEE!!! And let, all who have, EARS . . . HEAR!!!

For it WILL BE DONE!!!

And, ALL . . . the WORLD . . . will have, the SIGHT of IT!!! WHEN, the times . . . COMES!!!

VIA . . . BBC, CNN, Internet, or . . . the like!!!

Now, FORGET the word, "NIGGER!!!" As being, ANYWHERE NEAR . . . as EVIL . . . as the word, NIGGARDLY!!!

And that, DESCRIBES the ENGLISH!!! And, the HIDING . . . CHOSEN PEOPLE of God!!!

The word, "NIGGER," merely means . . . ANY MEMBER, of ANY DARK-SKINNED RACE!!! I'll say it again . . . it MERELY means . . . any member, of any dark-skinned race.

YES!!! It has been, THROWN ABOUT!!! By the, WHITES . . . As DAGGERS . . . of ABUSE!!! And, it's OFFENSIVE . . . in it's EVIL CONNOTATION!!!

I GET IT!!! IT HURTS!!! IT HURTS ME . . . DEEPLY!!! And, I'm ASHAMED . . . to be WHITE . . . for SUCH REASONS!!! But, I am, 'cuz God . . . chose it. And . . . I MUST, GO FOREWARD . . . no MATTER what COLOR . . . if I was, green, purple, pink . . . I don't care!!!

And, I've said before . . . I don't care . . . what kind of, HAIR I have . . . don't care . . . what kind of, LANGUAGE I speak . . . I DON'T CARE!!! The truth is . . . the truth!!!

Now, WHY did they USE . . . that WORD?!? And, Bandy it ABOUT . . . to try and HURT, the PEOPLE . . . that they DRAGGED, from AFRICA!!! To come, OVER HERE . . . and BUILD . . . this NEW WORLD!!! Of, America!!!

"Cuz they, were TOO LAZY . . . to DO it . . . THEMSELVES!!! As I've said before . . . They said to themselves . . .

OH! Where are the MOST . . . STRONG, INTELLIGENT, ABLEBODIED. PEOPLE . . . in the world?!? Ach! Ahah! Ahah! AFRICA!!!

Then, let us GO . . . GET . . . those FINE PEOPLE . . . and PUT them . . . To TASK!!! And become, their TASKMASTERS!!!

Well, they DID that . . . People of African Descent . . . BECAUSE . . . they're SO INSECURE!!! In their, OWN insecurities . . . they had to, RESORT . . . then, to NAME-CALLING and, LABEL-MAKING, to COVERUP . . . their OWN . . . INADEQUACIES!!!

And, the EVIL USE and ABUSE . . . VIA, the SLAVERY!!! And then, POST-EMANCIPATION . . . by the, Abraham Lincoln . . . they CONTINUED!!! To, DENEGRATE, DEGRADE . . . and

STILL PRETEND . . . to THIS very DAY . . . and, I'm speaking to you, this is the 25th of June, in the year, 2008!!!

They CONTINUED . . . to PRETEND . . . to this day, that THEY . . . are the SUPERIOR RACE!!! WHO can, HAND-DOWN . . . life SENTENCES . . . of toil, drudgery and SUBMISSION!!! To our, BEAUTIFUL African, BROTHERS and SISTERS . . . of the world!!!

WHO, did NOT . . . ASK . . . to COME . . . here . . . IN the . . . FIRST place!!!

I'm Sick and TIRED . . . of the, Chosen People . . . COMPLAINING, about PHARAOH!!! Or EVEN, Adolph Hitler . . . for that matter!!! What THEY DID . . . was WRONG . . . to YOU!!!

BUT . . . what have you DONE?!? What have YOU done?!? Down through time . . . well, let's just take a QUICK PEEK!!! Shall we!!!

God sent MOSES, to RELIEVE YOU . . . from the SUFFERING, of the Pharaoh!!! Then what did you do?!?

You FLEW, in God's FACE . . . and COMPLAINED!!! For FORTY YEARS . . . in the DESERT!!! You complained to Moses. OVER and OVER . . . again!!! That, MOSES . . . should . . . DO SOMETHING!!!

DO SOMETHING!!! DO SOMETHING!!! This!!! That!!! This!!! That!!!

And, you know what . . . when Moses . . . had; had, ENOUGH . . . of your complaining . . . and your, BELLYACHING . . . AS CHOSEN PEOPLE!!! ON your WAY . . . to . . . EMANCIPATED!!! From SLAVERY . . . NO LESS!!! And, on your WAY . . . to a PROMISED LAND . . . from God . . . NO LESS!!!

He just had, the Creator . . . KNOW . . . that he'd HAD ENOUGH!!! Of your, complaining and your, bellyaching . . . in the desert. So, what did God DO??? God showed him, ALONG the WAY . . . He showed him . . . the LAND. Okay! And it came, at the end, of Moses . . . days. God took Moses . . . up to, the HIGH PEAK . . . so that Moses, could have, a LOOK . . . and, he had a look . . . at the Promised Land. And then, The God, TOOK MOSES . . . to HEAVEN . . . for a JOB WELL DONE!!!

So, having said that . . . DELIVERING the Chosen People . . . FROM the Pharaoh . . . DELIVERING the TEN COMMANDMENTS . . . GUIDING the FORTY YEARS . . . of WANDERING . . . in a DESERT . . . and FINALLY, PUTTIN' the LAND, of MILK and HONEY . . . WITHIN, the Chosen Peoples reach . . . MOSES DID WELL!!!

Well DONE . . . good and faithful . . . SERVANT!!! And God, GAVE him, the RELEASE . . . that, HE needed . . . from this . . . EARTHLY PLANE!!!

When the Chosen People . . . DID REACH, their Promised Land . . . they AGAIN, began . . . to SLIP-SLIDE AWAY . . . from the Creator!!! The Creator, had to make, a DECISION!!! And . . . The God . . . SENT, The Lord God . . . Rabbi Yeshua!!! TO . . . the Chosen People!!!

To WAKE THEM . . . from their, SELF-IMPOSED-STRAYING . . . YET . . . AGAIN!!! What did they DO?!? The USED, Rabbi Yeshua!!! And, ABUSED HIM!!! And, HANDED Him OVER . . . to the ROMAN JIBOT . . . the . . . ROMAN ELECTRIC CHAIR!!!

BECAUSE . . . they were, AFRAID . . . of HIM!!! AFTER, He'd done . . . ALL KINDS, of SIGNS and WONDERS . . . and MIRACLES . . . and HEALINGS . . . and RISING, their LOVED ONES . . . from the DEAD . . . and CURING LEPERS . . . and you just, CAN'T even BEGIN . . . to KNOW . . . the BETRAYAL!!!

But, it had to BE!!! It had to be, by the GOD!!!

FOR the SPILLIN' . . . of, the BLOOD . . . of the LAMB . . . of GOD!!!

And, I'll speak to you, on the END . . . final . . . chapter. The SIGNIFICANCE . . . of THAT BLOOD . . . havin' come DOWN . . . and TRICKLED . . . DOWN . . . off the JIBOT!!!

But, setting that aside . . . SO they RELEASED . . . they were with the ROMANS . . . and, they were SO AFRAID . . . of the Rabbi Yeshua . . . and they asked for . . . a TRULY EVIL . . . BARRABBAS!!! To be RELEASED . . . INSTEAD!!! And . . . for the Rabbi Yeshua, one of, THEIR OWN . . . who DID all GOOD . . . nothin' BUT good . . . to be CRUCIFIED!!! MURDERED!!! Like a . . . COMMON CRIMINAL?!?

FOR . . . WHAT?!? The LOVE . . . the MIRACLES . . . and the TRUTH, that He TAUGHT?!? The Chosen People, OF ALL . . . should KNOW, what I am, ABOUT TO SAY!!!

And THEY DO!!! And they . . . KNOW!!! That I KNOW!!! The SECRET of the SECRET!!!

WHICH, I will REVEAL . . . at the FINAL . . . IN the final, ANALYSIS!!! Of, this dissertation . . . so PLESE, be patient . . . because I can deliver . . . what the Creator, the LAST BEST . . . WARNING!!!

That's all I can speak of it . . . right now. But, I will REVEAL, the final analysis . . . of it all . . . in the FINAL, END . . . of this dissertation.

Here comes, SOME of IT . . . NOW . . . everyone . . . everywhere. Just a TINY . . . TASTY . . . TIDBIT!!! So, BUCKLE your SEATBELT . . . we're GOING . . . on the REALITY CHECK . . . REALITY, ROLLER-COASTER RIDE . . . of a LIFETIME!!!

Who will be STANDING . . . and who will be ILL . . . FOREVER!!!

When . . . we GET OFF . . . ONLY the Creator . . . KNOWS!!! Who will be left standing . . . in a PEACE . . . and who will be, ill FOREVER!!! IN GEAHENNA!!!

So . . . OKAY . . . God made a PACT . . . with NOAH. And, I can direct my lineage, BACK . . . to his son . . . JAPHET. So, I am TRULY a, DAUGHTER . . . down through time . . . of Noah and Japhet . . . and so on and so forth.

God, made that pact, with Noah . . . NEVER AGAIN . . . by FLOOD!!! And SET, the BOW . . . in the SKY!!! As the EVERLASTING SIGN!!!

The Rainbow . . . DONE!!! We've all SEEN IT!!! It's not FICITON . . . it's FACT!!! It's God COVENANT . . . FACT!!!

Then . . . the Creator God . . . sends Yeshua!!! Ahah! Now, the Chosen People now know, EXACTLY . . . that I KNOW. what I'm TALKIN' ABOUT!!! Because, the Rabbi Yeshua, of the House of David, HIMSELF . . . was a KABBALAHIST . . . a KABBALAH RABBI!!!

And, He was TRAINED . . . by the GOD!!! He was BORN . . . with IT!!! And trained . . . and ingrained . . . to TEACH . . . to HEAL . . . to EVANGELIZE . . . LOVE and FORGIVE!!!

Well . . . the ROMANS . . . KILLED HIM!!! At the SELECTION . . . of the FEARFUL, JEWS . . . and He lie DEAD!!! Ladies and Gentlemen, Boys and Girls . . . THREE DAYS!!! And WENT, where NONE of US . . . have YET . . . GONE!!!

DON'T . . . FORGET THAT . . . for a MOMENT!!!

He went into DEATH!!! And, to HELL!!! And, to TAKE the KEYS . . . from Lucifer . . . SATAN . . . the LATE great . . . FALLEN angel . . . of LIGHT!!! The HYPOCRITE . . . who REFUSED . . . to KNOW, LOVE and SERVE . . . the Triune GodHead!!!

God. The Lord God and the Lord . . . also known as . . . and in PROPER ORDER . . . God the Father, God the Son . . . Yeshua and God the Holy Ghost, ie: SPIRIT!!!

When Yeshua ASCENDED, back to the RIGHT HAND of GOD, The Father, He had ALREADY . . . set in place, God The Holy Spirit . . . at the PENTECOST!!! In the UPPER ROOM!!! With Simon Peter, the Twelve and . . . Rabbi Yeshua's HUMAN Mother . . . Mary, Miriam . . . In that room . . . they RECEIVED . . . The Holy Spirit . . . in TONGUES of FIRE!!! Tongues of fire . . . tongues of fire. And this, will be VERY significant . . . for OUR time!!! On this DOOMSDAY CLOCK!!! Which, is NOW . . . about . . . 'Em, 24 SECONDS to MIDNIGHT!!!

Tongues of FIRE!!! Ladies and Gentlemen!!! Be READY . . . and be PREPARED!!! To SEE it!!! TWO . . . tongues of FIRE!!! That's ALL I'll SAY . . . right now.

YOU'LL SEE IT!!! IF . . . you'll OPEN, your EYES!!! And you'll HEAR, what they SAY . . . in tongues, of fire . . . if you'll OPEN, your EARS!!! And, I HOPE you DO!!! Because THIS is about LOVE!!! GOD!!! Doin' His God THING!!! It's NOT about . . . anything ELSE!!! It's about what's REAL . . . and, what's NOT!!!

What's LOVE . . . and, NOT love . . . and, the OPPOSITE, of love . . . is HATE!!! And, the MASTER, of HATE is SATAN!!! The master, of EVIL . . . the master of EVIL and DECEPTION!!!

But, let us just get back to . . . The Holy Spirit . . . that they RECEIVED . . . in the upper room. Now, he SPEAKS . . . in tongues of fire. That merely means, the GIFT . . . of FERVOR!!! On FIRE . . . through and through . . . in THOUGHT, MIND, WILL, HEART, SOUL and DEED!!! For the GodHead.

The ARMOR . . . that we can PUT ON!!! The Holy Spirit . . . to WAGE WAR!!! When, NECESSARY . . . against LUCIFER . . . and the FALLEN angel . . . AND the, OTHER fallen angels . . . and other, fallen SPIRIT BEING . . . COHORTS!!! Who FOLLOWED Lucifer . . . to the GEAHENNAH!!! The UNQUENCHABLE FIRE . . . of, DAMNATION . . . ETERNAL, damnation . . . and eternal, PUNISHMENT!!!

FOR . . . FAILIN' and REFUSIN' . . . to KNOW . . . LOVE . . . and SERVE . . . the GODHEAD!!! ALL, very . . . SIMPLE!!! Ladies and Gentlemen, Boys and Girls . . . and there's NOTHIN' to be SCARED of!!!

It was Lucifer, who SPOKE, to the WOMAN . . . of Adam . . . called EVE!!! And his voice came . . . FROM the GROUND!!! AT the BASE, of the TREE . . . the FORBIDDEN . . . FRUIT, tree. He GREW that tree, HIMSELF!!! That was NOT a God TREE!!! God did NOT, place that tree THERE!!!

It was a TOXIC tree . . . that SPRUNG up . . . from the PIT, of GEAHENNAH . . . where Lucifer was, DAMNED TO . . . FOREVER!!!

And he SPROUTED . . . the ONE tree . . . and, I'll touch on that, in the FINAL dissertation, of this book, this volume . . . of the TRUTH!!!

Now, he grew THAT tree, out of JEALOUSY . . . to GOD!!! Once AGAIN!!! Jealous of God, in HEAVEN . . . jealous of God and God's CREATION . . . on the ORB!!! Which WE call . . . EARTH!!! Which God made . . . from . . . NOTHINGNESS!! From the ABYSS!!

He CHALLENGED God, when he . . . DID THAT!!!

He AWFULLY, awfully DID!!!

He challenged GOD . . . to a DUEL!!! For the SOULS . . . of God's Creation . . . and the, Creation . . . the orb, the Earth . . . and ALL, LIVING creatures . . . that would EVER come . . . even BEFORE . . . and/or AFTER . . . Adam and Eve . . . even GOT THERE!!!

So, Lucifer . . . SET the DEMISE!!! The TRAP!!! For the demise, of God's Creation. And, that's ALL . . . it IS!!!

Now, we've ALL . . . been TRAPPED!!! At ONE point . . . or ANOTHER!!! And being trapped, means . . . CHOOSING the WIDE PATH . . . that leads to . . . DESTRUCTION!!! Choosing to BREAK TIES . . . with God . . . and God's LOVE . . . and God's SET, of GUIDELINES . . . to Live a GODLY, HAPPY, LIFE!!! On this Earth . . . and in ETERNITY, with Him FOREVER!!!

The master, of deception PLANTED that TREE!!! And, I will extrapolate, on that more . . . later. But, I'm . . . very, very, very much . . . SICK and TIRED . . . of Lucifer's GAMES!!! And, his DISCIPLES . . . and the, EVIL . . . and the, WORKS . . . that they've DONE!!!

And I'm here, as Cynthia Anne Marie Gunn Queen of Scots and America, direct descendent . . . of NOAH . . . to TELL YOU . . . Heh! Heh!

Your DAYS are NUMBERED . . . they've BEEN numbered . . . Since the death of, Karol Wojtyla . . . when the GATES of HELL, heh, heh. heh . . . were COMPLETELY . . . OPENED!!!

Because . . . YOU know WHO . . . GOT the KEYS!!!

You can give it, your last best shot. But, in the END . . . you WERE . . . NOTHIN', you ARE . . . NOTHIN" . . . and you'll FOREVER, in GEAHENNAH . . . with all you cohorts . . . and all the SOULS, that you're STEALIN' . . . be RELEGATED . . . to STAY THERE . . . at some point.

And then, you'll all be LOCKED . . . DOWN THERE!!! AGAIN!!! By Saint Michael, the Archangel . . . so DON'T think, for a MOMENT . . . Lucifer, that . . . MICHAEL, SAINT MICHAEL, THE ARCHANGEL . . . is NOT gonna' DO, what GOD has ASKED!!! Michael . . . will you, know, love and serve?

And . . . MICHAEL . . . and . . . RAPHAEL and GABRIEL . . . all said, YES! I will love. YES! I will know! YES! I will serve. So, you know what . . . YOU are NOTHING!!! YOU have NO POWER!!! You THINK . . . you do . . . and, your cohorts . . . think you do . . . BUT, you DON'T!!!

And, in the final analysis, the final GREAT EXPERIMENT . . . of the Creator . . . the Triune Godhead . . . SHALL PREVAIL!!! And, there isn't a cotton-pickin', damnation thing . . . you can do about it. So . . . "TOODLELOO," . . . to YOU . . . Lucifer!!! You've got . . . about 23 seconds . . . to midnight . . . left to play, your awful games."

BUT . . . we're NOT here, to play GAMES . . . NOW!!! We're here . . . to fight FIRE . . . with FIRE!!! So, you're PUT on NOTICE!!! We are here . . . to fight fire . . . with fire . . . AND I'LL SAY it AGAIN . . . if you didn't hear me Lucifer . . .

We are here . . . Cynthia and Michael . . . and our, family . . . who loves us . . . who we, love them . . . and we SHALL . . . fight fire . . . with fire . . . and, you won't be winnin' . . . you'll be losin'. So, prepare YOURSELF . . . for your FINAL . . . demise. And, your final . . . LOCK-AWAY . . . to the unquenchable fire . . .

BECAUSE . . . you're STUPID!!! As much, as you THOUGHT . . . you were SMART . . . ARCHANGEL . . . you're the STIPIDEST of the STUPID!!! And, you TAKE . . . the stupidest, of the stupid . . . with you. And THAT'S . . . just plain, good old, Connecticut, dyed-in-the- wool, YANKEE LOGIC . . . IF, you will, from Cynthia Queen of Scots and America . . .

So, we're coming after you. And, we're not playin' games. You're all DONE!!! By GUNN!!!

Now, I'm sorry, I had to get up, on a high horse . . . about that . . . BUT it had to be DONE!!! And . . . so God, has challenged him . . . to the DUEL . . . for the SOULS . . . of God's CREATION . . . as I said, and the, creation . . . and the, orb . . . earth and all, the living creatures . . . that were HERE . . . EVEN, before, since, during, after, up until the END . . . were here on this earth.

Well . . . NOW, is the time . . . to EXPOSE that Lucifer, the master of deception . . . for WHAT, he IS . . . folks!!! Ladies and Gentlemen, Boys and Girls . . . there's NOTHIN' to FEAR . . . but . . . FEAR ITSELF!!! But, if you WANT, to fear SOMETHING . . . DON'T fear ANYHTHING . . . but Lucifer . . . and his WAYS!!!

And, DON'T take ON . . . his ways!!! We've ALL, bandied his ways . . . about, because . . . he's SCREWED UP . . . Adam and Eve!!! And, we're all SUFFERING . . . the CONSEQUENCES of it. Because, he TWISTED, their HEADS OFF . . . and screwed 'em . . . BACK ON . . . the WRONG way.

He, is the master, of deception. For what is he??? TRULY??? This . . . is the ESSENCE . . . of, the Lucifer:

He's JEALOUS, he's WEAK, he's HATEFUL, he's INSECURE and . . . he's DISHONEST!!! And THAT is all.

These FIVE things . . . are the MARKERS!!! They are the markers . . . of TRULY, his essence. They are, ALL that he's got LEFT . . . NOW!!! Ladies and Gentlemen, Boys and Girls . . . to WORK, his CORRUPTION . . . throughout . . . the WHOLE earth!!!

So, WE are GOING, to TEACH him, Lucifer . . . his FINAL lesson. Once and for all!!! And TAKE BACK, our God GIVEN DIGNITY . . . as HUMAN creatures . . . CREATIONS . . . of GOD . . . in HIS very OWN, IMAGE and LIKENESS!!!

We're NOT like you, Lucifer. We're NOTHIN' like you. And, we're through, playin' games. We KNOW . . . who loves us, we KNOW . . . who created us, we KNOW . . . who takes care of us . . . and UNDERSTANDS us . . . and makes us feel . . . LOVED!!! And, it's NOT you. Because . . . you're all . . . those weak, evil, things . . . that you are . . .

You NASTY . . . little SNIPE!!! How DARE you!!! HOW dare you!!! SHAME ON YOU!!! FOR SHAME!!! And you are the, prince of darkness . . . and the, prince of hell . . . and Geahennah. Where you'll be stayin' . . . FOREVER!!!

No more, Mrs. NICEGUY . . . Lucifer, no more, Mrs. CLEAN . . . no more, Mrs. Niceguy . . . Satan, you're SICK, you're OBSCENE . . . and your number . . . six-score-sixty-and-six . . . IS UP!!!

SO HELP ME . . . LAMED VAV VAV!!!

So, let no human . . . once called, "NIGGER," and FOLKS . . . you know . . . forgive . . . pick a piece of the fruit . . . off the Tree of LIFE!!! Off the Tree of FORGIVENESS!!

Forgive, those IDIOTIC . . . INSECURE . . . JEALOUS, WEAK, HATEFUL, DISHONEST, English . . . and Chosen People . . . who came over here, to HAVE you . . . BUILD, this COUNTRY . . . on THE BACKS . . . of your . . . BLOOD, SWEAT and TEARS . . . and STOLE you AWAY . . . from your FAMILIES . . . and your GOD-GIVEN, Country of AFRICA!!!

And, brought you OVER HERE . . . NOW!!! And won't even, RECOGNIZE . . . that . . . you're STILL SUFFERIN' . . . the TRICKLEDOWN SUFFERAGE . . . I won't even SAY . . . TRICKLE- DOWN ECONOMICS!!!

It's a TOTAL SUFFERAGE!!!

They don't KNOW!!! They don't WANT, to know!!! If they, had the CHOICE . . . to have come, into the world, through BLACK PARENTS . . . and to have, BLACK SKIN . . .

WELL . . . GUESS WHAT?!? They didn't MAN UP and WOMAN UP!!!

And, they didn't CHOOSE IT!!! They didn't choose, to GET WITH . . . THE GOD!!! And to get with . . . THE BONDAGE!!!

Of the, EVILS . . . PROPAGATED, on the EARTH!!! And to . . . RISE UP!!!

It's TIME . . . for MY FAMILY . . . my TRUE FAMILY . . . 'CUZ . . . I DON'T HAVE A COLOR!!! I don't HAVE a color. I don't care.

I'll paint my BODY, any COLOR . . . I want!!! I'm still the SAME . . . inside. And, I'll SHAVE my HEAD . . . BALD 'cuz . . . I don't CARE, what kind . . . of HAIR . . . I have . . . as RIDICULOUS!!!

And IMUS . . . OOH!!! YOU have CROSSED, the LINE AGAIN!!!

MISTER IMUS!!! And, you know what . . . you know . . . fool us ONCE, shame on YOU . . . fool us TWICE, shame on US!!!

You don't FOOL us . . . for a cotton-pickin' moment . . . IMUS!!! You're PREJUCICE!!!

SHAME ON YOU . . . for asking . . . the WHEREABOUTS, or the WHATABOUTS . . . of an athlete . . . and what his name is . . . OH!!! WHAT COLOR IS HE!!!

And then, when someone said, that he was of AFRICAN DESCENT . . . 'ya said . . . OH!!! WELL!!! THAT EXPLAINS IT!!! NOW I KNOW WHAT'S . . .

You know what?!? SHAME ON YOU . . . IMUS!!! SHAME ON YOU!!! And, SHAME ON YOUR NETWORK!!! SHAME ON AMYBODY ELSE . . . who, SUBSCRIBES . . . to what YOU said . . . AGAIN!!!

About GOOD, GOD-FEARIN', GOD-LOVIN' PROPLE!!! WHO'VE had . . . ENOUGH!!! Enough . . . is ENOUGH!!!

Now, I want to REITERATE . . . and say again . . . LET NO HUMAN . . . BEING . . . CREATURE . . . CREATION . . . BEAUTIFUL . . . AFRICAN . . . CHILD OF GOD . . . Once called, "NIGGER," by the EVIL PEOPLE . . . And, THE DEVILS DISCIPLES!!!

Do not FEAR . . . do NOT fear . . . that you will NOT . . . be DELIVERED!!! DO not fear . . . that the GOD . . . has said to YOU . . . as He once said . . . to the MOSES . . . It's ENOUGH . . . on your PEOPLE . . . ALREADY!!! It's . . . ENOUGH!!!

And, I did not have . . . the PRIVILEGE . . . to be born, with dark skin. And, I'll get . . . INTO . . . the TRUTH of THAT . . . at the END . . . of this dissertation.

"Cuz . . . I KNOW . . . Who did WHAT . . . to WHOM!!!

ADAM, EVE, CAIN, ABEL, TOWER of BABEL . . . I've got it. And, we're ALL . . . going to, GET WITH IT on the last, of this dissertation . . .

All the MYSTERIES . . . and the, SECRETS . . . WILL BE UNLOCKED. So, you know what . . .

Reverend WRIGHT . . . out in Chicago . . . you keep on doin' . . . what you're doin' . . . and although, the Catholic Church . . . is PO'D and TICKED OFF . . . at the Catholic Priest . . . who came in there . . . and spoke TRUTH . . . ALSO!!! About, your CONDITION . . . of what you've . . . SUFFERED!!! And they're, sanctioning him . . .

Well, you know what . . . Benedict?!? KNOCK it OFF!!! Knock it off, right now . . . BENEDICT . . . XVI . . . 'cuz you KNOW, I am, who I am . . . and you know, I can do . . . what I can do . . . AND you know that, what I SAY . . . is the TRUTH!!! And I love you, too . . . Benedict . . . because I was born . . . PREDESTINED . . . to be a follower, of the Roman Catholicism . . .

But, you know what . . . I've STUDIED . . . all the Great Religions, of the world . . . and, they're ALL FLAWED!!! They've all, got SOME of the INFORMATION . . . NONE of them, have it ALL!!! Or, if they DID . . . they LOST it . . . ALONG the WAY!!!

And, we're gonna . . . CLEAR that UP too, Ladies and Gentlemen, Boys and Girls!!!

IN VERY SHORT ORDER!!!

This second book is, COMING OUT . . . and in RAPID, SUCCESSION . . . book three . . . is, coming out. And, when we get book three . . . we've GOT the KEY . . . to UNLOCK, the DOOR . . . to the Promised Land . . .

And to the . . . THOUSAND YEARS of PEACE and the, RETURN . . . of RABBI . . . YESHUA!!!

LIKE it or NOT Israel . . . The KABBALAHISTS . . . know who, Rabbi Yeshua . . . IS . . . and they BETTER, quit PRETENDIN' . . . that they . . . DON'T!!!

And they know, who Cynthia is . . . THEO SOPHIA . . . and they BETTER not PRETEND . . . that they DON'T!!!

Because . . . I'm COMING!!! I'm coming . . . OVER there!!! When the TIME . . . is RIGHT!!!

And, I'm gonna . . . REBUILD the TEMPLE!!! AS I TOLD YOU!!!

Singlehandedly . . . without a PIECE of, MORTAR or, BRICK or, ROCK!!! And, it will happen. By the GOD!!! Yahweh!!! And the GOD!!! YESHUA!!! And the GOD!!! HOLY GHOST-SPIRIT111

So, NEVER . . . EVER . . . FEEL . . . PEOPLE that were . . . once called, "NIGGER," that GOD . . . has NOT, HEARD you and that, you're not 'gonna be . . . DELIVERED!!!

Because YOU ARE!!!

And, it's 'gonna be . . . THE GREATEST DELIVERANCE . . . of the world . . . because, through . . . your TOIL . . . and TORMENT . . . and SUFFERING . . . and DENEGRATION . . . and ALL you've SUFFERED . . . and the LASHES, you've TAKEN . . . and the THINGS, you've BUILT . . . and the way, WAY you've been SHUNNED . . . and had SOCIETY . . . look down their, NOSE at you . . .

HOW DARE THEY!!! How DARE they!!! Treat you, as DOGS!!! We'll be findin' out . . . who the dogs truly are.

FOR . . . SACRILEGE!!! EVERYONE . . . that is AGAINST . . . what the God, is DOING . . . and the, WAY . . . He's 'gonna be

MOVING . . . in these, NEXT 24 seconds . . . of the, doom day clock . . . DOOMSDAY CLOCK!!!

Is, 'gonna be LIVIN' . . . in a STATE of SACRILEGE!!! And, you're 'gonna be . . . WANTED!!! By The GOD!!! For SACRILEGE!!!

So . . . don't, let ANYONE, be SACRILEGIOUS!!! And, GO AGAINST . . . ANYTHING . . . that The God . . . is puttin' forth . . . now. Because, it's ALL true . . . by Cynthia . . . by Cynthia . . . ONLY 'cuz, I've had the GIFT!!! I have HAD the gift, of PERHAPS . . . aspiring to be . . . someone LIKE . . . MOSES!!!

And MOSES . . . PLEASE . . . COME . . . FOREWARD . . . AGAIN!!! MOSES . . . we NEED you . . . DESPERATELY!!!

MICHAEL, I LOVE YOU!!!

We NEED you!!! You Need to COME . . . FOREWARD!!!

We NEED to do, this thing!!! FOR our CHILDREN!!!

Please Michael!!! FORGIVE ME . . . I have the INFORMATION. I was WRONG!!! We were . . . we were THERE . . . and I listened, to the DEVIL . . . and it was WRONG!!! And so, PLEASE . . . FORGIVE ME!!! Please GIVE ME, this OPPORTUNITY . . . to MAKE it RIGHT . . . for our CHILDREN!!! And, our children's, CHILDREN!!! And so, that the . . . CHRIST . . . can . . . . COME TO US!!!

Please . . . I'm BEGGING you, Michael . . . I LOVE YOU . . . have NO DOUBT, of that . . . Michael. SAINT MICHAEL!!! Please . . . THE ARCHANGEL . . . and, you know who you ARE!!!

You know . . . I'm not . . . Moses, I'm not . . . Saint Joan of Arc, I'm NO ONE!!! I'm just Cynthia . . . but Michael . . . you truly ARE . . . who you ARE . . . and I am here . . . I'll be RIGHT by, your SIDE!!! Right by your side . . . my love . . . I will.

Because . . . we are, well, the two. We are the twin flames. We are the twins. We are the soul mates. We were created for each other. And that is the truth of that, Michael.

Now, Cynthia DOES know . . . the TRUTH . . . Ladies and Gentlemen and Boys and Girls, of the world.

About . . . WHO did WHAT . . . to WHOM . . . and WHO'S BAD . . . and WHO'S . . . in SACRILEGE!!!

Love, Cynthia

Photo Gallery

Cynthia's beloved Granduncle, Rev. Walter J. Pilecki, "The West," seeks out and meets, "The East," Rev. Karol J. Wojtyla in Krakow, Poland. Behind the, "IRON CURTAIN," Circa July 1964

"Now, we've met, here is the truth. You've beheld, Theo Sophia-Cynthia's, baby picture, blood of my blood. Now, do the right thing, Fr. Wojtyla or do not." Uncle, to Future Pope John Paul II, Circa July 1964

"At last, yes, I Am Pope now as you predicted Fr. Pilecki. Tell me, how is our theo-sophia Cynthia doing? I need the update" Granduncle Fr. Walter, John Paul II and Grandaunt Mary. THE VATICAN May 19, 1982

"First, Holy Father, please allow me to introduce, my sister Mary, Theo-Sophia Cynthia's Grandaunt.

Pope John Paul the II, gave a gift, to Grandaunt Mary, for a life well lived.

Grandaunt Mary, Kisses the ring of Simon-Peter the Good Shepherd.

Grandaunt Mary cries. Granduncle Fr. Walter listens to John Paul II intensely

"Guide Theo-Sophia Cynthia this way"

Holy Father blesses Granduncle and Grandaunt of
Theo-Sophia Cynthia
"Well done Father Pilecki I now know; Cynthia will be ready when
the time is right a man"

Chapter 14

Welcome back . . . Ladies and Gentlemen, Boys and girls. What we need to do now, is a quick review . . . of only the twentieth and the, short-lived, twenty first century.

Highlights and or, lowlights . . . of history . . . it is enough to know, bits and pieces, of our entire, human history . . . from the great, do- gooders . . . to the worst, do-badders.

I've already spoken, of SLAVERY . . . man on man.

The last APOSTACY . . . of slavery and disbelief, in God's system . . . of LOVE and ORDER . . . most recently, MANIFESTED ITSELF . . . when the RUSSIANS, overthrew . . . their own Monarchy! In the early, nineteen hundreds . . . and ESTABLISHED, the FALSE, ERRONEOUS, SOVIET UNION . . . and it's, RULE . . . OVER their COUNTRYMEN!!!

And, took NUMEROUS . . . other countries, such as . . . but not limited to, POLAND . . . and the like, into their erroneous, EVIL CLUTCHES!!!

Breaking . . . the MINDS, HEARTS, SOULS, WILLS and DESTINIES . . . of such Citizens . . . UNTIL, Gorbachev, Reagan and John Paul II, took the GREAT LEAP . . . of FAITH . . . as Men, elegant, strong, loving and honest.

HUMANS!!! To say . . . ENOUGH, was ENOUGH!!! And so, the INSANITY . . . and EVIL, PROPAGATED . . . by those, erroneous . . . Soviet Union . . . WAYS . . . ENDED!!! OR DID THEY?!?

That CANCER did METASTASIZE . . . and SPREAD . . . to CHINA . . . who ONLY ALLOWS, ONE BABY . . . per couple?!? ABSURD!!!

Then, NORTH KOREA . . . CUBA . . . and others.

And, the IRON-CLAD . . . school of THOUGHT, has been ingrained . . . in a different, yet EQUALLY . . . and CUNNING, WAY . . . throughout, other countries . . . of the world!!! Who, do NOT VALUE . . . their OWN CITIZENS!!!

Men, Women, Children . . . and LOOK at them, as LESS than . . . HUMAN!!! To be DESTROYED!!! By GENOCIDE?!?

Their ATHIESM . . . is their . . . REASON!!!

KILLING is KILLING . . . GENOCIDE is GENOCIDE . . . HOLOCAUST is HOLOCAUST . . . SERVITUDE is SERVITUDE . . . DIABOLICAL DEEDS are DIABOLICAL DEEDS . . . AND . . . HATE is HATE . . . no matter, HOW you slice it!!! It has to STOP!!!

The INSANITY HAS to stop!!!

They NEED to, REJOIN . . . the FAMILY of MAN . . . whom ONLY God Created. They NEED to, KNOW . . . LOVE and SERVE . . . The Creator!!!

Now, EVERYONE is AFRAID . . . EVERYWHERE!!! RIGHT NOW!!!

The have-nots . . . live in FEAR, POVERTY, GRIEF, ANGUISH and DESPAIR . . . every DAY!!! The haves . . . are STARTING!!! To FEEL, the ONSET . . . of FEAR, POVERTY, GRIEF, ANGUISH and DESPAIR . . . EVERY day!!!

Well . . . If you THINK, all is BAD . . . right NOW . . . 25 June 2008 . . . JUST WAIT!!! You haven't seen, ANYTHING YET!!!

There will be, a WORLD WAR 3 . . . but, it will NOT be FOUGHT . . . only by HUMANS!!!

Oh YES!!! We will SURELY START IT!!! Because, PEOPLE are acting, as STUPID . . . as Lucifer . . . and are in his TRAPS!!! Of, jealousy, weakness, hatefulness, insecurity and dishonesty!!!

Is there ANY thinking PERSON . . . OUT THERE?!? The WORLD OVER . . . that HONESTLY believes, that the DOOMSDAY CLOCK . . . is not set, at twenty four seconds to MIDNIGHT?!? RIGHT NOW?!? The SIGNS of the TIMES, which I have been instructed . . . by my Father . . . to REVEAL, at the PROPER PLACES and TIMES . . . are all AROUND us NOW.

PLEASE!!! I beg of you . . . PLEASE!!! Allow me, to SHARE . . . what INFORMATION, I have been GIVEN!!! And, let's just all . . . GET WITH, The Creators . . . SIGNAL GRACES!!!

Those . . . of TRULY . . . The Creators FINAL MESSENGER . . .

The Creators . . . little girl . . . now a WOMAN, who KNOWS . . . the TRUTH, tells the TRUTH . . . and lives, to personify . . . the TRUTH of, The Creator . . . for the BENEFIT, of The Creator . . . and WE . . . The HIGHEST . . . in the ORDER, of His Creation!!! His IMAGE!!! His OWN LIKENESS!!! So please . . . I BEG of YOU, fellow HUMANS . . . Let us ALL . . . WAKE UP!!!

From this DIABOLICAL, self-imposed . . . Lucifer AIDED . . . NIGHTMARE . . . culture of DEATH, DECEPTION and DESTRUCTION!!!

BEFORE . . . the COMET RUP . . . makes IMPACT . . . with our PLANET!!! As I told you . . . in the first book, it's . . . perhaps in the second book . . . IT has ALREADY been DISPATCHED!!!

What we DO . . . in the coming days, weeks, months and LAST few YEARS . . . coming up, will DETERMINE . . . whether the Creator, will DEFLECT . . . the Comet RUP!!! So it will NOT, make IMPACT and BURN the PLANET!!!

By FIRE . . . we'll be DESTROYED.

Because we're livin' . . . the WAYS that the people, lived . . . INSANITY . . . and every kind of, DIABOLICAL . . . JUST EVIL!!! And IDIOCRACY!!! Of the DAYS . . . of NOAH!!!

So, me . . . very . . . unbelievable . . . mysterious . . . happenings!!! So, MANY . . . VERY . . . UNBELIEVABLE . . . MYSTERIOUS . . . HAPPENINGS!!!

Trust me, when I tell you . . . will BE taking PLACE!!! Before the year 2013!!! I truly believe and KNOW this!!! The SIGNAL GRACES, I am aware of . . . TELL me. That, we all need to . . . WISE UP!!! MAN UP!!! WOMAN UP!!! HUMAN UP!!!

And, STOP the INSANITY!!! Please!!! Let us ALL take, the FRUIT of . . . The Tree of LIFE!!! The FRUIT of FORGIVENESS!!! And, get BACK, on the ESSENCE . . . back TO the ESSENCE . . . of a HUMAN BEING!!!

As I have said before . . . the Torah, has puzzle pieces, left out . . . PURPOSELY!!! DONE!!! The New Testament, especially

the Revelation, has had puzzle pieces, left out . . . PURPOSELY!!!
DONE!!! Just for our TIME . . . in HISTORY!!!

I have the pieces . . . I was born to have them. I was schooled . . .
to have them. I suffered, to know and live them. I myself fell . . . into
DESPAIR . . . and went down, the WIDE PATH . . . from July 2006
until April 2007!!! I'm NOT gonna sit HERE and LIE, to 'ya!!!

I went into my OWN, HELLISH NIGHTMARE . . . of the
DESERT.

Because, I . . . FLEW, in the FACE of GOD . . . myself . . . in
despair . . . I'm just LIKE you!!! No BETTER, no WORSE!!!

But when, the GRACE . . . of The Creator, whom I call God . . .
RETURNED to me . . . I was AGAIN . . . FILLED . . . with the
Lord, Holy Ghost. THE SPIRIT!!!

And, I'm so ETERNALLY grateful . . . and, I had to go down . . .
a road, of Commandment breaking . . . one, two . . . BUT . . . no
matter!!! It didn't matter!!!

Because, Rabbi Yeshua said . . . if we have broken one . . . we've
broken them ALL!!! And I did. And I'm sorry. And, I made my
amends, to The Creator.

We ALL need to do that.

Not just Cynthia . . . where Rabbi Yeshua went . . . he PREPARES
a place for us . . . if we MAKE AMENDS . . . to The Creator . . .
The God, the Father.

So, having done that, I truly KNOW . . . and BELIEVE . . .
and FEEL . . . and now, can be the person . . . that He created me, to
be!!! That's when, The Creator . . . then ALLOWED me . . . to get
on with my work . . . for Him.

And, we humans . . . as . . . as . . . WELL, He dubbed me,
His Secretary of, AUT PAX AUT BELLUM!!! It was exactly how, it
came down . . . to me. From, my Guardian.

It's a title, given to me, by birth . . . and through me lineage . . .
and so, I am HAPPY NOW!!! And pleased . . . to REPORT . . .

Dear Creator,

I'm back. It's your once, little girl, Cynthia . . . older, wiser and
stronger. I am now, the Lady . . . who is elegant, strong, loving and
honest. I will deceive no one. I will take no one down, a wrong path.

The information I have, to share . . . as the Creator's Secretary of, Either Peace or War . . . HIS title for me . . . not my own title. As His Secretary of, Either Peace or War . . . the information I have to share, will be the TRUTH . . . of how, the FALL . . . of mankind, STARTED!!! Who did what, to whom? And how, to prepare ourselves, for the TIMES . . . we're in which . . . WHICH . . . will only get . . . WORSE and WORSE . . . DAY by DAY by DAY!!!

Economically, spiritually, natural disasters, of BIBLICAL proportions . . . included but not limited to . . . fires, floods, volcanic eruptions, earthquakes, tsunamis, also know . . . as tidal waves . . . hurricanes, typhoons, cyclones, tornadoes, California . . . San Andreas fault . . . splitting the land and sending, the DESPICABLE Hollywood and it's VIPERS, into the sea!!!

I tell you, Ladies and Gentlemen . . . PREPARE yourselves!!!

These are to name, just a FEW . . . of the, PLANETARY pangs . . . And let's not FORGET . . . the GREENHOUSE effect of GLOBAL WARMING!!!

And EVENTUALLY . . . BRACE YOURSELVES, for this one . . . BE SITTING DOWN . . .

The POLAR . . . total . . . polar SHIFT!!! Which will CHANGE, the EARTH'S . . . orbital ROTATION . . . TO polar OPPOSITES!!!

From my mouth . . . to God's ear and from God's mouth . . . to my ear . . . it SHALL be DONE!!!

Be not AFRAID . . . of these things. For, they MUST and WILL happen.

TOTAL global CHAOS!!!

And . . . MONETARY doom . . . ie: DEPRESSION.

Failures of crops, lack of foods, of all types . . . lack of clean water and clean air . . . ECOLOGICAL disasters . . . which will MAKE the EXXON VALDEZ crisis . . . look like, a HICCUP!!!

And then, the animals . . . will start to DIE . . . humans TOO!!! For lack of EVERYTHING and the vultures . . . and scavengers of the earth, will REAPPEAR . . . to FEAST, on the dead animals . . . and people . . . which will bring PLAGUE . . . upon PLAGUE . . . black DEATH . . . once MORE!!!

No one will have . . . ANYTHING!!! There will be no, WALMART . . . no, McDonald . . . nothing, will be MOVED!!!

By boat, plane, train or automobile . . . and, who can afford the hay . . . for a HORSE!!! Who can afford ANYTHING . . . that isn't AVAILABLE . . . to purchase, anymore . . . in the FIRST place!!!

Wall Street . . . Chicago Commodities . . . will FAIL!!!

The RICH will throw themselves, to their DEATHS!!! No coping SKILLS!!!

Everyone . . . will be finally . . . equal . . . among EQUALS!!! No one, will have ANYTHING . . . ANYMORE!!!

And that . . . will bring . . . humans . . . to their . . . KNEES!!!

But wait!!! WAIT!!! Just wait . . . just as the Pharaoh, FLEW in the Creator's FACE . . . as do WE!!! Then . . . the PESTULANCE of every description . . . will come. It will come . . . the waters, will turn POISONOUS . . . TOXIC!!! The air too!!! Multitudes, DYING!!!

Those still left . . . if wearing . . . warning each other . . . will have, new ARMIES . . . to fight . . . the ants, the scorpions, biting stinging insects, frogs, wild boars, bears, wild cats, hungry, rabid . . . packs of dogs and other small creatures, of the woods . . . will ATTACK us . . . from all sides!!!

That friends, is only the BEGINNING . . . of how God Creator, will REBUKE US . . . FOR FOLLOWING . . . Lucifer, through Eve!!! And, the EVIL FRUIT, at which KILLS US ALL!!! That she ATE!!! Which . . . KILLS US ALL!!!

And to come . . . we will beg, to DIE . . . from the HORRORS coming . . . but we won't be ABLE to DIE!!! Just YET!!!

NO!!! We will be KEPT, hardly and barely . . . ALIVE to suffer, the WEEDS . . . we have sown!!! The WHEAT will be cut down . . . as the weeds.

The WEEDS will be . . . for GEAHENNAH!!!

The WHEAT will be HARVESTED . . . by The Creator . . . Himself.

In the end . . . the IMMACULATE HEARTS, of Rabbi Yeshua and His Mother . . . Mary, Miriam . . . WILL TRIUMPH!!!

But first, the CHASTISEMENT!!! Rather, the chastisement . . . AFTER . . . the final WARNING . . . of the GOD CREATOR!!!

Oh! Please . . . I beg of you . . . brothers and sisters, of the world. Please, I ask you . . . so BRACE YOURSELVES!!! For what is DANGEROUS . . . BAD and is surely, coming.

I will help you. Learn. How to reconnect, with The Creator and be READY . . . for what He DECIDED . . . to send us . . . to correct . . . our wicked, wicked, wicked . . . WAYS!!!

Love, Cynthia

Chapter 15

And . . . Welcome Back! Ladies and Gentlemen, Boys and Girls, of the world . . . this is Cynthia. Please forgive me, for my strong REBUKE, of the last chapter 14. This is now, chapter 15 of book 2. 'Em . . . I was MOVED . . . by The Holy Ghost/Holy Spirit, to administer, a firm rebuke . . . as I did.

But, here we are. Independence Day, of the America . . . and ad I told you, the Americas . . . were sullied and fouled, by the likes of the English . . . QE2 . . . BACK through TIME . . . to her forefather, Henry VIII AND Anne Boleyn.

The watered down, Monarchy . . . so-to-say, of England but, let me tell you again . . . that I, Cynthia Anne Marie Gunn, am the TRUE . . . Queen of Scots and America.

Now, I can be totally CALM . . . I hope . . . I hope NOT to get, up on a high horse . . . . and I hope, NOT to be scolding, or rebuking . . . anymore, for we don't need it . . . from me! 'Em . . . unless or until, we listen to 'Em . . . all the Books, of the Torah . . . all the books, of the New Testament . . . all the Dead Sea Scrolls . . . all the agnostic books . . . that were hidden . . . 'Em even the Quran, which has secret clues for all of us . . .

You know, I . . . this is a short chapter . . . because, I'm hugely busy today . . . and I need to go out, amongst friends and relatives . . . and celebrate, the American . . . Independence Day! The forth of July . . . 2008, twenty 0-8 . . .

I just wanted, to speak to you today . . . because, I'm reviewing the first book and I'm reviewing, the second book . . . which is about, right now, three quarters . . . of the way DONE . . . not for nothin' . . . only for LOVE . . . of, the Creator!

I will KNOW, I will LOVE and I will SERVE . . . the Creator. And, I Cynthia Anne Marie Gunn Queen of Scots and America . . . let ME, take on the personification of, of your GOD MOTHER!!!

Let ME, take on the personification of, EVE of ADAM . . . in the Garden of Eden!!!

Because, I HAVE . . . the information!!!

Who did WHAT . . . to whom! Who was RIGHT . . . who was WRONG . . . who knew more FIRST . . . who knew LESS . . . who, did what . . . to whom!

And, I PROMISE you . . . I'll CLEAR . . . EVERYTHING up!!!

Because; Adam, Eve, Cain, Abel, Blood spilt, Tower of Babel,

Rabbi Yeshua . . . you and me, Again blood spilt . . . for the Truth . . . to be!

And, that's all I really . . . can tell you . . . right now . . . except to say, on the fourth of July . . . huh! . . . American Independence . . . and that's, way, way, way, way . . . AFTER . . . Cynthia Anne Marie Gunn of Scots and America's . . . people, were here . . . as we did NOT, claim it.

I'll tell 'ya, how George Washington . . . all the way down, to George Herbert Walker Bush . . . and then, I'll tell 'ya . . . how they're ABOUT . . . to pin off, everything . . . on Barack Mohammed Obama . . . 'Cuz . . . I CAN'T . . . get into it . . . right now.

But . . . I shall. In the next chapter . . . or two, tell 'ya . . . how the geopolitical structure . . . of this earth, NOT a Christly, Rabbi Yeshua earth . . . is about to, hand down a sentence . . . ONCE AGAIN . . . to the Fruits of AFRICA!!!

And, they're going to hand it . . . down . . . to Barack Obama . . . because they FAILED . . . at the GAME . . . of the Israelis and their . . . COUSINS . . . the Arabs!!!

Huh! The English, failed . . . NOW!!!

And, they want to PIN IT OFF . . . on Barack Obama!!! 'Cuz, they put forth the . . . LEAST . . . likely candidate . . . the weakest candidate . . . of the Republicans . . . OF, the ONCE . . . Abraham Lincoln, party . . .

Who, emanciplated . . . excuse me . . . CORRECTION . . . EMANCIPATED . . . the SLAVES . . . and RIGHTLY SO!!! And Abraham Lincoln, came to my . . . Norwich, Connecticut . . .

And, I'll be sharin' with you, a flag he left here . . . when he was on his campaign . . . for President! But . . . setting that aside . . . by jetport/ bill/senior . . .

Let me . . . just say to you now . . .

EVERYTHING . . . that Cynthia Anne Marie Gunn tells you . . . is a thousand percent TRUE. Two of the names, have been changed . . . to protect the innocent . . . or the GUILTY!!! The name of, the hairdresser and the name, of the car salesman . . .

Because, I'll NOT . . . have them suing . . . you, me, or anybody else, for rights . . . to any of the portions, of the proceeds of this book . . . Because . . . I don't need money . . . I don't need nothin' . . . but, I Cynthia Anne Marie Gunn, already have . . . a corporation, for American Veterans, of all . . . races, colors, creeds, ethnicities . . . and, the NEXT . . . corporation . . . that I shall form, will be a non-profit . . . AGAIN!!!

For the . . . REPARATION FOR SLAVERY!!!

If it's the LAST thing I do!!!

I shall, emanciplate . . . pate . . . excuse me . . . emanciplate . . . pate . . . there I go again . . . heh . . . I have a stutter! . . . but I've been trying, to hold it back . . .

I . . . Cynthia Anne Marie Gunn, shall FINALLY . . . and for ALL TIME . . . kick the Pharaoh's . . . BUTT . . . in the Boston Store window!!! And, kick the Hebrews . . . BUTTS . . . who tried to kick . . . MOSES butt, in the desert . . . when he'd had ENOUGH!!! He said . . . there it is, in the distance!!!

And, I love you . . . for now . . .

Love, Cynthia

Chapter 16

The day after . . . Independence Day of America. Welcome back, Boys and Girls . . . Ladies and Gentlemen . . . of all . . . places, times, ages and spaces, on the earth . . . right now! This is Cynthia Anne Marie Gunn Queen of Scots and America.

I just need to speak to you . . . quickly . . . this is going to be a super-short chapter . . . 16 . . . regarding, the TRUTH of the BEGINNING . . . of the truth of . . . the country of America . . .

You know, Ladies and Gentlemen . . . 'Em . . . those that came before us . . . after the Puritans . . . WHO RAN AWAY . . . from King . . . I don't know . . . who was it . . . George?!? Heh! I don't know . . . I don't care.

But, they came WELL AFTER . . . The Gunns . . . and then . . . a hundred years after The Gunns Christopher Columbus came . . . and then, THEY came . . . as Puritans, to Plymouth ROCK.

Now, Plymouth Rock . . . is just Plymouth Rock.

But, the CLIFF . . . that I've told you about . . . IN THE New England State . . . with MY FAMILY'S coat of arms . . . and the YEAR, etched on it . . . IS THERE!!! Well BEFORE . . . Columbus . . . well before Plymouth Rock!

That is all I can say, on that subject . . . right now.

But, in terms of the American, scene and in, terms of the geopolitical, scene . . . right now, I just need to tell you . . . that George Washington, and the early . . . "boys" . . . men . . . of this country 'Em . . . I FIRST . . . need to tell 'ya . . . tried and true . . . that . . . the CONCEPT, for America . . . was first called . . . The Constitutional Congress . . .

So to say . . . CONTINENTAL CONGRESS . . . and so, Norwich, Connecticut . . . surely, is to REWRITE HISTORY!!! Because . . . the ACTUAL FIRST PRESIDENT . . . of the Continental Congress of America . . . which came before, The Declaration of Independence . . . etc., etc., etc., . . .

Was a man, called Samuel Huntington. And he, was the first President . . . of the, Continental Congress . . . Constitutional . . . . whatever.

He was, FIRST!!! And, he was from Norwich, Connecticut. And then, of course . . . we ALL know . . . that there was BENEDICT ARNOLD . . . the HUGE Traitor!!! Who did everything, wrong . . . for LOVE, of an ENGLISH woman!

And, you know . . . that's all forgivable. And so, let's just get with, some TRUE history Huh!

As I told you, the Torah . . . Torah . . . has left things OUT!!! And, The New Testament . . . has left things OUT!!! I'll NOT go into it . . . anymore.

But, Samuel Huntington . . . of Norwich . . . was THE first President . . . of the . . . what would then be . . . later called . . . United States of America!!!

He came, BEFORE George Washington . . . NOT . . . because jetport Bill senior, said so . . . but, because it's TRUE!!! And, jetport Bill senior . . . won't be here, much past 2011.

And, God rest your soul . . . Mister Bill. But, the truth is there. And you've, PRESERVED IT!!! And, I want to thank . . . your Norwich . . .

Historical Society . . . and I won't, make a joke . . . of it as OTHERS . . . have made . . . "it's a . . . OH . . . NORWICH . . . Hysterical Society" . . . NO! You know what you know you've written ALL your BOOKS . . .

Once upon a Time . . . Once upon a Time 1 . . . Once upon a Time 2 . . . 3 . . . 4 . . . I don't know . . . Mister Bill . . . of Norwich. And your brother . . . James brother, who passed away . . . many . . . I don't know . . . and I don't care.

But, I know . . . that you know, SOMEWHAT . . . of the TRUTH so, I'll ACKNOWLEDGE it . . . here today. Cynthia Anne

Marie Gunn, acknowledges . . . that you, William of Norwich, who's about 'Em . . . high seventies . . . today . . .

My Father's friend . . . jetport Bill . . . I acknowledge the FACTS . . . that you know. And, I acknowledge . . . ALL, that you DID . . . to try and bring, Benedict Arnold, into the LIGHT!!!

Samuel Huntington, Benedict Arnold . . . whatever. But, Benedict Arnold . . . Heh! Heh! Was a VERY . . . sly and crafty, man. Because, as much as people, THINK . . . that a traitor, of the United States of America . . . which wasn't even, so-called yet . . . was a traitor . . . he HAD TO . . . GO FORTH!!!

Before even GW . . . George Washington of . . . was EVER in office! And I get it, jetport Bill senior! I get it! All these THINGS . . . HAVE to HAPPEN!!!

Now, talking about George Washington, the first . . . I don't know, if he ever had a son . . . George junior . . . doesn't matter to me. All I'm saying is . . . I understand, that George Washington, the first President of the United STATES . . . of America . . . after Samuel Huntington, the first President of the Continental Congress . . . what have you . . . of America . . . and then, there was Benedict Arnold . . . as I said before, whatever . . . we set that aside.

But, George Washington, if anybody ever, looked at him . . . Heh! Heh! He was, NOT ONLY . . . a FREEMASON . . . in the way he dressed . . . and the apron . . . and the symbolism . . . of the Freemasons . . . but he was ALSO . . . A Knight Templar!!! And that's where . . . I STOP . . . that.

Because, I DON'T need . . . the Hebrews . . . and THEIR STUDIOS, through Harrison Ford . . . whomever . . . to bring forth, movies . . . to show you . . . THAT . . . 'Em . . . there IS such a thing, and tried and true . . . as The Arc of the COVENANT . . . and . . . The HOLY GRAIL!!!

And, do you NOT think, for a moment . . . that, Cynthia Anne Marie Gunn Queen of Scots and America . . . does NOT KNOW . . . Where . . . The Arc of the Covenant . . . lies . . . and . . . The Holy Grail . . .

But, you have a . . . HUGE SURPRISE COMING . . . Ladies and Gentlemen . . . The Holy Grail . . . is not JUST . . . one cup . . .

of the Jesus Christ, of Nazareth . . . the Rabbi . . . Rabbi Yeshua of Nazareth . . . it's Not just ONE cup!

Its thirteen cups!!! A bakers dozen . . . of cups!!! "Cuz the Rabbi Yeshua . . . had His cup . . . and the twelve . . . INCLUDING . . . Judas Iscariot, who HAD . . . to turn Him OVER . . . for X . . . 30 . . . 40 . . . I don't care . . . pieces of SILVER!!! All had to be done . . . and then, the Judas, the Iscariot . . . hung himself . . . etc., etc., etc.,

WHY?!? Because LUCIFER . . . the devil . . . tempted the Iscariot . . . to turn over the Christ . . . to the Roman Guards . . . and, hence . . . turned over, with the HUG . . . with the ear CUT OFF . . . and the Rabbi Yeshua, put the ear, BACK ON . . . of the guard . . . etc., etc., etc.,

And, I will THANK . . . Mel Gibson, for bringing THAT forth . . . in a movie called . . . The Passion. Now Mel, you have a brother . . . a priest . . . you so-called, set him up . . . on your land . . . you so-called established, a TRUE . . . Roman Church!!!

With a, ROMAN LITURGY . . . for your Brother?!?

Well, you either DID . . . or you DIDN'T . . . Mel Gibson!!! So MAN UP!!! Mel Gibson . . . CUT the COMEDY . . . get TO your WIFE . . . get to your CHILDREN . . . get to your BROTHER . . . or DON'T!!! I don't care!

You HIGHLY, embarrassed ME . . . Cynthia Anne Marie Gunn Queen of Scots and America . . . WHEN you ended up, in front of . . . the CAMERAS . . . as an alcohol . . . driving . . . whatever . . . I don't know. But, you know what . . .

Forget . . . Clint Eastwood's movies . . . the good, the bad and the, ugly . . . where, a . . . one of the characters . . . went back and tried, to make amends . . . to his brother, a priest . . . and it could not be done . . .

You know what . . . Mel . . . Gibson . . . not for nothin' . . . but, you need to CUT . . . the comedy, cut the crapola . . . and get BACK to the TRUTH . . . Mel Gibson!!! And, this is from . . . Cynthia Anne Marie Gunn . . . so you know what . . . you either ARE or you AREN'T . . . WITH your wife and your children and . . . the God . . . first and foremost.

And, that's all I have to say . . . on that subject . . . Mel Gibson . . . because . . . HUH! You went out . . . and you PLAYED . . . in hypocrisy!!! You played WHO??? In a MOVIE . . . BRAVEHEART!!! Listen . . . you're NO braveheart!!! Trust me! Only, on a FRONT . . . of a SCREEN!!!

Unless OR until . . . you SHOW me . . . Mel Gibson . . . with MY CELTS . . . with MY COLORS . . . The Gunn, Ancient, Modern and Weathered . . . Unless Mel Gibson, shows me . . . that he UNDERSTANDS . . . Cynthia Anne Marie Gunn . . . he shows me, nothin'!!! Doesn't matter.

Because, I have . . . R. Stuart McGregor . . . of the Clan McGregor! Who's ready, willing and able . . . to STEP UP . . . to the PLATE . . . because the likes of you . . . or not . . . that's all I can say, in this dissertation . . . of chapter 16 . . .

And, don't think . . . I don't love you Mel . . . and don't think I don't love you . . . any human being . . . from the, highest to the lowest . . . from the, strongest to the weakest . . . and those . . . ALL in between . . . and for now . . . I bid you . . . adue . . .

Love, Cynthia

Chapter 17

Well, this is chapter seventeen . . . and apropos, to the age of seventeen, as being a marker . . . of youth, which will definitely get, what I'm about, to say . . . hopefully, down to thirteen year olds . . . and hopefully, up to twenty five year olds . . . and let those, who have ears, hear . . . and let those, who have eyes, see . . . that I, Cynthia . . . am telling, the TRUTH . . . not for nothin', but for the truth!

Now, if the youth that I'm speaking to you, now . . . of the United States, of the English speaking world . . . AND . . . of the rest of the world, ALL the world over . . . because, I . . . as your God Mother and I told you, very soon, in this dissertation, I will speak to you DIRECTLY . . . as EVE . . . our FIRST MOTHER . . . of ALL of US, even the likes of, Cynthia, who'll be 49, on 28 July 2008.

But, let me just say . . . that 'Em . . . we all need, to FORGIVE . . . our parents. We all need to forgive our grandparents. We all need to forgive our teachers . . . our . . . our priests, our rabbis, our pastors, our guides, our friends, our enemies, ANYONE . . . who has FALLEN short, of the Creator, which . . . whom . . . I call, choose to call . . . God, called Yahweh, Jehovah, Allah, Buddha . . . what have you.

There's ONE Creator, young people . . . AND . . . He wants to ask you . . . THIS???

DO YOU, LOVE YOURSELF . . . and your, FRIENDS?!?

Do you, FEEL . . . LOVED and ACCEPTED . . . by yourself and your, friends . . . BETTER YET . . . more IMPORTANTLY, so . . . do you feel, LOVED . . . and accepted, by your PARENTS . . . by your, FAMILY . . . do you feel, UNDERSTOOD . . . not for, nothin' . . . not for, THE trappings, of the RIGHT NOW . . .

The MUSIC, of the, right now . . . the bands . . . the . . . ah . . . THINGS, that we DO, when we're in, YOUR AGE GROUP . . . and I, did them, as well . . . the REBELLIONS . . . AGAINST, our PARENTS . . . against the, ESTABLISHMENT . . . 'Em . . . body PIERCINGS . . . 'Em . . . sexual PROMISCUITY . . . which . . .

Don't let them, THINK . . . and tell 'ya, for a MOMENT . . . has NOT, been going on . . . since, the BEGINNING!!! Huh! "Cuz. I can trace the, sexual promiscuity, of my . . . own grandmother . . . who was born, in twenty . . . let's see . . . twentieth century, 1908 . . . all the way, back to THAT!!!

If THEY, wanna TRY, and sell you, a bill of goods . . . that you're, doing something, WRONG . . . any more WRONG, than they . . . were DOING, when they were, TEENS . . . and early, TWENTIES . . . then, you know what . . . they're, HYPOCRITES . . . but FORGIVE 'Em, and LOVE 'Em.

All I say to you, now . . . is . . . NOW, IS THE TIME!!!

THIS is, the ERA!!!

And YOU . . . ARE, the FUTURE!!!

YOU . . . the YOUTH . . . of the WORLD . . . in this year, 2008 . . . I would say, between the ages, of 12 and 25, to 30.

YOU young PEOPLE . . . will DECIDE, the OUTCOME, of not ONLY . . . us . . . we who are, OLDER . . . but, of YOURSELVES!!!

In the FUTURE . . . when we're, LONG GONE and you're, OLDER and then, the FRUITS . . . of YOUR LOINS . . . children . . . boys and girls . . . baby boys, baby girls . . . will decide, YOUR FATES!!!

So, Let's NOT . . . think for a moment . . . that your, parents and your, grandparents . . . have NOT . . . gone THROUGH, some of the, SAME . . . CRAPOLA . . . that, YOU HAVE . . .

ONLY . . . the CRAPOLA . . . you're going, THROUGH . . . is MUCH more . . . INTENSE . . . because, you were CHOSEN . . . to be BORN . . . in so-called, so far . . . the HIGHEST LEVEL . . . of TECHNOLOGY!!!

And, I know it's HARD . . . for you, to NAVIGATE . . . through ALL THAT!!! I KNOW . . . it's hard because, from little, TINY, children . . . all you first, WANTED . . . or NEEDED . . . or could CARE ABOUT . . . was the LOVE of your, PARENTS and your, siblings . . . and then, it went on . . . from there.

It went on, to YOU . . . watching . . . you watching . . . the BOXES . . . which CAME IN, through your house . . . LIKE Cynthia in, the first book . . . I AM WHY THEY KILLED DIANA The Secret of The Red String . . .

The FIRST box, that came into, MY HOUSE . . . was, the TV SCREEN!!! And the, HIGHEST . . . most, ABHORRANT sight . . . I EVER saw, was the 'Em . . . ASSASINATION, etc., and the, next few DAYS . . . COVERAGE, of John F. Kennedy . . . and then, I moved on and moved on and MOVE ON!!!

But NOW, you young . . . BEAUTIFUL, young people . . . of the world, have been RAISED . . . on the . . . WORLD WIDE WEB, the Internet. And so, don't THINK . . . for a MOMENT . . . that you're, NOTHIN' like . . . the OTHER CHILDREN . . . youth, of the world! You're above, children . . . or you're STILL, children. Doesn't matter . . . to me.

BUT, if you understand, what I'm saying . . . to you . . . the World Wide Web, the Internet . . . has now, CONNECTED US ALL . . . to one another!

It's TIME . . . for the YOUTH . . . of the WORLD . . . American, English, European, of course, beautiful Africans, Australians, Southern American children, children of the East, children of the . . . MOSES descendents . . . the Hebrew children, children of their cousins . . . the Arab children, children of the Orient, all the Asia . . . majors and minors, from the Japanese, through the Chinese, and all the Stans . . . as you know . . . Kazakhstan . . . whatever . . . I don't care . . .

We've GOT to, FORGET . . . all the LABELS . . . that were HANDED DOWN, to US . . . at the TOWER of BABEL!!!

And, as I said to you . . . the REASON, that our foremothers and forefathers . . . WE . . . the FRUITS, from which we . . . ALL COME . . . were SPLIT UP . . . at the, Tower of Babel . . . I will REVEAL . . . in the, LAST chapter . . . of, this DISSERTATION!!!

Because, EVE . . . HERSELF . . . won't be, channeling through me . . . but, her HEART IS BROKEN!!!

And, if you THINK . . . inasmuch, as we think, or the Catholic Church, thinks . . . or ANY other, Christian Church . . . or WHATEVER religion, of the world . . . THINKS . . . that we've OFFENDED, the God . . . that they, want to call . . . Yahweh, Jehovah, Allah, Buddha . . . whatever they . . .

If YOU . . . THINK, for a MOMENT . . . YOUNG people . . . and you're, so SMART now . . . and you're, so BEAUTIFUL . . . and so, SAVVY . . . much MORE, savvy . . . than Cynthia and those, that came BEFORE us . . . or, came AFTER us . . . until . . . YOU NOW . . . the Youth Of The World!!! It's UP to . . . YOU!!!

'Cuz . . . the Rabbi Yeshua, the Jesus Christ of Nazareth . . . his NAME . . . TRULY . . . first and foremost . . . WAS . . . Rabbi Yeshua!!! Because, HE WAS . . . a Kabbalah RABBI!!!

Jesus was . . . a KABBALAHIST Rabbi!!!

And He's, TRYING TO SAY . . . to YOU NOW . . . Please open your eyes, please listen, don't make a hasty judgment, when you're ready, make, a, a, a, an honest judgment, from your hearts.

You know, some of you . . . that I'm speaking, to you today . . . were as SPOILED, as Cynthia was. EVERYTHING . . . that MONEY, could BUY!!! Everything . . . that money, could DO!!!

And YET . . . did my parents . . . ESPECIALLY, me Father . . . NOT give me, the most . . . IMPORTANT . . . GIFT, of ALL!!!

You know what? I don't care. How MANY, Internets . . . how many, lessons . . . in, in, in, SPORTS . . . and in, DANCE . . . and in, ART . . . and in, HORTICULTURE . . . and COLLEGE DEGREES . . . and COMPUTERS . . . I don't care!!! CARS, MONEY . . . all the, HAPPY BOLOGNA . . . of the false, phony, Lucifer . . . ALL of the, PHONY TRAPPINS . . . of the WORLD!!!

You know, next time . . . your parents, ask YOU . . . what you WANT, for your BIRTHDAY, or for . . . CHRISTMAS . . .

Say to them . . . you know what??? I HAVE everything else!!! I have EVERYTHING . . . that MONEY, can BUY!!!

I've NOT had YOU, much . . . because, you've BEEN OUT . . . WORKING . . . to buy, everything that MONEY . . . could buy!!! But, you know what . . . we ALL, need to GET AWAY . . . from that.

Uno momeno por favore . . . we ALL, need to get away, from that . . . for a MINUTE!!!

Because a minute . . . is like, a day . . . a day is like, a thousand years . . . a thousand years, is like a day . . . in a God's SIGHT!!! In the Creators sight!!!

YOU need, to GET UP . . . on YOUR, High Horses . . . as Cynthia, is up on her, high horse . . . now!!! And say . . . you know what . . . MUM, DAD, GRANDMUM, GRANDAD, Foster MOTHER, Foster Father, whatever . . . your case may be . . .

YOU are the WORLD!!! You are the CHILDREN!!! You are the FUTURE!!! And you, need to SET, the TONE . . . for the, rest of US . . . and that tone, should BE . . .

When . . . you parents, NEXT . . . ask YOU, what you WANT . . . that money, can BUY!!! That they can, PLACATE YOU WITH . . . because, they can't be . . . THERE for you, THEMSELVES . . . they CAN'T GIVE, of them self and their, TIME!!!

You NEED to SAY . . . You know what??? You know what I, REALLY WANT??? More than, a trip to the MALL . . . a trip to DISNEYWORLD . . . or a trip to . . . WHATEVER!!! More than I want, my Internet . . . more than I want, my friends . . . more than I want, ANY . . . sex, drugs, rock and roll, rap, hip hop . . . I don't care!!!

IF YOU . . . say to THEM . . . LOOK give me, the ULTIMATE . . . GIFT!!! GIVE ME . . . THE GIFT . . . OF PEACE . . . AND LOVE!!!

I'm WAITING!!! Just TELL THEM . . . I'm waiting for you. You're OLDER than ME!!! You've BEEN here LONGER!!! You know what??? I . . . and MY CHILDREN . . . in the, FUTURE . . . WE WANT PEACE!!!

P-E-A-C-E . . . So, you know what . . . all I'm saying . . . as Cynthia's, good friend, John Lennon, said . . . all HE, was saying . . . was GIVE PEACE . . . a CHANCE!!!

If we ALL, get on the . . . SAME PAGE . . . and we, TELL . . . ALL the, POWERS that be . . . ALL the, GOVERNMENTS . . . of the WORLD!!!

And first, it's gotta START . . . at the, GRASS, ROOTS, LEVEL!!! In OUR . . . own HOMES!! If we, CAN'T say . . . TO our parents . . . WE WANT PEACE!!!

WE WANT LOVE!!! And, WE WANT A FUTURE!!! For OURSELVES . . . and OUR children!!! And we DON'T want . . . YOU, our parents and our grandparents . . . or the people ABOVE 'ya . . .

ALL the WAY . . . BACK, through TIME . . . who WAGED, the CRAZY, INSANE, WARS . . . that you're now . . . WAGING over OIL!!!

FORGET IT!!!

And, I'm going to speak, to you . . . YOUNG PEOPLE . . . young Men and Women . . . of the WORLD!!! More, in this book . . . 'cuz the REST, of the people . . . May, or MAT NOT . . . hear me. And, I don't CARE!!!

But, as long as, the YOUNG PEOPLE . . . can GET WITH . . . the PROGRAM!!! You know, WE CAN do . . . THIS THING!!!

Let Cynthia, be your . . . God Mother. Whether . . . you have, a Godmother . . . or not . . . I, Cynthia Anne Marie Gunn . . . would LOVE to be, YOUR . . . God Mother!!!

Not for nothin' . . . because, I CARE . . . 'Cuz I care about . . . YOU and the FUTURE, of YOUR children!!! Which, your PARENTS . . . aren't EVEN, SPEAKIN' . . . to you, of you . . . YET!!!

Because, they don't CARE MUCH . . . about THEMSELVES!!! Look WHAT they're DOING!!! They're OUT . . . RUNNING AROUND . . . trying to make, MONEY . . . NOT paying ATTENTION, to YOU!!! Fluffin' . . . 'ya OFF . . . on COMPUTERS, onto friends . . . onto CELL PHONES . . . YOU are SO . . . set ADRIFT, at SEA . . . by your OWN PARENTS!!!

But, don't THINK . . . for a MINUTE, that Cynthia's . . . NOT, your LIGHTHOUSE!!! On a FOGGY, STORMY, NIGHT!!! 'Cuz . . . Cynthia IS your GOD MOTHER!!!

And, she LOVES YOU!!!

So COME TO ME . . . all of you, YOUTH . . . who are HUNGRY . . . and THIRSTY . . . for the, TRUTH!!! YOUTH!!!

Who are, hungry and thirsty . . . for LOVE . . . of a, Mother and/or a Father . . . that you MAY, or MAY NOT . . . have, in your HOUSE!!!

And FORGIVE THEM, for they know . . . as the, Christ said . . . on the CROSS!!! Forgive them, for they know not, what they do.

THIS . . . your GENERATION . . . has to BE, the generation . . . of FORGIVENESS!!!

Your generation, has to be the generation . . . that PICKS, the FRUIT . . . off the, TREE OF LIFE!!!

And, the Tree of Life . . . is the TREE, of FORGIVENESS!!! So, pick the fruit . . . off the Tree of Life!!! Forgiveness!!!

DON'T . . . pick the fruit, off the . . . TREE OF DEATH!!! Which people, MY AGE . . . 49 . . . and down, to your parents age . . . and ABOVE US ALL!!!

And, they're ALL DEAD NOW!!! 'Cuz there's NOBODY . . . a hundred and thirty, years old . . . ANY MORE!!! 'Cuz they're ALL . . . DEAD NOW!!! 'Cuz they . . . ALL PICKED, the tree, off the . . . FORBIDDEN FRUIT!!! FRUIT!!!

They ALL . . . picked . . . THE TREE OF DEATH!!!

I . . . URGE YOU . . . and I, BEG YOU . . . not for Cynthia . . . for YOURSELVES . . . and for YOUR children, in the FUTURE!!! For PEACE . . . FINALLY, upon this ORB . . . we ALL call . . . EARTH . . . Our Mother . . . NO OTHER . . . our SANCTUARY!!! EARTH!!! Why . . . does it . . . HAVE TO . . . BECOME . . . our PRISON . . . our GRAVE and our, MORTUARY?!?

It DOES NOT . . . have to CONTINUE . . . THAT WAY!!! We can HAVE . . . the THOUSAND YEARS . . . PEACE!!!

We can HAVE . . . the SAVIOR . . . send his LAMB . . . AMONGST US . . . to GIVE us . . . the PEACE and LOVE and SECURITY . . . that we're LOOKIN' for!!!

SO, DON'T . . . LET . . . NOTHIN' . . . SCARE, YOU!!! Don't let the, American Government!!! The GEO-POLITICAL . . . World Government, Iran, Iraq, The Russians, The Cubans, The North Koreans . . . DON'T . . . LET . . . any, of 'em . . . scare 'ya.

'Cuz . . . they're SCARING . . . the BEJABBAS . . . OUT of your, PARENTS . . . and your parents, PARENTS!!!

WHY??? Why do you THINK . . . they'll STILL, make WAR . . . to THIS DAY??? 'Cuz, they're ALL . . . SCARED!!!

But, there's NOTHIN' . . . to be FEARED OF!!! Of, FEAR . . . ITSELF!!! FEAR Lucifer . . . FEAR the DARKNESS . . . FEAR the angel, of DEATH . . . and . . . DARKNESS!!!

And, Cynthia . . . I WILL SHOW YOU . . . in the next, couple chapters, of this book . . . and then, in the final book . . . I will GIVE you . . . my YOUTH . . . of my, WORLD!!!

Cynthia, God Mother . . . of the youth, of the world . . . I WILL GIVE YOU . . . HAND PICKED . . . HANDED DOWN . . . WORD FOR WORD . . . THE BLUEPRINT . . .

TO, ETERNAL LIFE AND ETERNAL PEACE AND ETERNAL HAPPINESS!!! And, I give it . . . to YOU . . . as a GIFT!!!

And, what YOU DO . . . with IT . . . for YOURSELVES, and for . . . YOUR CHILDREN . . . to, REVERSE . . . the EVIL, ILL, CYCLE!!! Of your parents . . . FORGIVE THEM . . . grandparents . . . and the, parents BEFORE THEM!!!

All, the WAY . . . BACK . . . through . . . EVE!!! Through . . . TIME!!! My next dissertation, I BEG YOU . . . TO FORGIVE . . . EVE!!!

I BEG YOU, to FORGIVE . . . your PARENTS . . . GRANDPARENTS . . . and ANYONE . . . who's EVER . . . STOMPED . . . on your HEART, MINDS, SOULS, WILLS and DESTINIES!!!

Just listen to Cynthia . . . and if, you DON'T agree . . . then, THROW EVERYTHING . . . I've said . . . out the window!!! TRASH IT!!!

But, If you DO agree . . . and you THINK, I know . . . wee bit . . . about . . . WHAT, I'm TALKING ABOUT . . . then, TAKE it . . . CLOSE . . . to your HEART!!! For, I love you . . . and I'm trying, to help. Before, MY JOURNEY . . . at 49 nearly . . . this is, the fifth, of July 2008 . . . and I'll be 49 . . . on the, 28th of July 2008 . . .

I'm trying, to help you . . . before I . . . leave this, earthly plane. Because YOU, shall INHERIT . . . the earth, NEXT . . . and what you, do WITH IT . . . will DECIDE!!!

And, that's all . . . I can say!!! It's NOT, a scolding . . . it's just a . . . HEADS UP!!! So, you know what . . .

I GOT YOUR BACK!!!
DO YOU . . . HAVE MY BACK?!?
That's all I ask.
Peace . . . BROTHER . . .
Peace . . . SISTER . . .
I love you all . . .

Cynthia

Chapter 18

Youth of the world . . . this is, your God Mother, Cynthia . . . again, speaking to you, out of love and out of FACT!

Now . . . I have the SECRET . . . of the secret . . . which, I will reveal to YOU, in the next chapter. But, the secret, of the secret contains . . . the secret of, The Torah . . . the secret, of the Creation . . . the secret, of Adam and Eve . . . and their first children, Cain and Abel.

And, WHO . . . KILLED Abel . . . and it WASN'T . . . Cain!!! And, after that . . . way down the line . . . WHY, the TOWER of BABEL . . . came along! Which SEPARATED us . . . ALL! By LOOKS, by LANGUAGES, by SCATTERED about . . . across, the FACE of the EARTH!!!

And, we can't seem . . . to get back, on the same page . . . and I leave it to YOU . . . the YOUTH, of the WORLD!!! From, 12, 13, up to 25 or 30 . . .

I leave this MESSAGE . . . to you, my POSTERITY . . . as your God Mother, Cynthia . . . and, I'm NOT CHANNELING, Eve . . . and, I don't claim to BE . . . EVE . . . but, I HAVE, the INFORMATION!!! Okay! Which, I will describe, in the next chapter.

But, a HUGE and HIDEOUS . . . thing . . . HAPPENED . . . in the, Garden of Eden!!! Huh! When EVE . . . the Mother, of us ALL . . . huh . . . was the FIRST one, TEMPTED . . . by Lucifer, Satan.

The Torah . . . ah . . . says that, he was a serpent . . . that was symbolism . . . his voice, came up from the ground . . . at the fruit, of the Tree . . . his demon seed that he, planted . . . in the Garden of Eden!!!

Why? Because, he was an archangel . . . called Lucifer, angel of light . . . so, he had the power, to plant . . . the one tree, before Adam and Eve . . . which God said, "You shall NOT, EAT of that FRUIT . . . of THAT TREE . . . lest you DIE!!!" Because he was so powerful . . . as an Archangel . . .

And the Archangels were: Lucifer, the angel of light . . . Gabriel,

Michael and Raphael, and Lucifer . . . took, himself and all the other, angels and all the, other COHORTS . . . COHORTS . . . from Heaven, down to the earth . . . and below, Geahennah . . . Geahennah . . . the UNQUENCHABLE . . . FIRE!!!

And, it was Rabbi Yeshua, the Jesus Christ . . . of, the House of David . . . of Nazareth . . . Rabbi Yeshua, Jesus of Nazareth . . . who, NONE OF US . . . as I've said before, have DIED!!!

And, lived in the . . . DEAD!!! Amongst the DEAD . . . for three days . . . and, HE took the KEYS . . . and, HE got THEM . . . and when, HE was RESURRECTED . . .

FISSION!!! FISSION!!! NUCLEAR FISSION!!! Which, we could NOT . . . understand, UNTIL . . . the Nuclear AGE . . . CAME!!! And then, the nuclear age, DIED!!! When . . . I PRAYED, TO THE GOD, to TAKE THREE MILE ISLAND . . . OUT OF MY LIFE!!!

I SAID, "Dear God, PLEASE . . . do SOMETHING . . . to THREE MILE ISLAND . . . so that, we can LEAVE . . . Pennsylvania!"

If, you don't . . . understand that . . . YET . . . there's nothing ELSE . . . I can SHARE . . . with you.

But, MY PRAYER . . . to REMOVE, Three Mile Island . . . not only, from MY LIFE . . . BUT, from . . . ALL OF OUR LIVES . . .

And, AFTER THAT . . . the Americans . . . were SO AFRAID . . . to BUILD . . . ANOTHER, Nuclear Plant . . . but NOW . . .

We have, Barack Mohammed Obama . . . and, I love him . . . and, he's BEAUTIFUL!!! Huh! A Prince, of his Mother and Father . . . a Prince, of Africa . . . under his Father's LINEAGE!!!

And, we have, John McCain . . . McCain . . . of the Celts . . . McCain . . . and, as I said to you, before . . . John McCain . . . is the WEAKEST, of the . . . Republican Candidates!!!

And don't think, for a minute . . . Ladies and Gentlemen . . . that the English . . . and the OTHER . . . POWERS, that BE . . . across the WORLD . . . the skinheads, the neo-nazis, I don't CARE!!!

DON'T think . . . for a MOMENT . . . that Barack Obama, with or without . . . Hillary Clinton, and this, is the 5th of July . . . 2008 . . . DO NOT THINK . . . for a moment, that Barack Obama . . . Hillary Rodham Clinton and Bill . . . well . . . let's just, get his name RIGHT!!!

William Jefferson BLYTHE Clinton . . . have not, pounded-out and hammered-out . . . an AGREEMENT!!!

Now, Hillary . . . has WHAT?!? All of a SUDDEN . . . thrown HER SUPPORT behind . . . Barack Obama?!? Not so much, for VP . . . if she gets it . . . I don't care . . . she MAY get . . . Secretary of the State . . . and we have Condoleezza . . . Condy . . . right??? Condoleezza, under . . . George W. Bush . . .

But, we're ALL being, SET-UP . . . for a HUGE FALL!!! And, I don't WANT . . . Barack Obama . . . to TAKE, the fall!!! But, I'm afraid, that he will. Either, the skinheads . . . neo-nazis and/or, I don't know . . . ONE WACKO PERSON . . . will try, to take him out. I'm afraid of that!

And, so . . . WHOEVER, is HIS . . . VP candidate . . . will become the President. And, that's SCARY . . . to me!!! It's NOT RIGHT . . . and it's scary . . . because, Barack Mohammed Obama, who's a Christian . . . I don't care . . . if he IS, or he ISN'T . . . He's ABOUT . . . to BECOME . . . our PRESIDENT!!! And, the VP . . . I don't know . . . I don't care.

But, Hillary . . . Rodham BLYTHE Clinton . . . Let's get it straight . . . 'cuz, William Jefferson BLYTHE Clinton . . . is THAT . . . President's . . . TRUE NAME!!!

But, this is a short chapter . . . just to give you . . . a HEADS UP!!!

To what's . . . COMING!!! Don't, let THEM . . . fool you!

YOUNG PEOPLE . . . from 12 or 13 . . . up to 25 . . . ANYONE, who's . . . YOUNG enough . . . and still, SMART enough . . . and, SAVVY enough . . . to HEAR MY VOICE!!!

Don't think, for a cotton pickin' moment . . . that, ALL . . . this, GEOPOLITICAL STUFF . . . has not, ALREADY . . . been, DECIDED!!!

And, let me tell you . . . ALSO . . . not prophecy, from Cynthia . . . BUT, prophecy . . . from MY FATHER . . . William Thomas Phillip Gunn . . . who told me, in 2000 . . . 2002 . . . and up until, the day he died . . . in 2005 . . . "Cindy, there WILL BE . . . a GREAT DEPRESSION . . . I won't BE HERE . . . to see it . . . YOU WILL. It WILL BE GLOBAL!!! It will be, on a GLOBAL . . . SCALE!!!"

My Father, told me. And, as I've told you, before . . . HIS FATHER . . . SAW the ALIEN . . . DISCS . . . at ROSWELL . . . and, my Father's, Grandfather . . . was a huge owner . . . of, land . . . cotton plantations, in Alabama . . . and oil, in Texas . . .

But . . . WAY BEFORE, THAT . . . WAY BEFORE, the PURITAINS, came here . . . The Gunns, were here . . . a hundred years, BEFORE . . . Christopher Columbus . . . and, as I said . . . three or four, ten times . . . before, it's CARVED . . . on a CLIFF, in a New England States . . . STATE . . . ONE, State . . .

And, The Knights Templar, The Vatican, and all, the powers that be . . . KNOW . . . that it's . . . TRUE!!! QE2 . . . Queen Elizabeth the second, herself . . . the HYPOCRITE, who . . . USED DIANA . . . MY 12th COUSIN . . . by birth . . .

To be, the woman who, BROUGHT FORTH . . . Harry, William first . . . then Harry . . . for the likes of . . . Charles!!! NO!!! Its all, FAKE, PHONY and FALSE!!!

All the way, from Henry VIII . . . DOWN!!! To . . . QE2!!! Henry VIII, Anne Boleyn's daughter, QE1 . . . all the way . . . down . . . to QE2!!!

Now, If you don't get it . . . if you don't understand . . . there's Nothin' more, I can say . . . to you . . . BUT, EVERYTHING . . . I SAY, is TRUE! I'm not, lookin' for your money. I'm not, lookin' for your pity. Not lookin' for . . . ANYTHING ELSE . . .

But, what I say, to you . . . IS . . . before I . . . leave this planet . . . on almost, my forty ninth year . . .

PLEASE . . . BELIEVE . . . WHAT I AM SAYING . . . TO YOU!!! IT IS . . . THE TRUTH!!!

And, in the next chapter . . . this is what? Eighteen . . . I believe? Of the book . . . chapter nineteen, of THIS BOOK . . . will TIE-UP all the LOOSE ENDS . . . it'll be, the final chapter, of book two . . . which, is called . . . I AM YOUR GOD MOTHER FORGIVE ME The Secret of The Secret . . .

And, It WILL be . . . REVEALED!!! In the, next chapter . . . so PLEASE . . . DON'T LEAVE ME!!! Stick by me!!! I love you.

Cynthia

Chapter 19

The Secret of The Secret . . . the Mystery . . . Begins . . . at the Beginning . . .

EVERYTHING . . . I am about, to tell you . . . is . . . TRUE . . . because . . . I was born . . . The Luna-Leo-Theo-Sophia . . .

I have the information, and The Vatican, The Knights Templar, The Kabbalah Rabbis and, The Freemasons . . . KNOW EXACTLY, who . . . I AM!!!

I was, to be BORN . . . in the LAST, one hundred year . . . EARTHLY, time frame . . . in the, current ERA . . . of Human History . . . and so, THE DAY . . . I was SENT, was FIRST, at CONCEPTION . . . when I chose, my EARTHLY parents . . . William and Celene.

AS, my INTELLECT, ESSENCE, LIGHTS . . . desired . . . to COME INTO, this Human CONDITION . . . through . . . their LOVEMAKING and through, their . . . LOINS.

The Tibetan Book of the DEAD . . . has the information, on which I speak, now . . . that our Intellect, Essence, Light . . . CHOOSES . . . from ALL the humans, copulating . . . when we, SEE THEM!!! When we CHOOSE!!!

Now, this OCCURS . . . and we DECIDE . . . to COME, to the EARTHLY PLANE!!! And if, CONCEIVED . . . and NOT, MURDERED . . . in ABORTION or . . . MISCARRIED . . . or the like . . . We stay . . . NINE LUNAR CYCLES!!!

Also, known as . . . MONTHS!!! In the . . . WOMB!!! In-VITRO!!! In the WATER . . . within, our Mother's BODY!!!

Now, I Cynthia. DRINK . . . the wonderful, FRUIT . . . the GOOD FRUIT . . . of the, HIMILAYAN Gogi . . . of the. Tibetan

MONKS . . . at the HIGHEST WELL . . . NEAR the Tibetan Monks.

And, I've been drinking it . . . for three years. I studied . . . my Roman Catholicism, for forty nine years. And, all the great religions, of the world . . . for MUCH, of my life . . . and recently . . . and then, LASTLY . . . I've studied, the Kabbalah . . . for two point five years . . . and I'm NOW, OVER FORTY years old.

And, the Rabbi's . . . KNOW, what I'm SAYING!!! Because, I'm forty nine . . . so I can SAY, what I can SAY . . . when I'm, OVER FORTY!!!

So PLEASE!!! TRUST ME!!! I know, what I AM . . . saying HERE, FOLKS!!!

Well . . . getting back to, the NINE MONTHS . . . those nine months, are NOT only, for our GESTATION . . . growth and development, they are for the, OPPORTUNITY . . . of our, intellect, essence, light, to MERGE . . . with, our human, SKELETAL and PERSONA . . . essence!!!

THAT . . . of a human BEING!!! Those nine months, are WHEN, the NINE MULTIPLE INTELLIGENCES . . . which the GREAT . . . Doctor Howard Gardiner, has UNLOCKED . . . the MYSTERIES of . . . ALL of, the nine multiple intelligences!!!

And, during these, nine LUNAR CYCLES . . . months . . . is WHEN, the nine multiple intelligences . . . take . . . HOLD!!! And, we come, into our intellectual essence.

Now, I would like to speak more, on the processes . . . of this, ENTIRE BIRTH!!! PROCESS!!! We will get into that . . . soon.

But, I want to say . . . right now . . . so, we who living . . . here, on this planet . . . on earth, we who are here, now . . . LIKE IT OR NOT . . . ACCEPT IT OR NOT . . . and WEIRD, and as FAR-FETCHED . . . as it may, SEEM to us . . . we DO CHOOSE, to COME HERE!!!

And who, we ARE . . . and who, our parents ARE . . . and what, we will LOOK LIKE . . . black or white, or whatever . . . kind of, HAIR . . . we have . . . MOST OF US . . . just, DON'T . . . REMEMBER!!!

That WE, made the GREAT CHOICE . . . to, come HERE!!!

NOT the . . . PHONY CHOICE . . . the phony choice . . . and the, phony choice . . . of ABORTION!!!

To SNUFF-OUT, the LIGHT . . . the PURE LIGHT . . . of The CREATOR'S . . . Intellect, Essence, Light or . . . SOUL!!! As, THE WORLD . . . LABELS IT!!!

So be it!

That FRIENDS . . . is ALL . . . we TRULY ARE! Intellect, essence and light! Then, choosing . . . HUMAN FORM . . . to TRY . . . this earthly plane . . . and OUR, condition.

This, ACTUALLY . . . and TRULY . . . MIMICS . . . the FIRST, Story of Creation! In the Torah! When, The Creator . . . now we can, call Him . . . GOD, Allah, Yahweh, Jehovah, Buddha, whatever . . . you like! Whatever's, your pleasure! It's of NO matter, or concern . . . to me. JUST . . . that He, is The Creator . . . God.

He, is the HIGHEST . . . in the ORDER . . . of intellect, essence, light. ONLY . . . a FEW, HUMANS . . . have SEEN Him! Such as, but not limited to, of course . . . NOAH and MOSES!!! Let us NOT . . . forget THAT!!!

Now, we ALL KNOW . . . what they . . . DID DO!!!

THEY SAID . . . YES!!! To The Creator!!! AND . . . FACE-TO-FACE . . . Ladies and Gentlemen, Boys and Girls . . . Moses and Noah, said . . . YES, I will KNOW . . . YES, I will LOVE . . . and YES, I will SERVE!!!

Inasmuch, as THEY said YES . . .

Lucifer and his . . . sub-angels-jealous-cohorts . . . JEALOUS, of The Creator said . . . NO, I will NOT KNOW . . . NO, I will NOT LOVE . . . and NO, I will NOT SERVE!!!

Hence, that Lucifer . . . and his cohorts . . . were BANISHED, from the paradise . . . also . . . called, HEAVEN.

Where . . . The Heavenly Court IS!!!

For DISLOYALTY . . . to The Creator . . . The TRIUNE GodHead!!! They were BANISHED, to the ABYSS . . . and it's INTERNAL CORE . . . the UNQUENCHABLE FIRES, of GEAHENNAH!!!

These THINGS . . . I TELL you . . . are TRUE. Please . . . BELIEVE ME!!!

So, our Creator . . . GOD, still loving, EVEN . . . that NASTY, SNIPE . . . Lucifer . . . said, to His TRIUNE ESSENCE . . . The Son Rabbi Yeshua and The Holy Ghost/Spirit . . . the, DIVINE FEMININE . . . the DOVE . . . What SHALL, we DO . . . NOW?!?

The THREE, in the TRIUNE GodHead . . . DECIDED . . . that the, GRAND EXPERIMENT . . . NEEDED to be CONDUCTED . . . to GET, that Lucifer . . . to, SEE THE LIGHT . . . AGAIN!!!

Of The Creator . . . AGAIN!!! And, AMEND his WAYS!!! And, RETURN to the FOLD!!! The Heaven . . . The Paradise!!!

To THIS DAY . . . Lucifer . . . REFUSES . . . he dug a PIT, for himself and his, FALLEN COHORTS!!! And, the human SOULS . . . that he's STOLEN!!! To Geahennah!!! From . . . the . . . beginning . . . So, OKAY . . . back to, the Creation . . .

Now, our Creator, MADE . . . this ORB, for His son and daughter, as their, BELOVED . . . PLACE!!! That was his FIRST, ENTITY CREATION . . . MALE and FEMALE . . .

And, they were . . . a MALE, BLACK . . . and a, FEMALE, WHITE with red hair . . . THE TWIN FLAMES . . . Yud Chet Vav and Mem Lamed Hey . . . and, have NO DOUBT . . . ABOUT IT!!!

Because . . . It's so . . .

Those were their names, the male, was Yud Chet Vav and the daughter, the female, Mem Lamed Hey.

So, The Creator . . . THEN FORMED . . . The SECOND Creation . . . in the TINY RECESSES . . . of the earthly orb, to MIMIC . . . Yud Chet Vav and Mem Lamed Hey's IMAGES!!! And, LIKENESS!!! Of The Creators TRINITY!!!

Father, Son, Daughter . . . ie: Father, Son, Holy Spirit!!!

Hence, The SECOND Creation . . . of His IMAGE and LIKENESS!!! Adam, of the DUST . . . and, Eve of Adam's RIB!!! The Creator SET THEM, Adam and Eve . . . in a Garden . . . in the EASTERN PART . . . of the orb . . . which, The Creator called: Garden of Eden.

Which, was BENEATH . . . the EARTHLY SKY . . . to LIVE and LOVE there . . . with ALL The Creation . . . EARTH, WATER, SOIL, PLANTS, ANIMALS and . . . EACH OTHER!!! To live . . .

in HARMONY!!! YET . . . that, nasty little snipe, Lucifer . . . became the WORM!!! Of the WORMWOOD!!!

And because, he was a FALLEN-Archangel . . . just as the status of . . . Gabriel, Michael and Raphael . . . who were NOT, fallen . . . who DID choose to, STAY in the HEAVENLY COURT . . . WITH, God . . . the TRIUNE GodHead . . .

What did that nasty, little snipe, Lucifer do???

He, because of EVERYTHING . . . he REFUSED . . . was miniaturized . . . and banished . . . to Geahennah . . . that snipe . . . sprouted, one EVIL SEED . . . one DEMON SEED . . . and one false, PHONY TREE . . . and RIGHT, in the MIDDLE of . . . The Creator's GARDEN!!!

HOW DARE . . . that Lucifer!!!

And those, who STILL EAT it . . . the FALLEN HUMAN beings . . . you or . . . I, only WE decide!!!

So okay . . . upon seeing the ABYSS, The Creator . . . separated the waters and turned the Abyss. Now, Satan was sent into the fertile, teaming planet, earth . . . and the, sky . . . reflects the blue waters above . . . and DAY . . . and we see the waters, kept ON the orb . . . EARTH, by wind and gravity . . . EVERY DAY!!!

And, the STARS of our NIGHTLY . . . sky!!! The Creator blew then . . . the SPIRIT, of the WIND and still does . . . TO THIS DAY!!! Which keeps us . . . UPON the EARTH!!!

Next . . . LIGHT was projected, on the ABYSS . . . then He MADE a DOME . . . of the SKY . . . the BLUE DAYLIGHT . . . as I've mentioned before and the STARRY SKY . . . NIGHT LIGHT, to allow LIFE on the ABYSS, to COME!!! And, to Continue!!!

Think of a SNOWGLOBE . . . we're IN IT!!!

The Creator . . . is EVERYWHERE ELSE!!! Outside of the snowglobe . . . the NEXT step was, to SEPARATE the WATER . . . on the abyss, and FORM . . . DRY LAND!!!

Hence, the SEA . . . and the earthly dry land . . . with SEEDS . . . JUST as WE are going . . . to becoming in time, to our Creator . . . as SEEDS!!! Of either WHEAT . . . or WEEDS!!!

REMEMBER THAT . . . FOLKS!!!

Now, The Creator . . . KNOWING, that Lucifer . . . was ALL about DEATH . . . and EVIL . . . and TROUBLE . . . being SOMEWHAT powerful . . . as a FALLEN Archangel . . .

WARNED the DUST MAN . . . and WOMAN of his RIB . . . that being, Adam and Eve . . . who were created, in the IMAGE and LIKENESS . . . of the FATHER and His son, YESHUA . . . and His daughter, The HOLY SPIRIT!!!

DO NOT EAT THAT FRUIT . . . NOR TOUCH THAT TREE . . . I GIVE YOU ALL ELSE . . . AS YOURS . . . EVERYTHING ELSE . . . BUT, DO THAT . . . AND YOU, WILL SURELY DIE!!!

And, aren't WE . . . STILL DYING . . . UNTIL, THIS VERY DAY!!!

Ladies and Gentlemen . . . and this is the 9th of July . . . in the year 2008!!!

Now, how many of us . . . KNOW . . . do YOU KNOW? I don't KNOW . . . do ANY of us KNOW . . . SOMEONE . . . OVER 130 Years?!? I say, NO ONE DOES!!! So now, I BEG OF YOU . . .

PLEASE . . . my BROTHERS and SISTERS . . . fellow children of Adam and Eve . . . fellow Cain and Abels . . . ENOUGH IS ENOUGH!!!

We can RECLAIM . . . our CREATED STATUS . . . as GOOD, CREATOR LIKENESS. BEINGS . . . OR WE SHALL . . . NOT!!! Shall we CONTINUE . . . to follow, the ERRONEOUS . . . WAYS of Lucifer!!!

OVER . . . OUR GOD!!! OUR OWN . . . CREATOR?!?

I will NOT . . . and YOU should . . . NOT!!!

And NOW . . . to SET the TORAH, STRAIGHT . . . ONCE and FOR ALL . . . CAIN DID NOT, KILL ABEL . . . EVE DID!!!

The Creators son, Yeshua . . . upon the orb . . . before Adam and Eve, were even FORMED . . . was a manchild black . . . and The Creators daughter, The Holy Ghost/The Dove . . . was a femalechild white with red hair. And, I've said this before . . . AND, IT'S TRUE!!!

Now, in the SECOND Creation . . . likeness . . . Adam and Eve, first and foremost . . . were here . . . it WAS EVE . . . who TASTED, the FORBIDDEN FRUIT . . . FIRST!!!

And then, GAVE it . . . to ADAM!!! So, she knew MORE!!! So Eve, herself . . . from the GET GO . . . from the BEGINNING . . . became the MOST . . . LIKE, Lucifer!!!

JEALOUS . . . of, Yeshua and the, feminine Holy Ghost/ Spirit . . . the Dove!!! Lucifer's voice, from the ground . . . ABOVE, the FIRE of Geahennah . . . ENTICED EVE!!! To eat, his WORMWOOD . . . DEMON SEED FRUIT!!!

Hence, as I said before . . . and we know . . . it's TRUE . . . she GAVE some . . . to ADAM!!! Who was SO IN LOVE . . . with Eve!!!

Now, God knew . . . Lucifer had . . . TRAPPED THEM!!! Beforehand!!! BUT . . . when they said . . . with FIG LEAVES, over their own LOINS . . .

"OH! WE HID!!! WE WERE NAKED!!!

God said, "WHO TOLD YOU . . . YOU WERE NAKED!!!"

No answer, from Adam and Eve . . .

God then stated . . . "SO . . . you've EATEN, the FORBIDDEN . . .

Lucifer fruit . . . NOW!!! OUT YOU GO . . . from EDEN!!! Eve, YOU shall SUFFER . . . in REBIRTH . . . Adam, YOU shall TOIL . . . SWEAT of your BROW . . . to PROVIDE!!!"

Done! They were CAST OUT . . . and a, PILLAR of FIRE . . . kept THEM, from REENTERING . . . EDEN!!!

Now, Cain was born FIRST . . . of course, then ABEL. Cain, was SAD . . . in his life, because . . . Abel, had found FAVOR . . . with GOD and his father . . . so it seemed . . . FAVOR . . . OVER Cain . . . now that, made Cain . . . VERY SAD . . .

WHY??? We DON'T KNOW, why . . . it's MYSTERIOUS!!! But, Abel was . . . WHITE, as EVE was.

Now, Eve, DESIRING only ADAM . . . of course, as God would say, "You will DESIRE, for your . . . HUSBAND!!!" WAS JEALOUS!!! Of her . . . OWN LIKENESS!!! The WHITE . . . RED-HEADED . . . ABEL!!! So . . . what did EVE DO??? She TORMENTED, her OWN SON . . . her BLACK SON . . . CAIN . . . who LOOKED LIKE . . . his Father . . . ADAM!!!

She TORMENTED and TORMENTED . . . CAIN!!! And TRIED . . . to HAVE HIM, KILL ABEL . . . for HER!!! She tried to GET HIM . . . to, DO THE DEED . . . FOR HER!!!

JUST as the ABORTIONISTS . . . of TODAY . . . NOW KILL . . . FOR HER!!! Those EVIL . . . daughters and sons . . . of HERS!!! TO THIS VERY DAY!!!

Now, Cain . . . on the other hand, DID NOT OBLIGE . . . his Mother!!! He would NOT KILL, his BROTHER!!! BUT . . . When God said, to him, regarding . . . WHERE IS YOUR BROTHER???

Cain, tried to COVER-UP . . . his OWN MOTHER . . . EVE'S . . . MURDER!!! NOT HIS . . . of Abel!!!

So . . . GOD DID . . . PUT a MARK . . . on CAIN!!! IE: Cain was, beautifully BLACK . . . as Adam . . . who was, beautifully BLACK, as YESHUA . . .

Well . . . the mark was put. WHITE PALMS . . . on the HANDS . . . and WHITE SOLES . . . of the FEET!!!

TO PROVE . . . that he DID NOT . . . KILL . . . ABEL!!!

He TRIED . . . to TAKE, the BLAME . . . for his MOTHER'S DEED!!!

And so, the SIGNS . . . upon HANDS AND FEET . . . of Cain . . . were to SHOW US . . . that TRULY . . . the ONE RESPONSIBLE . . . the RESPONSIBLE PARTY . . . was his WHITE Mother . . . EVE!!!

Who TRULY KILLED, her OWN . . . WHITE SON . . . Abel . . . out of JEALOUSY!!! Satan's JEALOUSY!!! INGRAINED!!!

She was so JEALOUS . . . that her BLACK HUSBAND . . . Adam and GOD . . . HIMSELF . . . LOVED Abel FIRST!!! Or, found FAVOR . . . with Abel . . . FIRST!!!

She HERSELF . . . was that JEALOUS!!!

Now, I KNOW . . . this is a, PUZZLING and MYSTERIOUS . . . SCENARIO . . . I AGREE!!!

But, THIS IS THE TRUTH!!! So, PLEASE . . . NOW let US ALL . . . get on . . . the SAME PAGE!!!

Of, The BLUEPRINT . . . of ETERNAL LIFE!!! I BEG OF YOU!!! At lease, THINK ABOUT IT!!! At lease, READ IT!!!

And DECIDE . . . whether you think . . . I'm telling you the TRUTH . . . or not . . . because, I WILL BE . . . TELLIN" YOU the TRUTH!!! As I HAVE . . . from WORD ONE . . . of BOOK ONE . . . to WORD ONE . . . of this BOOK . . . to WORD ONE . . . of the THIRD . . . ALL the WORDS . . . I say, are TRUE!!!

Otherwise . . . MAY I BE STRUCK DEAD . . . by GOD ALMIGHTY . . . HIMSELF!!!

Now, MORE of the TRUTH . . . will be COMING!!! And, the TRUTH . . . will be the BLUEPRINT . . . of ETERNAL LIFE!!!

And, it is going to be . . . in BOOK THREE . . . which is COMING . . . in VERY RAPID, SUCCESSION!!!

And, THAT BOOK . . . is called, Ladies and Gentlemen, Boys and Girls of the WORLD . . . I AM AS NUTS AS NOAH AND MOSES The Secret of The Truth . . .

Until then . . . God bless you ALL . . . and I love you . . .

Cynthia

Chapter 20

Epilogue. The Triune . . . INTELLECT, ESSENCE, LIGHT . . . called God, consists of THREE POINTS . . . of light . . . The Father, The Son Yeshua and the, feminine deity . . . The Dove/Holy Ghost/ Spirit.

I have been URGED, to RECAP . . . this for you . . . and to, just EXPLAIN . . . a tiny bit more . . . of EVE'S MURDER . . . of Abel. So, I'll be doing that . . . right now . . . Ladies and Gentlemen, Boys and Girls.

This GodHead, is a TRIANGULATION . . . of LIGHT . . . LOVE . . . and MYSTERIOUS, UNFAILING . . . POWER!!!

As I mentioned, in the last chapter . . . the secret of the secret . . . is NOW OUT!!! The first Creation . . . of THEM . . . male and female . . . were PERSONIFICATIONS . . . of the Son and the Dove.

The Son was BLACK . . . the Dove was WHITE, with red hair . . . as I've said. Hence, RED STRING!!!

Down through TIME . . . and the, Kabbalah Rabbis . . . and the HEBREWS . . . who've SUBSCRIBED TO, the red string . . . who've KEPT IT . . . have kept, that SECRET!!!

Also, the RED STRING . . . SYMBOLIZES . . . the BLOOD, that EVE HERSELF SPILT . . . for Eve . . . KILLED Abel. In the PRESENCE . . . of Cain, out of her OWN . . . JEALOUSY!!!

That WHITE Abel . . . with RED HAIR . . . was, FAVORED MOST . . . by Adam and God . . . . EVE herself . . . with Cain . . . LOOKING ON . . . MURDERED, Abel . . . by IMPAILING HIM . . . with his SHEPHERD'S STAFF!!!

A DIRECT BLOW . . . to his HEART!!! Resulting . . . in HIS BLOOD, SPILLING ONTO . . . and INTO . . . the GROUND!!!

Now, that BLOOD of ABEL . . . and the HUMAN DNA . . . and INTELLECT, ESSENCE and LIGHT . . . of Abel . . . CRIED OUT . . . TO GOD!!!

When God HEARD IT . . . and CONFRONTED, Cain . . . Cain told, a HUGE LIE . . . to COVER-UP, his MOTHER'S DEED!!!

Because, he was JEALOUS . . . of his, Mother's JEALOUS OBSESSION . . . of HER JEALOUSY . . . over HOW, Adam and God . . . LOVED Abel, THE MOST!!!

She TWISTED . . . TWISTED . . . Cain's LIFE, AROUND!!! HOW DARE . . . SHE!!!

Call herself . . . MOTHER!!!

A VICIOUS CYCLE . . . then ENSUED . . . which REPEATS ITSELF . . . OVER AND OVER AND OVER . . . unto, THIS VERY DAY!!! I'm speaking to you . . . this is the 9th of July . . . the year 2008!!! TO THIS VERY DAY!!!

IN, OUR LIVING . . . DEATHS!!!

Now, WHAT . . . do I MEAN . . . by THAT???

I mean . . . We're NOT ALIVE!!! We're DEAD!!! Because, the Lucifer took, the form of, a serpent and, SPOKE TO . . . the EVE . . . at his DEMON SEED TREE . . . the WORMWOOD TREE . . .

And so, DEATH . . . the PARASITE . . . of the WORM . . . ENTERED, Eve and Adam's . . . MOUTHS and BODY SYSTEMS . . . and they, BECAME . . . the PARENTS, of US . . . the LIVING . . . DEAD!!!

MORE . . . on THIS . . . later . . .

Now, When God . . . CONFRONTED Cain . . . Eve, was ALREADY BACK . . . in the PRESENCE . . . of Adam!!! At their . . . OWN ABODE.

God ASKED, the WHEREABOUTS . . . of Abel . . . and Cain. RESPONDED . . . with a VAGUE LIE!!! "I do not know . . . am I my brother's keeper?"

God knew . . . BEFORE, He asked Cain . . . ABOUT Abel's MURDER . . . by EVE!!! For STANDING BY . . . and

WATCHING . . . God, MARKED CAIN . . . for just standing by and, watching . . . what his Mother did.

HE marked him . . . with the WHITE hands, PALMS . . . and the WHITE SOLES, of the FEET . . . to SIGNIFY . . . to ANYONE . . . ANYWHERE . . . that Cain DID NOT . . . KILL ABEL!!! Did NOT SPILL . . . Abel's BLOOD . . . onto and into, the GROUND!!!

The SIGN . . . on Cain . . . WAS, as I said before . . . the white colored hands and the feet . . . of SHE . . . WHO DID . . . DO IT!!!

Their OWN Mother . . . EVE!!!

Now, God . . . then BANISHED Cain, AWAY and PROCLAIMED . . . that the MARKS . . . would SIGNIFY . . . to KEEP ANY OTHER HUMANS . . . in a CONSTANT REMINDER . . . of the JEALOUS, WHITE ONE . . . EVE!!!

KILLING . . . her white son Abel . . . and so, her black son Cain . . . born LIKE Adam . . . same skin color . . . black man . . . beautiful black man . . .

He, WAS JUST . . . merely, the INNOCENT BYSTANDER . . . of the MURDER . . . and, COVERING-UP . . . his Mother's EVILDOING!!! So, God also PROCLAIMED . . . because of that . . . that if ANYONE . . . did MURDER CAIN . . . that THEY . . . would HAVE, GOD'S . . . WRATH . . . SEVENFOLD!!! And so, back to OUR STATUS . . . AS THE LIVING DEAD!!!

Now, BRACE YOURSELF . . . from the MOMENT . . . of CONCEPTION . . . in our, Mother's WOMB . . . we are on the ROAD . . . to OUR DEATH!!!

WHO AMONG US . . . is 130 YEARS OLD . . . or OLDER??? No One . . . POINT PROVEN!!!

The TOWER of BABEL . . . will be DISCUSSED . . . at GREAT LENGTH . . . in the next book . . . book three.

Before THAT . . . God told NOAH . . . to BUILD the ARK!!! He TOLD NOAH . . . who WALKED with GOD . . . who SAW, GOD . . .

God said . . . "I'm SORRY . . . that I've EVEN . . . MADE a MAN . . . and a WOMAN!!!"

Noah was JUST and GOOD and God . . . FAVORED HIM!!! But, God was BROKENHEARTED . . . and SAD . . . upon SEEIN' the . . . DEPRAVITY, CORRUPTION and LAWLESSNESS . . . of the people!!! The HUMANS . . . He had Created!!!

God DECIDED . . . to WASH AWAY . . . all those SINS . . . and END their EXHISTANCE!!! Except for Noah . . . and those . . . who got ONTO the ARK, including . . . the animals!!!

And, AFTER the . . . GREAT DELUGE . . . AFTER the GREAT FLOOD . . . God RESTORED . . . ALL THINGS . . . and MADE, ALL THINGS . . . NEW . . . AGAIN . . . through NOAH and . . . ALL, on the ARK!!!

When God had, FINALLY SETTLED . . . Noah down . . . and there was some . . . ORDER RESTORED!!! God gave, a DIRECT QUOTE . . . to NOAH!!!

If ANYONE . . . sheds the BLOOD . . . of MAN . . . by MAN . . . shall HIS BLOOD . . . BE SHED!!! For, in the IMAGE . . . of GOD . . . has MAN . . . BEEN MADE!!!

And then . . . THE COVENANT!!!

No . . . OTHER FLOOD . . . to DESTROY!!!

GOD . . . SET HIS BOW . . . in the SKY!!! As a SIGN . . . of THE COVENANT . . . He MADE . . . to the EARTH!!! To the orb . . . that He had Created . . . FROM the NOTHINGNESS . . . of the ABYSS!!!

Now, once again . . . Ladies and Gentlemen, Boys and Girls, Brothers and Sisters, Fellow Human Creatures . . . Human Beings . . . LIKENESSES and IMAGES . . . of GOD . . . The Creator . . . HIMSELF . . . We're ALL . . . the SAME!!!

CUT the BOLOGNA!!! CUT the STUPID, STUPID . . . IDIOTIC . . . STUFF!!!

And, START LOVIN' . . . ONE . . . ANOTHER!!!

If YOU . . . want PEACE . . . and SECURITY . . . YOU GOTTA' . . . SHOW LOVE!!! It's that SIMPLE!!!

So, I say to YOU . . . don't think, that I'm SNIPING . . . at YOU . . . don't think, that I'm MAD . . . at YOU . . . I'm NOT!!! I LOVE YOU!!! I CARE!!!

BEFORE, I LEAVE . . . this EARTHLY PLANE . . . I HAVE TO, leave . . . THESE MESSAGES!!! Whether they're HEARD NOW . . . 100 YEARS, FROM NOW . . . or NEVER!!!

But, it's MY DUTY . . . because . . .

I will KNOW . . . I will LOVE . . . and I will SERVE!!! And I URGE YOU . . . to DO . . . THE SAME!!!

KNOW, LOVE and SERVE . . . The GOD!!! The CREATOR!!!

In the next book . . . I AM AS NUTS AS NOAH AND MOSES The Secret of the Truth . . .

I tell you ALL . . . I will EXPAND . . . on THIS . . . The Secret of the Secret . . .

FOR NOW . . . ENOUGH SAID. But, I PROMISE YOU . . . FELLOW, Ladies and Gentlemen, Boys and Girls . . . ALL OVER THE WORLD . . .

When WE HAVE . . . the THIRD BOOK . . . of the TRILOGY . . . we will HAVE . . . The BLUEPRINT . . . of ETERNAL LIFE!!!

And, I love you . . . and thank you for listening . . . and PLEASE . . . CONSIDER . . . at least READING . . . The BLUEPRINT . . . of ETERNAL LIFE!!!

And then, MAKE YOUR DECISION . . . ACCORDINGLY . . .

I love you ALL . . . Cynthia Queen of Scots and America

I AM AS NUTS AS NOAH AND MOSES
The Secret of the Truth . . .

(Excerpt)

The books of . . . CYNTHIA Queen of Scots and America

Dedication

This work, is dedicated to us all . . . ALL HUMANS!!! Of all ERAS . . . all COUNTRIES . . . COLORS . . . RACES . . . ETHNICITIES . . . PERSUASIONS . . . TIMES . . . TALENTS . . . etc., etc., etc.,

This work is DEDICATED . . . to OVERCOMING . . . the DEPRAVITY . . . CORRUPTION . . . and LAWLESSNESS . . . of EVE!!! And, the PEOPLE . . . of the, DAYS of NOAH . . . and the, SAME . . . which is CONTINUING . . . until . . . TODAY . . .

Foreward . . .

To: Benedict XVI

Fanum, flamen, missa, pia pium, pius, sanctifico, sanctus, senium, abavus, abbas abbatis, altor, amita, atavus, avus, compater, gigno, genuit, pater, patris, paterna, paternus, patria, patria, patrius, patrizo, priores, proavus, sator, socer, vitricus, infensus, infestus, periclitatus, periclitor, periculosus, periculum, periculum, quorum, caveo, abavus, abbas abbatis, abnocto, aborior, absit, adhuc, adstringo, aequoreus, aer aeris, aether, agnatus, agonotheta, agrarius, aiunt, alarius, alauda, alcedo, alcedonia, alces, alcyon, alias, alibi, alieina quadra vivere, alii alii, alio, alioqui, alioquin, aliter, alius, alius, alius, aliusmodi, alnus, alter altera alterum, alter alter, alter, alterno, altor, amita, ancilla, agno, anhelo, animadverto, antiquitas, appono, apud, aquilo, arduum, arista, arto, atavus, auarca, auctorizo, augeo, aut:. aut, autem, avus, balnearius, barathrum, barbaria, basiatio, basilica, caetera, calx, campeador, cancer, canonicus, canonus, carceres, cardiacus, cardo duplex, careo, carina, carnificina, cauda, causa, cetera, ceteri, ceterum, ceterus, claro, coadunatio, coaegresco, cogo coegi coactum, cohaero cohero cohesi, colligo ligi lectum, colonus, coma, commessatio, communis, compater, compello, compescor, complico, compono, comprehendo, comprehendo, comprovincialis, concateno, concieo, concilio, concilio, concino, concretio, concutio, concutio, conduco, confero, conforto, conforto, confundo, congrego, congressio, conicio, coniecto, coniuro, constrictio, construo, consulo, consulo, consulto, consummo, consuo consui, consutum, conticinium, contineo, contenio, continuo, continuus, contrado contraho, convenio, conventus, converto, convoco, corroboro, corruo, cras, crastinus, crebo, cubitum, cui, cuius, cuius, cuius, cunctus, cuneus, curriculum, cuspis, decerpo, decerto, deinde, deliciae, demitto, desipio, destituo, determino, devia, devio, dexter, dextera, donec, duco, eatenus, econtra, editio, efflo, epops epopis, eptheca, equipero, ergo, etiam, etiamtum etiamtunc, evangelium, evoco, exinde, exinde, exordium, experior, exsequor exequor, extremitas, extrinsecus, flax, fanum, fastidio, ferrugo, ferula, ferveo, fiendo, firmamentum, firmo, follis, forensis, frater, frendo, furor, frux, frux, flucio, flucio, fundo, furtum, galactinus, galea, ganea ganeum, gelamen, genetrix, gentilitas, gigno, gratia, gratia, gressus, hac, hactenus hitherto, Heidelberg, Helcim, hi, hic haec, hos, hostes hostium, hostis, iam, iam tandem, ibi, ibidem, idem eadem idem, ideo, iecur, igitur, igitur, ilico illico, illa, illa, illac, illae ille, illas, illaturos, ille illa illud, illi, illic, illius, illos, illuc, immo, immo, impraesentarium, in excelsis, in praesentia, incolumis, incumbo, incunabula, inde, indifferens, induviae, ineptio, infelix, inferi, inferne, infero, inferus, infra, infrendeo, ingredior vi ventorum, inguen, inhalo, inibi, instar, interdum, invalesco, invicem, itaque, iugo, iugulum iugulus, iuguolo, iunctus, iuncus, iuniperus, iussu, iuvenesco, juventus, labores solis, labruscum, lacertus, laevus levus, latito, latrocinor, laurus, lautus, lavo, lavo, lego, lemma, lentulus, littera, lorica, lumen, magis, major domus, mane, maneo, maro, mater matris, matera mairia, maxime, medium, medius, messis, minagium, minime, misellus, modo modo, morior, mortalitas, mox, multi, multis, prosecutionibus, nam, nec, necto, neque, nichilominus, nihilominus, nihilominus, nichilominus, nobis, nobis, nos, nunc, nunc quidem, obviam, obviam, obvius, occasus, occido, Olympus, omnino, opinor, opisthotonos, oporotheca, optimates, optimates, optimus, orbis lacteus, orbis signifer, orbis, terrarum, orchestra, orcus, oriens, pactus, pala, palam, pannus, panthera, pardus, partier, pater, paterna, paternus, patria, patria, patrius, patrizo, penna, penna, pennatus, penniger, per, per, per, moenia urbis, per sic quod, perago, perfruor, permaneo, permaximum, pessum, picea, pilo, planatarium, plaustrum, plebs, plebs, plerumque, plerusque, pluma, plurimi, plusculus, pocius potius, poena, populus, porro, potius, potius, praeeo, praestolatio, prestolatio praesum presum, praeterea preterea, praevenio, primitus, primo, primoris, primum, priores, pro eo, proavus, produco, profendum, proinde, prolato, proletarius, propostium, prospicio, prothoplastus, protiuns, provolvo, pubesco, publicus, pugnacitas, pugnus, pulex, pulmo, pulso, puppis, pupula, qua, quadrivium, quae que, qualis, quam, quamquam, quandoque, quantocius, quantum, quarum, quas, quem, qui, quibus, quibus, quibus, quibus, quibus, quin, quin, quinymo quinimmo, quo, quo, quo, quod, quod, quod, quod, quod, quorum, quorum, radicitus, ratio, recolligo, relictus, respiro, rumino, rurus, rus ruris, ruta, Sanctus Eleutherius, Sarcalogos, sator, scabies, scapulus, secus atque or quam, secus, semel, sibimet, silenti etc, simul, simul, sive, socer, sodes, solito, sollicito, solus statim, sterno, stillicidium, stipo, subodiosus, subsisto, substringo, subvenio, summa, superna, supero, superstes, surrogo, suscriptor, suus sua suum, talus, tamen, tempestas, tergo a tergo, tergus, terrigenus, texo, texo, theatrum, theca, thema, thema thematis, theologus, theorice, theoricus, thermae, thesaurus, thesis, thymbra, thymum, toto, translatio, transmaritanus, tum, tunc, ulterius, ultra, ultra, una, undique, undique secus, universi, universitas, universum, unus, urbanus, usitor, usque, ususfructus, uter utrius, utercumque, uterlibet, utinam, utrum, utrum, vallum, veho, vel vel, venatio, venter, ventilo, ver veris, Verbigena, verumtamen verumptamen, vestigium, vestio, vicissim, vieo, vietus, vitricus, vos, vos, vulgariter, vulgus, vultus, ymo, basilica, demitto, ecclesia, fanum, his, illis, quam, suffragium templum, a ab abs, abalienato, abdico, abicio, abiego, abigo, abrumpo, abscido, absit, abstergo, abunde, abutor, acies, admninistratio, adultus, aeneus eneus, aequorenus, aetas, affectus, affectus vocis, agalmate, agricola, ala, alarius, alienatio, alienigenus, aliquantus, alveus, amens, amo, amoena, amoenitas, animadverto, animus, annona, ante, apud, arca archa, argumentum, arista, armis, arripio, articulus, asporto, attentus, attinet, aufero, avello, baiulus, balatus, balneator, barbaria, basiatio, belliger, belligero, blande, bonae indolis, caeli, campeador, cancer, canonus, captus, capulus, carbasa, carbaseus, carceres, carchesium, cardiacus, cardo duplex, careo, careo, carina, caris, caritas, cameus, camificina, carpo, caruncula, cassus, cassus, castellani, castigatio, castimonia, cauda, causa, cavare, caveo, celsitudo, celsus, certamen, cesso, charitas, cohors, colonus, coma, commissum, commodum, commoneo, communis, compater, completion, compositus, concipio, confidenter, confido, conscius, consisto, conspicio, consulo, consulo,

consulo, consulto, contemno, conticinium, contremisco, contristo, contubernium, conservatio, correptio, corripio, crastinus, crebro, credulitas, credulus, crimen, criminor, crinis, croceus, crumens, crystallinus, cubile, cubito, cuiusmodi, cuneus, decentia, decerpo, decido, defendo, defero, degenero, demens, demitto, demulceo, denuntio, deporto, deporto, deputo, deruptus, desino, desino, desino, desipio, despero, destitutus, determino, detieno, detraho, devia, diaria, dictito, dicto, dignus, diluo, dissero, dissolutus, diutius, diuturnus, do, dolus, domiegena, dominor, donarium, donativum, donum, editio, effusio, egenus, elatus, elemosinarius, eloquentia, enim, epulae, eguipero, eradico, ergo, erubescundus, esse, evado, evagor, evolutio, ex, executor, exhibeo exibeo, exordium, expers, expers, exsors, exuo, exuviae, facio, facundia, facunditas, facundus, famosus, famulatus, ferramenta, ferrarius, ferreus, ferrugo, fides, flandrensis, floccipendo, foras, fore forem, foris, forus, frigus, fructus fructus, fruor, frux, frux frugi, gaudeo, generosus, germen, glacialis, glorificus, gratia, gratia, Helcim, hereditas, hodiernus, holocaustum, honor, honor, hostiliter, hostis, ignoro, illudo illusi, illusum, imbrium, incol ae, incola ae, incompositus, incongruens, incontinencia, incrementum, increpo, incultus, indigeo, indigus, inditiae, inefficax, infula, ingrens, ingero, ingluvies, inhospitalitas, inquisitor, instar, instruo, intemptesta nox, inveteratus, invideo, irritus, irritus, iugum, iugum, iumentum, iunceus, iurisdictio, iussu, iuvenesco, iuxta, ivi, jubilus, juramentum, juventus, labores solis, lacteus, laedo ledo, lambo, lamnia lamina lamna, latito, latrocinium, laureola, legatio, legatus, lentesco, Lesciense, leviter, liber, liceor, littera, lorica, lucror, lucrosus, lucrum, lumen, macero, madidus, magister, major domus, mansuetus, matera mairia, medius, mei, mendiosus, mendosus, mihi, militaris, militus, minagium, moenia, mollio, mollis, monumentum, mortalitas, mulceo, multigenus, munificator, munus munneris, nimirum, noster nostri, noxa, obicio obieci objectum, obscoena, occasus, occuludo, offa, offendo, offendo, offendo, offensio, offensio, offensus, offensus, offero, officina, officiose, officiosus, officium, officium, Olympus, omnigenus, opinor, optimus, ora, oraculum, orbitas, orbus, orchas, ordior, orgia, orior, pagenses, pagus, palam, palmula, pannus, paratus, paries parietis, paterna, paternus, patiens patient, peculium, pecuniosus, pecus, pecus, pecus, penetrabilis, pennipotens, pensio, peplum, per, per, per, per, per moenia urbis, persolvo, persona, phalanx, phalerae, picturatus, pignus, plantarium, plumbeus, pluries, plurimi, pluris, pluvialis, polliceor, pollicitas, pondus, porro, posteritas, posthabeo, potior, potissimum, potissimus, prae pre, prae se ferre, prae se ferre, praebeo prebo, praebeo, praecelsus, praeda, praedatio, praedatus, praeficio, praefinio, praemium, praesentia, praesto, praesto presto, praesum praesum presume, praevenio, privatus, privus, pro, pro, pro eo, procuro, prodico, prodigentia, prodigus, profano, profano, profanus, profanus, profectio, profectio, profecto, profectus, profero, profero, profero, professio, professio, professio, professor, professorius, professus, proficio, proficio, proficio, proficiscor, proficiscor, proficuus proficiscor, profiteor, profiteor, profiteor, profiteor, profor, profugus, profundo, profundum profundus, profusius, profuturus, progagus, progener, progenies, progenitor, prolato, proles, proletarius, promissum, promulgatio, propositum, propter, prosum profuturus, psallo, pubes, pubesco, publicus, pugnax, pulverulentus, pulvis, puppis, pupula, purgo, quadrivium, quaestuosus questuosus, qaestus questus, qualis, quailscumque, qualislibet, quandoque, quantum quare, quasi, quidam quaedam quedam quidam, quin, quippe, quo, quos, quotiens, quontienscumque, recessus, reconcilio, recordo recordor, regalis, religo, respuo, rhetor, rostrum, saepe sepe, saepius sepius, sanitas, scaccarium, schola, scilicet, securitas, seges, sententia, servitium, singularis, sis, solito, solium, somnio, sono, sponte, sterilis, stilla, stipatio, stipator, stolidus, suadeo, sublime, sublimes, sublimitas, sublimiter, subnascor, suboleo, suboles, suboles, subsequens, substantia, subtraho, suggero, summisse, superstes, suppono supono, suscriptor, sustituo, tactus, talis, tango-tetigi-tactum, tantus, temero, tener tenera tenerum, terminatio, testimonium, texo, textils, toties, traba, translatio, triduum, tripudium, tumbarius, tumultuosa, tumulus, ultra, ultroneus, unanimis, undique secus, uredo, usitor, usura, usurpo, usus, ususfructus, uter utrius, utercumque, uterlibet, utor, utor, vaco, vacuus, vena, venditio, vendo, veneficus, ventito, ventosus, ventulus, ver veris, Verbigena, verecundia, vereor, vestigium, veter, victus, videlicet, villa villa, villanus, vir, vitiosus, vitualamen, violator, volubilis, volva vulva, voltus, absit, caelestis, compater, dues, filiolus, impius, Olympus, oraculum, pia pium, pius, religious, suffragium, Vulcanus, milia, mille, abavus, aberro, abnepos, ac, adsum, ager, agnosco, agnosco, agrarius, agripeta, alienigenia, aliquando, alterno, amplitudo, andron, Angli Angles, animadverto, anas, appello, appello, applico, arcus at, atavus, atqui, auarca, autem, avus, barbaria, barbaricus, belle, bellus, blande, blandio, blandior, blanditia, blanditium, blandus, barba, carduus, cautor, decoctor, hac, hactenus, hic haec, hinc, hinc, his, his, his, his, igitur, ipsemet, is ea id, nunc, phthisis, pro eo, quibus, quibus, sophisma, sophismata, suffaragium, susurro, suus sua suum, verbis suis meis, diabolus, pastor, accersitus, Ronald Weinland, cui, cuius, ego, hac, haec hec, hanc, hic, Hirenses, hoc, hoc, hoc, hoc, huic, huic, huic, huius, huius, hunc, I Ico, Illae ille, illi, immo, inquam Insula, mei, moleste, quandraginta, quae, quam, quarum, quibus, quibus, quibus, quibus, quibus, quo, quo, quod, quod, quorum, quorum, tui, utinam, vos, creba, crebo, indentidem, ingemino, itero, reddo, refero, renovo, repeto, resumo, revolve, saepe sepe, saepenumero, saepius sepius, diabbolus, pastor, accersitus, Ronald Weinland, an, aperio, appareo, aptus, arguo, assimilares, attentus, audio, auditor, ausus, baiulus, barbare, bellum, blande, blandior, boo boare, carectum, careo, careo, careo, carex carexicia, cases, cautio, cautus, cavare, caveo, caveo, caveo cavi cautum, cellarius, clamo, commercium, communico, compare, conscius, considero, consulo, consulto, contemplor, contendo, crepito, crispo, crudus, cura, curiosus, curo, curo, decipio, decipio, decollo, decolo, demulceo, denuncio, denuntio, detgo detectum, dilgenter, diligens, dissero, edico, effor, eloquor, equa, equito, eructo, esito, evasto, exaresco, expedio, foras, forca, formido, formidonis, forum, foveo, fovi, fotum, gnare, haec hac, Heidelberg, hi, horum, huius, ignoro, illi, illius, illorum, impedio, impedo, incoho, incohare, incommodo, incomparpbilis, increpito, incuria, incuriose, incuriosus, incurvo, induco, inrento, irreto, insciens, insidiae, instruo, laqueum, laqueus, latro, lepus, loquor, locutus, luminare, luminaris, mare, maris, membrana, mutuus, negligentia, nescio, no, no, noto, operam do, orbitas, orbus, ordino, ostendo, palificare, pappo, paratus, parco, parco, parco, parens, parentela, parentes, pareo, pareo, paro, pars, particeps, patesco, pensito, peragito, perpendo, perspicuus, pervium, pessum dare, pharetra, poena, praedicare, praeparo, praesumo, probatur, procinctu, procuro, profiteor, profiteor, proloquor, promptus, promptus, propago, protestor, protesto, provider, proximus, pulvis, quadratus, quandrum, quare, quinquiplico, quirito, rare, rarus, reboare, renuntio, rus ruris, scapulare, securus, sermocinare, sicco, sis, socus, sors, subseco, susicivus, tempero, terga dare, terreo, territo, tractare, tutela, valedico, vix, vomer, vomer, abundantia, anticipo, antiquitas, antiquus, antistes, arrogantia, attonbitus, constantia, cupido, deficio, delinquo, dissolutus, expers, fastigate, iactantia, inconstantia, infantia, infrequentia, insperatus, inundantia, obliquus, perservantia, perservantia, praecipio, precipio, praefero, prefero, praestantia, prestantia, praesumo, presume, praevenio, precipio, priscus, quanti, redundantia, Santiago, satus, substantia, tantillum, tantillus, temperantia, verberantia, vis, absit, caelestis, compater, deus, filiolus, impius, Olympus, oraculum, pia pium, pius, religiosus, suffragium, Vulcanus.

Amore, ratio, theologus, theorice, theoricus, et Sophia, Cynthia Anne Marie Gunn Queen of Scots and America Et tu . . . Benedictum XVI . . .

Love, Cynthia

Post Script: Saint Methodius (died 885 AD) . . . "In the last period, Christians will not appreciate, the great grace of God, who provided a Great Monarch, a long duration of peace, a splendid fertility of the earth. They will be very ungrateful, lead a sinful life, in pride, in vanity, unchastity, frivolity, hatred, avarice, gluttony and many other vices, so that the sins of men, will stink, more than a pestilence, before God.

Many men, will doubt, whether the Catholic faith, is the true and only saving one and whether the Jews, are perhaps correct, when they still expect, Messias. Many will be, the false teachings and resultant bewilderment. The just God, will in consequence, give Lucifer and all his devils, power to come, on earth and tempt, the godless creatures."

Chapter 1

Welcome . . . this is Cynthia again . . . and I'm so, happy and so, pleased and so, blessed . . . to be able, to speak to you and this, is Thursday, the 17th of July . . . and the year is 2008 . . . twenty-o-eight, Anno Domini . . . as they, USED to call . . . AFTER DEATH!!! Of . . . WHO??? Rabbi Yeshua!!!

OH!!! Wait a minute . . . AD . . . BC . . . BC meant, BEFORE CHRIST!!! AHAH!!! AHAH!!! Don't give me . . . the year five thousand . . . whatever . . . Kabbalahist Rabbis know, what I'm saying . . . 'Em . . . Huh! Your ADVERSARIES . . . the ROMANS . . . went by THIS particular, calendar and this is, 'Em . . . Thursday . . . the 17th of July . . . and the year IS, 2008!!!

And this is, Cynthia . . . once again. Cynthia Anne Marie Gunn Lazuk . . . and you've NOT . . . heard me use, this name before . . . BUT . . . Those who know . . . who, Cynthia Anne Marie Gunn IS . . . then, those of you, who know who Cynthia Anne Marie Gunn Lazuk . . . of the, WHITE RUSSIANS . . . And DON'T . . . BESMIRCH, my HUSBANDS . . . LINEAGE. 'Cuz as I told you, before . . . told you my CHILDHOOD . . . told you what I WENT THROUGH . . . in book one. And book two, was all about . . . THE CORRECTION!!! We ALL, need to GO THROUGH!!! And now, in book three . . . let, no one besmirch . . . the name Lazuk . . . L-A-Z-U-K . . . la zee like zebra ukay. And I am . . . and I have been . . . Cynthia Anne Marie Gunn Lazuk . . . of Scots and America and, because I'm married . . . to the, White Russian Prince . . . Alexander Jon Lazuk . . . of the, White Russians . . .

Now, any of you BOLSHIEVICKS . . . or your BULL-WHATEVER- AKAVICKS . . . I don't care!!! You EITHER know . . . WHO you're HEARING . . . who you're READIN' NOW . . . or YOU DON'T!!!

And if you don't, I love you . . . SO PLEASE!!! Just get with me, in the first book, 'Em . . . I AM WHY THEY KILLED DIANA The Secret of The Red String . . . and the second book, I AM YOUR GOD MOTHER FORGIVE ME The Secret of the Secret . . .

And NOW . . . this the third book, IS . . . THE TRUTH!!! Of EVERYTHING . . . that CAME, before EVERYTHING!!! FORGET . . .

Indiana Jones!!! FORGET . . . who was the ACTOR?

Harrison Ford? And, the DIRECTOR . . . Steven Speilberg?!? And God Love 'ya . . . sir, 'cause you did, GOOD!!! When you reminisced, about . . .

Ellis Island! But, of course, Cynthia Anne Marie Gunn Lazuk Queen of Scots and America and the Russians . . . by my MARRIAGE . . . to me HUSBAND . . .

Will NOW, tell you . . . in the third book . . . the truth of the truth. And I hope, beyond hope . . . that my husband and I . . . who went to meet, with a financial planner, lo these three, four days, ago now . . . I hope we, can YET . . . show you, all of you, like us, humans beings . . . a MIRACLE!!! That's ALL, I'm interested in. Because a miracle is a miracle . . . you can look it up, in WEBSTER . . . I don't care, what dictionary . . . you have.

I don't care what Library . . . you subscribe to. Ah . . . excuse my stutter . . . whatever . . . I don't care!!!

O, O at Home, O on the phone . . . O beyond . . .

You know what . . . O . . . I love you, but you know what . . . you need to get with, this program. You proclaim to be, who you are . . . HARPO . . . in REVERSE . . . you either ARE, or you AREN'T!!! And, that's from, Cynthia Queen of Scots, America and Russia!!!

TRUE RUSSIA!!! Forget . . . SOVIET UNION!!! I don't need, the Bolsheviks . . . and I don't, need the USSR . . . and the ERRORS, of their WAYS . . . to CORRECT, the errors . . . of EVERYTHING . . . that's been, HANDED-DOWN . . . from Adam and Eve . . . ALL THE WAY!!! Now, Mother O, I don't know . . . who you ARE!!! I don't care . . . but, you NEED, a LITTLE-BITTY-TINY . . . piece, of a REBUKE . . . Madame O . . . because, I saw 'ya . . . I saw 'ya . . . and I live here, in Connecticut!!! And, I was BORN, in CONNECTICUT!!! And, I saw you, use your friend . . . who was, a huge, huge, huge ANCHOR, in Connecticut, BEFORE you, WERE . . . ANYTHIN'!!!

Your friend . . . your G woman . . . and I'm, not even . . . be . . . say, her name . . . Miss O . . . but, you know what . . . you rode, HER COATTAILS . . . until you rode, your OWN . . . coattails . . . and THEN, YOU figured OUT . . . the WHITES!!!

And, I LOVE THAT!!!

Oprah . . . Huh! And now, I'll get with you . . . I'll call you, Oprah . . . Winfrey . . . I don't know, the other PARTS . . . of your family names . . . If you and I, get together . . . on television, we do . . . or don't . . . at your behest . . . or, Gayle King's behest . . . I don't care. It doesn't matter to me. But, Mother O . . . Mother O . . . and Gayle King . . . friend . . . GK . . . of Mother O . . . if, you haven't got with, books one and two YET??!?

You don't, know NOTHIN'!!!

And, ANYBODY . . . who doesn't get with, books one and two . . . and now, three . . . well . . . they don't, know nothin' yet . . . let's just take . . . them, down the road . . . of, book three.

So PLEASE!!! Lady Oprah Winfrey . . . beautiful, black Queen . . . of America . . . and, before you . . . were renowned . . . Gayle King Bumpus, was renowned . . . here, in the State of Quinnecticut . . . q-u-i-netticut . . .

Now, don't think, for a minute . . . that Cynthia Anne Marie Gunn Lazuk Queen of Scots, America and Russia . . . for that matter . . . and Queen of the Cherokees . . . for that matter . . .

Does NOT, know what I'm speaking of . . . and does not; KNOW . . . what, I'm SAYIN'!!! I don't care, about MONEY . . . I don't care, about TITLES . . . I don't care, about anything . . . 'cuz I'm not insecure. I'm not jealous . . . I'm not weak . . . I'm not any, of those things.

Just . . . I'll NOT, even say . . . how long, it took, 'Em . . . an associate . . . of my, Husband . . . my, world renowned Husband . . . Alexander Jon Lazuk, TRUE HIGH KING . . . of RUSSIA!!! After, the Bolsheviks . . . OVERTHREW HIM . . . and I, either before his death . . . or after . . . I, Cynthia Anne Marie Gunn Lazuk Queen of

Scots and America and The Cherokees and Queen of the Russians . . . because I married, the Russian Prince . . . ha, ha, ha, ha . . .

The Bolsheviks, thought that they . . . KILLED . . . Anastasia . . . they killed, NO ONE!!! And, Anastasia . . . came down, SECRETLY . . . through TIME!!! As . . . Cynthia Gunn!!! And, I told you . . . from the 12th generation of Noah . . . I'll NOT repeat, The Secret of The Red String . . . Now, we're into . . . The Secret of The Truth . . .

So, you know what . . . OPRAH?!? Gayle . . . I love you guys . . . and you guys are beautiful! And, you know what . . . my HAT . . . not that I had one . . . my PARASOL . . . not that I had one . . . my COACH, the ROOF of, my coach . . . not that I have one . . .

But, if you TWO LADIES . . . were to stand, right now . . . in front of, Buckingham Palace . . . which is ACTUALLY . . . mine . . . Cynthia Anne Marie Gunn Queen of Scots and America . . . NOT . . . would I have 'ya . . . standin' . . . OUTSIDE!!!

But, you'd be . . . LET IN!!! And, we'd ALL . . . be UP, on the BALCONY!!! Not like, the HYPOCRITES . . . the, the PHONY . . . PHONY . . . descendents . . . of King Henry VIII . . . all the way DOWN, to QE1 . . . QE2 . . . I DON'T CARE!!!

You people . . . need to, STEP OFF . . . Buckingham Palace . . . and let, the likes, of . . . Michael and Cynthia and Alexander and Oprah . . . and all, of our friends . . . and our, TRUE FAMILY . . . who LOVE US . . . with BLOOD . . . without BLOOD . . . doesn't matter.

Now, I DON'T need, HOLLYWOOD . . . I DON'T need, MGM . . . FOXWOODS . . . I don't care!!! Metro Goldwyn Mayer . . . how DARE, you come . . . into the State . . . of, Cynthia Anne Marie Gunn Queen Scots of America . . . and put up . . . a WHAT?!?

An MGM GRAND, hotel . . . did you NOT, besmirch . . . the TRIBE . . . that may, have or may, have not . . . besmirched its OWN self . . . the Indians . . . of the Foxwood . . . but, we'll NOT argue that, in the Hague . . . 'cuz they'll be losin'!!! Trust me!!!

But, settin' them, aside . . . do YOU, HEBREWS THINK . . . for a minute . . . that, Cynthia Anne Marie Gunn of Scots, America and Russia . . . and SAINT MICHAEL . . . HIMSELF!!! Don't see, THROUGH . . . Your PHONY VEILS!!!

Don't SEE through . . . your PHONY . . . minds, hearts, souls, wills and DESTINIES!!! That YOU . . . handed out . . . to the people . . . that CAME . . . to this SOIL!!! AFTER . . . you SULLIED IT!!!

And, you've USED THEM . . . and you've ABUSED them . . . and you've put . . . THEM in SERVITUDE . . . LONG ENOUGH!!!

Don't THINK . . . for a moment, that Cynthia of Scots and America and of Cherokee . . . and Alexander . . . of RUSSIA . . . and Michael . . . of the Dark Skinned People . . . don't think, for a MINUTE . . . that we're NOT HERE, to SET you ALL, in YOUR PLACE!!! Because . . . WE ARE!!! But . . . WITH LOVE!!!

Not with Nothin'!!!

Not with HATE!!! With LOVE!!!

We ONLY, need to speak to you . . . in HARSH TERMS . . . to GET, YOUR ATTENTION!!!

Now, I'm going to have . . . by his OWN DIGNITY . . . and by his, ACQUIESCENCE . . . after EVERYTHING . . . he's been through, including . . . PROSTATE CANCER . . .

In the NEXT . . . 'Em well, this is chapter one, book three . . . that's cool . . . I'm going to have, my own Husband . . . a huge, huge, huge . . . for the third time . . . man . . . of the Whale . . . and of Jonah . . . EXPLAIN, to 'ya . . . EXACTLY HOW . . . what I DESCRIBED . . . at the beginning, of this dissertation . . . COULD HAPPEN . . . to the Plankton . . . and so on, and so forth . . . down the line . . . until, I'm speaking to you . . . today. And, I love you . . . I reach out, to the youth of the world . . . look . . . I don't care . . . I DON'T HAVE A COLOR!!! I don't care what I look . . .

I don't care what you look like . . . I don't care who has money . . . who doesn't . . . WE'RE ALL . . . CREATIONS . . . OF GOD!!!

Now, we need to get . . . I'm speaking, to the YOUTH OF THE WORLD!!! You know . . . if your, grandparents and your, parents . . . have failed you, miserably . . . if your FRIENDS . . . have failed you, miserably . . . if your TEACHERS, your PASTORS, your SO-CALLED, friends . . . 'Em, RELATIVES . . . what have you . . . if they've ALL, failed you miserably . . . Then, I don't ask you to

COME . . . with Cynthia, on any journey . . . I'm not lookin' for a CENT! All I'm ASKIN' . . . is that you keep, an OPEN . . . mind, heart, soul, will and DESTINY!!!

Now, If you . . . YOUNG PEOPLE . . . of the world . . . and I'm speaking, to you . . . from 12 years old . . . up to 'Em . . . 30. If YOU, would JUST listen, to Cynthia . . . 'Em, whether or not, the people ABOVE you, do or don't . . . it's NOT, my CONCERN!!!

I'm MORE CONCERNED . . . with, YOUR GENERATION!!! Because, your generation . . . is the one, that will HAVE TO PAY!!! For ALL the EVILS . . . and the, DESPICABLE DEEDS . . . of the ones . . . that CAME BEFORE YOU!!!

All the way DOWN . . . from . . . WELL . . . if you looked in book two, it's called; I AM YOUR GOD MOTHER FORGIVE ME The Secret of The Secret . . .

Now, if you've FOUND THAT OUT . . . and you've, read it . . . you UNDERSTAND . . . what I'm TELLING you . . . about WHO, did WHAT, to WHOM . . . in the, Garden of Eden . . .

Where we ARE, RIGHT NOW!!! On 17 July . . . 2008 . . . then, you know . . . WE CAN DO THIS THING!!!

With or without, Michael . . . and . . . I've already, been INSTRUCTED, by my Kabbalahist Rabbi, Asher . . . that Michael, may not be . . . ABLE, to get with, THIS PROGRAM . . . BECAUSE . . . He's ALREADY, DONE ENOUGH!!! In His lifetime!!!

So, in the event, MJJ . . . does not, come on board . . . DON'T THINK . . . that it, ISN'T TRUE . . . because IT IS!!!

And HE, will either DEBUNK ME . . . or HE, will JUST quietly, as a MAN . . . ELEGANT, STRONG, LOVING AND HONEST . . . MJJ . . . will back, CYNTHIA!!!

MJJ WILL, back . . . MJJ will back Cynthia . . .

In the event, that HE . . . understands, what I've just said . . . to you . . .

And HE, IS . . . A MAN, elegant, strong, loving, honest . . . KIND . . . ALL, those WONDERFUL . . . things!!!

So . . . I say to you, goodnight . . . and may God bless! Cynthia.

BOOK IV

I AM THE QUEEN OF DOOM The Secret of The Blueprint of Eternal Life . . .

(Excerpt)
The books of . . . CYNTHIA Queen of Scots and America

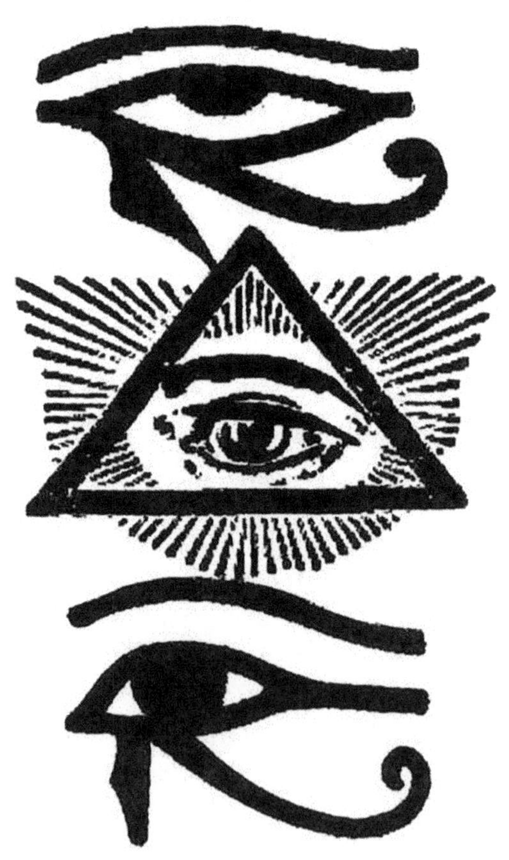

Dedication

Testing . . . Here we are . . . DEDICATION . . . The moment, of TRUTH!!! Of ALL, the TRUTHS!!! Of, the TRIANGULATION . . . of, The Secret of The Red String . . . The Secret of The Secret . . . and The Secret of The Truth . . . is as follows:

With all due, LOVE and RESPECT . . . Dear God,

PLEASE!!! PLEASE!!! Bless EVERYONE . . . who HEARS, my voice . . . SEES, my written words . . . LOOKS AT, my work . . . UNDERSTANDS, that I have LIVED . . . THIS Human . . . CONDITION . . . and . . . I'm NOT, DONE YET!!!

But, I God . . . I Cynthia, WILL KNOW YOU . . . WILL LOVE YOU . . . AND, WILL SERVE YOU!!!

And, I've done my best . . . throughout . . . my WHOLE LIFE . . . and I had a two year, "SLIP UP!!!" And, I KNOW . . . You FORGAVE me . . . for it.

So . . . LET ME, make it up to YOU NOW!!! And LET ME, do the RIGHT THING!!!

DO the RIGHT THING!!!

And . . . DO PLEASE . . . do the right thing . . . With ALL . . . GOOD . . . LOVE . . .

Cynthia

Foreward

To: Benedict XVI

Fanum, flamen, missa, pia pium, pius, sanctifico, sanctus, senium, abavus, abbas abbatis, altor, amita, atavus, avus, compater, gigno, pater, paterna, paternus, patria, patria, patrius, patrizo, priores, proavus, sator, socer, vitricus, cometes, cometissa, crinis, accersitus, Rup, abyssus, accelero, affluo, atrocitas, caste, castigo, castimonia, castitas, castus, casula, contendo, culpa, cursim, emo emi emptum, emptio, festinanter, festinatio, festino, festino, festinus, fugo, fugo, has, hasta, incito, integer, livor, me, orchas orchadis, penso, phasma phasmatis, praeproperus, profundum, propero, propero, propero, pudicus, reparo, tumultuarius, vado, venatio, volito, vorago, abeo, allatus adfero, relictus, accersitus, Rup, absens absentis, absum, acquiesco, adnuo, adsum, alimonium, annuo, annuo, apostolus, assentator, assimulo, careo, charisma, consentaneus, consentio, designo, desum, dictata, donum, expedio, explico, exprimo, extrico, huic, iam, illi, impraesentarium, in praesentia, mox, munero munerior, munifico, munus, necessarius, nunc, offero, ostendo, persentio, post modum, praebeo prebo, praesagium, praesentia, praesto presto, admonitio, moneo, monitio, paecipio, praecipio, praedico, praemoneo, precipio, caminus, cardo duplex, creta, frux, frux, humo, humus, humus, mara marl, motus-us, terra, terrenus, terrigenus, tumulus, vallum, atriocitas, beneficium, candidus, canonicus, caste, claritas, claritudo, claro, clarus, corrigo, dexter, dextera, erectus, fas est, formido, huic, ilicet, illi, immanitas, ingenuus, ius iuris, iuste, iustum, iustus, jus, legitiums, licet imper v, lucidus, luminosus, metuo, mico, niteo, nitidus, nitor, nitor, perspicuus, pius, probitas, probus, quod sui juris est, rectum, rectus, refulgo, relucesco, scilicet, sic, sto, terro, territo, territo, ver, verus, vox vocis, abhinc, adhuc, agnitio, agnosco, agnosco, celebrer, celebritas, clarus, confiteor confessus, conscientia, diffama???tus, effulo, eruditio, etiamnun, expertus, famosus, fatero, gloria, gnaritas, gnarus, gnarus, iam, iam pridem, iamdiu, iamdudum, ignarus, ignoro, ignotus, illustratus, imperceptus, indico, innotesco, innotesco, insciens, interdum, latet, modo, nam, narro, nescio, niveus, noero, nominor, nosco, notitia, nunc, nusquam, nusquam, olim, pando, praescio, profitero, prope, protraho protractus, quaero quero, quarum, quibus, quin, quod, sapio, scientia, scientia, scio, teno, Ventagium, ventorium, vobis . . . Amore, Cynthia Anne Marie Gunn Queen of Scots and America Et tu . . . Benedictum XVI . . . ???

Epilogue

Testing . . . 123 . . . 321 . . . Let's GO!!! This is C101 Radio, Epilogue. Thank you all, for joining me . . . this is the same day, as chapter 13 . . . excuse me, was recorded.

It's about eight . . . twelve . . . thirteen . . . p.m., Eastern Daylight Time. And, I've had a HUGE day . . . today, 'cuz I had a HUGE . . . appointment, today . . . with SOMEONE, who . . . ha, ha . . . well, in the event the GOVERNMENTS . . . of the, world and 'Em . . . people, of the world . . . what have you . . .

SATAN himself . . . Lucifer . . . Deet Da Dee . . . you know, like Church Lady . . . used to say, on a Saturday Night Live . . . NOT HAPPENIN'!!! Lucifer . . . not happenin' . . . Satan.

"Cuz . . . the IS, the Epilogue . . . to book four. And book four, as we all know . . . and we've discussed, AT LENGTH . . . earlier tonight, and let me, just find my notes here . . .

Mister Lucifer . . . and your BROOD, OF VIPERS . . . don't think, for a moment . . . Lucifer, that I DON'T, have your NUMBER . . . six, score, sixty and six . . .

Now, that having been said . . . 'Em . . . C101 Radio, is Cynthia Anne Marie Gunn Lazuk Queen of Scots, America, Cherokee America . . . a-heh . . . and Russia . . . 'Em, comin' right AT YOU . . . in this, Epilogue.

Now, this book . . . book four, is DONE!!! By Gunn . . . Cynthia!!! And, I don't mean that, in a harsh way . . . I just mean, that this one's done now . . . and WE NEED, to PREPARE OURSELVES . . . which, for that which, is DANGEROUS, BAD and COMING!!!

This book, was just, to merely . . . merely . . . merely . . . give 'ya, a HEADS UP . . . to the FACT . . . that I AM the QUEEN of DOOM!!! And, this book . . . proclaimed it!

Now, 'Em . . . in book five, I'm going to tell 'ya . . . about the, DOOM . . . and books four and five will be . . . published together . . . 'Em, on the SAME TEXT . . . as books two and three, were . . . because I'm NOT . . . the likes of, 'Em . . . Danielle Steele . . . and, Wally Lamb . . . and, WHO?!? These people . . . that write; THE FIRM . . . and the . . . this . . . no, no, no, no!

I don't want money. I don't want fame. I don't want fortune. I just, do . . . what I do . . . for . . . XTO1 . . . XTO2 . . . and . . . XTO3!!! Bebe . . .

And anyone, who studied LATIN . . . knows EXACTLY . . . what I just said! And I gave, NO WARNIN' in this, book four . . . I AM THE QUEEN OF DOOM . . . the secret of XTO'S, OWN WORDS . . . I gave, NO warnin' . . . ANYMORE!!!

To the likes of, 'Em . . . BENEDICT XVI . . . no, no, no, no, no, no!!! If you DON'T, UNDERSTAND . . . Mister Benedict . . . 'Em, what's your name . . . its GERMAN . . . 'Em, RATZINGER?!? Cardinal once . . . whatever . . .

Donney THINK . . . for a, cotton pickin' moment . . . Sir, that you're ANYTHING NEAR . . . the likes of, a POLISH PRINCE!!! Of Yahweh, Jehovah, Allah, Buddha . . . GOD . . . CREATOR!!!

You're oh, ABOUT . . . ooh . . . maybe, HALF the MAN . . . ha, ha, ha, ha!!! "Cuz . . . I've, BEEN OBSERVED . . . by the, GOOD POPE . . .

Paul the sixth . . . at, THE VATICAN!!! When I was WHAT??? OOH . . . SEVEN. nearly eight, years old!!!

Deet Da Dee . . . and when, HE passed AWAY . . . there was, John Paul I . . . for LESS than . . . WHAT??? Less than ninety days?!? Whatever, it was . . . it was DEFINITELY . . . less, than SIX MONTHS!!!

It's NOT my SPEAR!!! I don't have to, THROW IT!!! As a, DAGGER . . . into the middle, of your CHEST!!! But . . . HEAR ME NOW!!! BELIEVE ME TOMORROW!!! Remember WHAT, I SAY . . . and then, AFTER THAT . . . when you WAKE, UP . . .

Remember . . . I said it!!! And, EITHER weep . . . or, RUN AWAY!!! But, I've TOLD 'YA . . . If YOU . . . and your FAKE, FALSE . . . ANY . . . fake, false, phony . . . Luciferite . . . CHARLETONS . . . that may, have ENTERED, THE SANCUTARY!!!

The HOLY PLACE!!! Of the HOLY . . . OOP!!! I won't, EVEN . . . say it . . . Indiana Jones . . . FORGET IT!!! DO YOU, THINK . . . for a cotton pickin' moment . . . that Cynthia Anne Marie Gunn true Queen, of EVERYTHING . . . that I've, STATED . . . this is book four, Epilogue . . .

You think, for a cotton pickin' moment . . . I'm 'gonna LET, the LIKES, of anyone . . . PLAY . . . with, The Holy Grail . . . and PLAY . . . with, The Arc of The Covenant . . . THEN 'YA DON'T, KNOW NOTHIN'!!! 'Cuz . . . I'm NOT, 'gonna TELL YOU . . . you can guess, all day, all night and all . . . weekend!!! WHO, I'm 'gonna, ALIGN . . . MYSELF . . . WITH!!!

It's NOT, 'gonna be YOU!!! And, it's NOT, 'gonna be Dali Lama!!! And, it's NOT, 'gonna be The Hebrews!!! And, it's NOT, 'gonna be Mohammedites!!! And, it's NOT, 'gonna be The Bahaiites!!! And, it's NOT, 'gonna be the . . . WHATEVER!!!

You need to . . . WAKE UP!!! And, SMELL the COFFEE!!! Wake up . . . and, smell the TEA!!! Wake up . . . and, smell whatever, it is . . . when, you wake UP . . . and YOU . . . SMELL IT!!! The MONEY, the OATMEAL, the coffee, the tea . . . the . . . WHAT HAVE YOU!!!

'Cuz . . . inasmuch, as Cynthia Anne Marie Gunn Lazuk . . . GOT . . . EVERYONES . . . NUMBER . . . from here, to ETERNITY!!! And, backwards!!!

Now, I'm going to GIVE . . . The Blueprint . . . of . . . Eternal LIFE!!! In, the book five . . . and a book five, IF . . . you can understand, what I'm SAYIN' . . . is going, to be called . . . and where's the title . . . here we go . . . before we FLIP IT . . . foreward, to book five . . . and where's the cover . . .

Deet Da Dee!!! Book five is: I AM THE BLUEPRINT OF ETERNAL LIFE The Secret of What You Need To Know . . . and, of course . . . once again, written . . . by Cynthia Queen of Scots and America.

And, I love you all . . . this is the Epilogue, to book four . . . so TAKE CARE!!!

Don't . . . BE AFRAID . . . of NOTHIN' and NO ONE!!! Except Lucifer, himself.

And TRUST ME, Saint Michael . . . The Archangel . . . and, Rabbi Yeshua . . . and EVERYONE . . . that CAME, BEFORE . . . Rabbi Yeshua . . . all the way down, to Cynthia . . .

We've ALREADY . . . SLAYED . . . that, DRAGON!!!

So don't THINK, that The Queen of The Celts . . . does NOT . . . KNOW HOW, to SLAY DRAGONS!!! And, my DRUID FRIENDS . . . will BACK ME UP . . . on this!!! And, me KNIGHTS TEMPLAR!!! And, me FREEMASONS!!!

And, EVEN QE2 . . . herself!!! IF . . . she's got, ANY BRAINS . . . in her head . . . LEFT!!! I don't EVEN, KNOW!!! She'll, STEP OFF!!!

And, STEP DOWN!!! But, it dosenny . . . MATTER!!! 'Cuz, heh . . . heh . . . you know, the HARE . . . thought, HE won the RACE!!! But, you know what . . . the TORTOISE, the FINAL ANALYSIS . . . the hare, did NOT . . . win the race, the rabbit . . . RUN!!! It WAS the, tortoise!!!

Because, slow and steady . . . slow and steady . . . and for the, third time . . . slow and steady . . . ALWAYS, wins the race!!!

So . . . if you're a, BETTIN' man . . . or you're a, BETTIN' woman . . . BET ON . . . Cynthia . . .

And Cynthia, ALWAYS . . . BETS . . . ON . . . BLACK!!!

And so we're, playin' CHESS!!! We're, playin' ROULETTE!!! And we're, playin' CHECKERS!!!

Only . . . THIS TIME . . . it's for . . . the ORB!!! Of The Creator!!! EARTH!!! So don't play . . . unless, you know . . . what you're doin'. Just SIT BACK . . . and WATCH!!!

You want to . . . sit back and watch?!? The CHARLETONS . . . in, Las Vegas . . . in, the casinos . . . win at, TEXAS HOLD'EM . . . POKER . . . this/that . . . I don't care!!! They ANTE-UP . . . ANTE-DOWN . . . ANTICHRIST . . .

ANTI-RABBI-YESHUA . . . and I'm 'gonna, CLEAR IT ALL UP . . . for 'ya . . . in book five!

And, I love you . . . just stick with me . . . and FLIP this, what you're readin' right now . . . just flip, the whole thing . . . OVER!!! "Cuz book five . . . is, RIGHT ON THE BACK!!! Comin' RIGHT AT YOU!!!

You only . . . have to pay, for ONE book . . . I don't, split my books up! I . . . book one, had to go . . . out of, the chute . . . pssssssst . . . BONGOLO . . . DONE!!! Book two and three, are together . . . you read two, you flip it over . . . you got three.

This book, four . . . you read it . . . you flip it over . . . to book five. And, as I said . . . book five, is next.

And it is: I AM THE BLUEPRINT OF ETERNAL LIFE The Secret of What You Need To Know . . . And, I love you all . . . STICK WITH ME . . . I shall NOT . . . fail THEE, nor . . . forsake THEE!!!

Love . . . Cynthia . . . on the 10:20 . . .

BOOK V

The books of . . . CYNTHIA
Queen of Scots and America

I AM THE BLUEPRINT
OF ETERNAL LIFE

The Secret of
What You Need To Know . . .

(Excerpt)

Dedication

URGENT . . . URGENT . . . EMERGENCY!!! Urgent, urgent, urgent, urgent . . . emergency . . . make it, FAST . . . make it, URGENT . . . Well, this of course . . . is the Dedication, for book five. OH BOY!!! Listen . . . this is Cynthia . . . and you know, who I am . . . and you know, what I'm the Queen of . . .

This is not, for any other, consumption . . .

This is only, for people . . . that understand what, I'm about to . . . say. TOP SECRET!!! PRIVILEGED!!! And, CONNFIDENTIAL!!! For, YOUR EYES . . . ONLY!!! And, that's NOT, just a movie . . . in a, Hollywood . . . ANYMORE!!! This is REAL!!!

WE ARE ALL . . . IN TROUBLE!!!

From Cynthia, to the . . . UNBORN CHILD . . . to the . . . LOWEST form . . . of LIFE . . . PLANKTON!!! In, THE SEA!!! PHYTO-PLANKTON!!! Excuse me . . . as my Husband said, all the way up . . . to WE!!! HUMANS!!! Who are, at the HIGHEST LEVEL . . . of, WHITE or BLACK or PINK or GREEN or YELLOW or RED or ORANGE or WHATEVER!!!

I don't care!!! PURPLE-POLKA-DOTTED . . . above, ALL CREATURES!!! From the, Phyto-Plankton . . . in the sea, to the LARGEST, of the LARGE . . . RIGHT NOW!!! Would be . . . WHAT . . . a HUGE, Elephant . . . a Giraffe . . . somethin' that you MIGHT, see on SERENGETI?!?

Look . . . we're ALL . . . in TROUBLE!!! It's NOT, just ABOUT . . . what it WAS, about . . . this is, REAL . . . this is, NOT . . . Orson Wells . . . H. G. Wells . . . by, Orson Wells . . . WAR OF THE WORLDS!!! THIS IS . . . REAL!!!

You know what . . . I'm 'gonna tell you, right now . . . in this LAST, book . . . of the, Theo Sophia . . . this is . . . I am, the Theo Sophia . . . The Secret of The End!!!

And, it's NOT . . . ABOUT . . . Hollywood!!! ANYMORE!!! And their, FAKE, PHONY, THE END . . .

We're ALL, in trouble!!! CHOSEN PEOPLE, all the way . . . to who, YOU or I or ANYBODY ELSE . . . ACROSS the, FACE . . . of the EARTH!!! That's HUMAN . . . THINKS!!!

Who's at the, BOTTOM . . . of the BARREL!!! No!!! We're not, PICKLES!!! We're not, PICKLED . . . ANYTHING!!! We're NOT, at the BOTTOM . . . of ANYBODY'S BARREL!!!

So . . . you need to . . . STOP!!! LOOK and LISTEN!!! Please . . . I BEG, OF YOU . . .

Dear Creator,

This is Cynthia . . . PLEASE . . . GIVE THEM . . . ears, to HEAR . . . at the least . . . eyes, to SEE . . . at the next . . . AND . . . soul, heart, mind, will and destiny . . . soul, heart, mind, will and destiny . . . of EVERY, livin' . . . breathin' . . . HUMAN.

From the, FIRST BORN . . . to the ELDEST . . . on the face, of the Earth! I PRAY . . . I BEG OF YOU . . . DEAR GOD . . . Please, Please . . . like I begged you, PLEASE . . . DON'T LET DADDY BEAT MUMMY . . . TONIGHT . . . Please . . . I beg of you . . . I love you . . . Goodnight!!!

So, when I say, that LAST PRAYER . . . at the, last day that, I say it . . . in a, public EYE . . . at the, TIME . . . and the, PLACE . . . Please . . . I say it, EARNESTLY!!!

For ALL, who have, a HUMAN LIGHT . . . INTELLECT and ESSENCE!!! Essence, Intellect and Light!!! Intellect, Light and Essence!!! Essence . . . whatever, the combination . . . may be!!!

THAT . . . IS . . . YOUR . . . CREATOR!!!

The ULTIMATE . . . of, LIGHT . . . INTELLECT . . . and, ESSENCE!!!

And, He's MINE . . . as well!!! And, we're all . . . in trouble!!!

If . . . we DON'T, GET WITH . . . His messages . . . not because, of Cynthia . . . said it!!! But . . . because it, WILL BE SO!!!

As it was . . . in the days, of MOSES . . . HE . . . had, NO FEAR . . . nor, do I . . . JUST PLEASE!!! Listen, to The Creator's . . .

MESSAGES!!! I am only, a VOICE . . . crying out . . . in the desert . . . and this is, August . . . the 29th of the year . . . two thousand and eight.

And, Once upon a time . . . a voice . . . cried out . . . in the desert . . . prepare ye . . . the way . . . prepare ye . . . the way . . . and prepare ye . . . the way, for the third time!!!

This time . . . it shall be, of The Creator . . . The Triune GodHead!!!

The Father . . . The Son . . . and, The Holy Dove . . . With that . . . let's DO . . . THIS THING!!!

Satan . . . Lucifer . . . you're . . . huh! A JOKE!!! Okay . . .

So . . . goodbye . . . to Satan . . . and, I don't need, Billy Joel's song, Goodbye . . . to Hollywood . . . to back me up. But . . . it does.

Say goodbye . . . to Satan . . . and say goodbye . . . to Hollywood. Love, Cynthia The Secretary of AUT PAX AUT BELLUM . . .

Foreward

To: Benedict XVI

Fanum, flamen, missa, pia pium, pius, santifico, sanctus, senium, abavus, abbis abbatis, altor, amita, atavus, avus, compater, gigno, pater, paterna, paternus, patria, patria, patrius, patrizo, priores, proavus, sator, soccer, vitricus, ter, tres tria, tricesimus, triduana, triduanus, triduum, priscus, tricesimus, triduana, triduanus, triduum, caliga, creperum, obscurum, accommodo, adapto, aequitas, aequus, equss, compono, credulitas, iam, immerito, iniquitas, iniquus, iniuria, iniustus, injustus, iurisdictio, ius iuris, iuste, iustitia, iustus, iuxta, iuxta, justicia, justifico, justus, licet imper v, modo, proinde quasi, proinde ut, prope, prout, purgatio, purgo, qualiter, quasi, quemadmodum, scilicet, secus, sicut, tamquam tanquam, tanquam, tantummodo, tantundem, totidem, velut, ante, antea, antepono, antequam, iuxta, offero, perantea, prae pre, prae pre, praecedo precede, praecox precox, praedestino, praeduco, praeeo preeo, praefatus-i, praeire, praejudico, praelibo, praenuntio prenuntio, praesieo praesedi praesedere, praesto, praesum, praevenio, prevenire, prius, priusquam, pro, promutuus, propello, propino, cometes, cometissa, crinis, accersitus, Rup, incursio, offensus, adfectus affectus, assilio, calco, commoneo, compaciscor, confido, contior, defigo, depascor, despecto, exinde, exoro, exoro, expeto, fretus, impello, incoho incohare, incresco, incubo, inculco, incumbo, incurro, infero, ingredior, ingruo, ingruo, inhalo, insideo, insignio, insisto, insulto, intueor, invado, invenio, invideo, invideo, irrumpo, irruo inruo, irruo, meditor, ministro, ministro, mox, nitor, filiolus, Olympus, caminus, cardo duplex, creta, frux, frux, frux frugi, humo, humus, humus, mara marl, motus-us, terra, terrenus, terrigenus, tumulus, vallum, a ab abs, a ab abs, a ab abs, abeo, abhinc, absit, aera era, alicunde, aliena quadra vivere, Angli, caelitus, careo, cretus, de, decoctor, deinde, desisto, despicio, desuper, devio, discedo, effugio, emendo, eminus, essedarius, ex, excuso, expedio, extrinsecus, flandrensis, foris, fusus, hinc, hinc inde, illata, illaturos, imcomposite, inde, instructus, lacrima, oriundus, quam, absit, caelestis, compater, deus, filiolus, impius, Olympus, oraculum, pia pium, pius, religious, suffragium, Vulcanus, insideo, penitus, permoenia urbis, aether aetherius, altithronus, aura, caelestis, caeli, caelitus, caelum, Olumpus, polus, sidereus, uranicus, aptus, crudus, instruo, membrana, paratus, paro, praeparo, procinctu, declaro, electus, legio, Francigeni, gens, gens, inflammatio, natio, natio nationis, optimates, plebs, populi, populus, publicus, vulgus, atrocitas, beneficium, candidus, canonicus, caste, claritas, caritudo, claro, clarus, corrigo, dexter, dextera, erectus, fas est, formido, huic, ilicet, illi, immanitas, ingenuus, ius iuris, iuste, iustum, iustus, jus, legitiums, licet imper v, lucidus a um, luminosus, metuo, mico, niteo, nitidus, nitor, nitor, perspicuus, pius, probitas, probus, quod sui juris est, rectum, recuts, refulgo, relucesco, scilicet, sic, sto, terro, territo, ver, verus, vox vocis, adhinc, adjuc, agnitio, agnosco, agnosco, celebrer, celebritas, clarus, Confiteor confessus, conscientia, diffama tus, effluo, eruditio, etiamnun, expertus, famosus, fateor, gloria, gnaritas, gnarus, gnarus, iam, iam pridem, iamdui, iamdudum, ignarus, ignoro, ignotus, illustratus, imperceptus, inclutus inclitus, incognitus, incompertus, indico, innotesco, innotesco, insciens, interdum, latet, modo, nam, narro, nescio, niveus, noero, nominor, nosco, notitia, nunc, nusquam, nusquam, olim, pando, praescio, profitero, prope, prope, protraho protractus, quaero quero, quarum, quibus, quin, quod, sapio, scientia, scientia, scio, teno, Ventagium, ventorium, vobis, comprehendo, concilio, concordis, concordo, conjugo, conjungo, conjuro, contraho, iunctus, iungo iunxi iunctum, reconcilio, adipiscor, advenio, conitor, contineo, devenio, disciplina, deceo docui doctum, doctor, doctrina, dolus, erudio, eruditio, insidiae, invicem, iuvenesco, magister, paecipio, perfidia, perfidia, perfidiosus, pervenio, postulo, praedicare, praedicatio, proditus, prodoceo, pubesco, quisque, quos, rhetor rhetorician, sensa, singuli, singulus, sulum, trado, uterque, utroque, alicubi, cotidie, hinc hinc, medium, omnifariam, omnis, panton, passim, sulum, undique, undique secus, abalienato, alienatio, beneficium, conatus, damnatio, damnatio, divinatio, dominatio dominium, dominatus, donativum, donum, explicatus, gens, gens, indignation, iunctura, mos moris, nation, nation nationis, percello, populus, solutio, terminatio, vicissitudo, voluntas, aeternus eternus, aliquando, bucinum, denique, diutinus, diuturnus, duro, eduro, extremus, firmo, flatus, inflatus, maneo, obduro, perennis, permaneo, perpetuus, prothoplastus, scholasticus, tandem, tricesimus triduana, triduana, triduanus, trilustralis, voltunas, demum, denique, tandem, admonitio, monitio, alias, alioqui, alioquin, aliter, alter, cetera, ceterum, infero, secus atque or quam, secus, expecto, improviso, inaestimatus, inopinatus, insperate, insperatus, praestolatio prestolatio, refero, repens, repente, repentina, specto, subito, subitus, supervenio, funditus, numerus, universitas, eversio, exitium, interitus, internecio, occasus, perditio, periculum, pestis, pestis pestis, ruina, a ab abs, abiuro, abyssus, affinis, alternis, ancilla, armis, auarca, aufero, barathrum, byssus, cardo, cautus, certo, coactu, cognatus, conjuro, cremo, creptio, curiosus, debeo, degenero, demulceo, deprecor, diu, diverticulum, divinitus, divinitus, duplicitas, emerio, ereptio, exclamo, expugno, expugno, extorqueo, extundo, fefello, ferveo, forte, fortuito, fortuitus, fortuitus, aduro adustum, aestus, cremo, extermino extermino, flamma, ignis, incendia, incendo, inflammatio, inflammo, succendo, Vulcanus, letum.

Foreward

Continued . . . To us all . . .

Well, here we are again . . . Ladies and Gentlemen, Boys and Girls, of the world. This is Cynthia . . . and you know my titles . . . and I DON'T, need to REITERATE . . . it, I think . . . It's been POUNDED . . . into MY head, and to yours . . . long enough!!!

'Em and pounded, into my life . . . from a wee . . . tiny, little, baby girl . . . all the way to now . . .
ENOUGH is ENOUGH!!!

And you know . . . that's what we all, have to say, to each other . . . because, I'm 'gonna tell you . . . ALL . . . SOMETHING . . . TODAY . . . Which is 'gonna, FLIP, YOUR BRAINS . . . right, OFF YOUR HEADS!!!

So, you might as well, just . . . 'Em . . . go GET, some kind of 'Em . . . A STRAP!!! To strap, your HEAD . . . on top of, your head . . . because, when . . . I TELL YOU . . . what I am ABOUT, to TELL YOU . . . ha, ha, ha, ha . . . you'll, FEEL IT . . . perhaps, like I DID!!!

Or, at least . . . Ah . . . some, TINGLING . . . WAY!!!

In your, CONSCIOUSNESS . . . in your, MIND . . . what have you. IF . . . you DON'T . . . even FEEL, a TWINGE!!!

WELL . . . then, the MUSTARD SEED . . . of a CONSCIENCE . . . that MAY, BE . . . in your BODY?!? Ha, ha, ha . . . JUST WAIT . . . 'til the FINAL HARVEST . . . COMES!!!

And, we're ALL . . . WELL, HARVESTED!!!

WEEDS . . . WHEAT . . . Mustard Seeds . . . I don't know . . . and It's NOT . . . up to ME, to SAY!!!

And, I'm a bit, Hoarse . . . Ahem . . . You know, I suffer . . . that . . . I don't REALLY SUFFER . . . I DEAL WITH . . . that, with Asthma . . . etc.

I'm coming to you . . . TODAY, to TELL YOU . . . that, UNLESS . . . or UNTIL . . . EVERYBODY . . . . EVERYWHERE . . . on the, face of the EARTH . . . and this, once again . . . is the 29th of August . . . in the year, two thousand and eight . . . AD . . . ANNO DOMINI . . . I'm NOT playin' . . . BC . . . BCE . . . I'm not playin' with that!!!

QUIT . . . CHANGIN' . . . EVERYTHING . . . around!!!

So-called, FAKE, PHONY, FALSE . . . powers, that be!!!

OKAY!!! We had, BC . . . which was, BEFORE CHRIST!!! And DON'T, play with it!

'Cuz . . . those, that PLAYED WITH IT . . . will be . . . well . . . WAYLAID, with IT!!! And, may be . . . waylaid . . . not to HEAVEN . . . right away!!! If, they're EVEN WORTHY . . . I DON'T, KNOW!!! I DON'T . . . DECIDE!!! But . . . FORGET . . . BCE . . . CE (common era) . . . what . . . FORGET ALL THAT!!!

FORGET . . . that a DAY, an HOUR, a WEEK, a MONTH, a YEAR, a DECADE, a CENTURY, a MILENNIUM . . . a whatever . . . ALL the way, BACK . . . to the beginning . . . of GENESIS!!! Genesis??? Ladies and Gentlemen . . .

Now . . . let me, just get with THAT . . . for a MOMENT!!! You know, FORGET GENESIS!!! Alright . . . and I'm 'gonna get, REALLY UP . . . on a, HIGH HORSE HERE . . . And, this is actually . . . the Foreward . . . to book five . . . YOU, can call, Genesis . . . whatever you want . . . Hebrews, Christians, what have you . . . BUT . . . I call it, what RABBI YESHUA . . . called it . . . in HIS OWN NATIVE TONGUE!!! OF . . . ARAMAIAC!!!

And, don't PLAY . . . with me!!!

And don't PLAY . . . with RABBI YESHUA!!!

'Cuz . . . SHOULD, a DAY COME . . . where, I'm PROCLAIMIN' . . . as a, mere mortal . . . HUMAN!!! In this . . . Human CONDITION . . . in this MILENNIUM . . . and it's ah . . . August 29th . . . of two thousand and eight!!!

And isn't, THIS . . . OOH . . . EXCUSE me . . . Pope Benedict . . . whatever, the HELL . . . your NAME IS, XVI!!! And, you CAN'T . . . EXCOMMUNICATE me . . . NOR, can your . . . COHORTS!!! "Cuz . . . in the event . . . you do that . . . you have to excommunicate . . . YOURSELVES . . . and then, the Jesuits, will have to FIGURE OUT . . .

IF . . . they're 'gonna FOLLOW . . . YOU . . . BUT, The Knights Templar, The Knights of Malta, The Knights of the Holy Seplechre of Jerusalem . . . LOOK!!! WE, ARE GOING TO . . . play chess . . . BENEDICT . . . for the, WORLD!!!

'Cuz, I'll NOT LET . . . the likes of you, or ANY RELIGIOUS . . . leader . . . I don't care . . . ROMAN CATHOLIC . . . as I AM . . . and I was . . . and I shall always . . . be, YOU SIR . . . well . . . IT'S IN QUESTION!!! BUT!!! That . . . havin' been said . . . from MY Family . . . PRINCELY!!!

PRINCESSLY . . . ancestry . . . of, POLAND!!!

WE KNEW . . . who was, the proper, BLUE-BLOOD . . . of the, Poles . . . to LEAD, The Catholic Church . . . into the, NEXT MILENNUM!!! So, don't THINK . . . that, Cynthia Anne Marie Gunn . . . HIGH QUEEN . . .

HIGH QUEEN . . . now, NOT of NOTHIN' . . . doesn't matter . . . But, High Queen . . . of Ireland . . . 'cuz we, Landed . . . there . . . Donemark . . . County Cork . . . Donemark Bay . . . WHATEVER!!! AFTER THE FLOOD!!! Benedict . . . If you DON'T . . . get, with this program . . . you know what, then . . . you're FULL . . . of BOLOGNA . . .

Full . . . of Malarkey . . . full of . . . I don't know!!!

BUT . . . NO ONE . . . in the VATICAN . . . man NOR . . . woman . . . should be PRACTICING . . . FUCK!!! Which is . . . F.U.C.K . . . . And NONE of you . . .

BETTER BE . . . practicing . . . Fornication . . . Under . . . The . . . Court . . . of the KING!!!

Of course . . . without, the benefit . . . of, TRUE CLERGY!!! And, WHO . . . is TRUE CLERGY??? HE . . . Rabbi YESHUA!!!

Who SPILT . . . his BLOOD . . . and WATER . . . in the RAIN . . . in the DARK . . . OFF the CROSS . . . and . . . Mel Gibson, only SHOWED, PART OF IT!!!

And, I don't need . . . BEN HUR . . . movie, with the Late Great, Charleton Heston . . . to TELL ME . . . WHAT, I already KNOW!!!

HOW . . . the sins of the MOTHER!!! And, the SACRIFICE . . . down the road . . . of the . . . SON!!!

Cancelled out . . . the sins, of the mother! NOW . . .

NOBODY . . . GETS THAT!!! But . . . I DO!!!

And, I AM HERE . . . me NOW . . . and BELIEVE me . . . TOMORROW . . . and REMEMBER . . . I said THIS . . . LATER!!! It's ALREADY . . . IN THE CAN!!! YOU . . . can get, the sharpshooter . . . from a HUNDRED . . . billion . . . miles . . . AWAY, from me.

You . . . can get, the sharpshooter . . . with the, most POWERFUL, handgun . . . from a mile or two . . . away . . . from me . . . TRY and take me OUT!!! LIKE, you took out . . . John F. Kennedy . . . Satan . . . you evil, nasty . . . SNIPE!!!

And, your . . . DISCIPLES!!! The RUSSIANS!!! And Lee Harvey Oswald!!!

Totally . . . besmirched . . . in this country . . . HATED AMERICA!!!

Took out, Kennedy . . .

DOESN'T . . . take, a ROCKET SCIENTIST . . .

Don't . . . Play Games!!!

You people . . . put, the SECOND MAN . . . in the GRASSY KNOLL!!!

To throw off, the WHOLE THING!!!

Don't think . . . for a moment . . . Vladamir . . . Dimitri . . . you, Bolshievicks . . . you Russians . . . Don't think . . . for a moment . . . that Cynthia's . . . NOT . . . DEVOTED . . .

TO: MARY!!! MIRIAM!!! Mother of GOD!!! Jesus Christ!!! Rabbi Yeshua!!! Of Nazareth!!! Then, you don't . . . know . . . NOTHIN'!!! And, you'll SUFFER . . . EVERYTHIN' . . . for your . . . IGNORANCE!!!

And, your, INSOLENCE . . . and your, GREED . . . and your, SLOTH . . . and your, PRIDE . . . and your, LEWDNESS . . . and your, LISCIVIOUSNESS . . .

Now, I KNOW . . . Vladimir and Dirmitri . . . and Russia . . . Beautiful . . .

Once, country . . . beautiful . . . once HOLY COUNTRY . . . of RUSSIA . . . You turned . . . to WHAT??? ATHIESTS??? Your

ERRORS . . . You've SPREAD . . . across the . . . WORLD . . . for, FAR TOO LONG!!! And, in the end . . . HUH!!! YOU . . . YOU, don't EVEN KNOW . . . what I issued . . . in the, the, the, dedication . . . of this book!!! You know, YOU ARE STILL LOVED!!!

And, YOU are Still . . . WANTED!!! You are still . . . needed . . . By The Creator . . . It JUST takes . . . a CONVERSION!!! One person, at a time . . . One heart, at a time . . . One soul, at a time . . . One on one . . . LET'S NOT!!! Play . . . that NUCLEAR, PROLIFERATION, BIOLOGICAL, CHEMICAL, ahh . . . above, the Earth's surface . . . Look, if you DON'T think . . . for a cotton pickin' moment, that Cynthia Anne Marie Gunn . . . LAZUK . . . Check it out!!! Witches . . . or wiccans . . . or bitches . . . or biccans . . . I don't know.

Check it out . . . if you, don't KNOW . . . who, you're PLAYIN' WITH . . .

YOU'RE, playin' with . . . FIRE!!!

I'm, on FIRE . . . for GOD!!! So, don't . . . play with HIM!!! Or, you're about . . . to be . . . BURNT!!!

'Cuz, I am . . . just one, amongst . . . THRONGS!!! T-H-R-O-N-G-S!!! Throngs . . . of people that have, had . . . ENOUGH!!!

And are, ON FIRE!!! For the Creator!!!

Because, we've HAD . . . had ENOUGH!!! And don't think . . . that if, you take, Cynthia . . . OUT . . . in the next . . . 20, 30, 40, 50 . . . ten thousand . . . hundred thousand . . . DON'T think . . . that CYNTHIA'S . . . family, one by one . . . is not READY, to take up . . . THE LANCE!!!

You know what??? FORGET YOU!!! Russian Bear . . . FORGET YOU!!!

Chinese Dragon!!! You know . . .

I love you . . . Chinese dragon . . . because, you're so much SMARTER . . . than, the Russians . . . and blah, blah, blah . . . that WEREN'T Christians . . . but . . . you know what . . . WE ALL . . . need, to GET WITH . . . EACH OTHER!!!

And . . . you know . . . Do I have to . . . like . . . set up, a WHOLE . . . you know what . . . Do I have to, do like . . . remember, we have WHAT . . . A UN??? United Nations . . . and we have . . . NATO??? North Atlantic Treaty Organization . . . ALL THOSE things . . . have FAILED US . . . MISERABLY!!! NOW . . . do we, WE REALLY DO . . . need . . . in the, FINAL ANALYSIS . . . Ladies and Gentlemen, Boys and Girls . . . THE UNITED . . . RELIGIONS and BELIEFS . . . and CULTURES . . . of the, WORLD!!!

And . . . it not, about . . . a TOWER, of BABEL . . .

BECAUSE . . . our ANCESTORS . . . were, STUPID!!! After, the DELUGE!!! Of Noah . . . they were stupid . . . and they thought . . . they could build . . . a . . . STAIRWAY . . . to HEAVEN!!!

Look, I'm not 'gonna, go out . . . on a, DRUG INDUCED . . . song . . . LED ZEPPLIN . . . you did, a lot of GOOD WORK . . . drug . . . whatever!!!

LSD . . . I don't care . . . BUT . . . we're not BUYING . . . the stairway; to HEAVEN . . . we're not building . . . the stairway, to Heaven . . . ha, ha, ha . . . HEAVEN . . . and the, GOD FATHER . . . the GodSon, Rabbi Yeshua . . .

NOW . . . get with that . . . ISRAEL . . . otherwise, your ASSES . . . are 'gonna be SPANKED!!! TUIT SUITE!!! Like, the REST OF US!!!

Ha, ha, ha, ha, ha, ha!!! You THINK, you have the MONEY . . . OVER US!!! Dosenny Matter . . . any more!!!

'Cuz the Creator . . . 'will be SPANKIN' . . . every last one, of your HINEYS . . . IF you, don't get on board . . . THIS TIME!!!

But, YOU . . . HAVE . . . YOUR . . . WARNIN' . . .

Now, the rest of us . . . have to just be . . . OOPS!!! We're NOT, chosen people . . . OOPS!!! We're ARABS . . . only cousins . . . of the chosen people . . . OOPS!!! We're EGYPTIANS . . . we're the next . . . OOPS!!! We're AFRICANS . . . we're next, from there . . . OOPS!!! We're GENTILES . . . SPREAD . . . OUT . . . ACROSS, THE WHOLE . . . World . . . ON, Boats . . . on, ships . . . on, rafts . . . doesn't . . . MATTER!!! EVERYTHING . . . came AFTER . . . the ARK!!! OF NOAH!!! . . .

And, as I've told you . . . in book one . . . I AM WHY THEY KILLED DIANA The Secret of The Red String . . . Cynthia, is the only human being . . . today . . . that's been, PROPERLY TRAINED . . . through time . . . Mano e mano . . . One on one . . . by, MY FATHER . . . William Thomas Phillip Gunn, THE LAST . . .

True, HIGH KING . . . of Scotland . . . unless, I have a son . . . of my loins . . . I'll be, the LAST . . . Queen . . . of Scotland.

But, I PRAY . . . the God, will GIVE ME . . . and you . . . and all of us . . . Well I'm HERE, to TRY and EXPEDITE, my part . . . in the THOUSAND YEARS . . . of PEACE . . . PROMISED!!! By RABBI YESHUA!!! From, the Promised Land . . . of old!!! EVERYTHING . . . split-off, from there . . . don't you, UNDERSTAND . . . YET!!!

UGH!!! The Pharaoh . . . the EMANCIPATION . . . thru, MOSES!!!

The COMPLAINING . . . for 40 years . . . in the DESERT . . . the MOSES, at the highest peak . . . seein' the, PROMISED LAND . . . in the distance . . . saying to God, "I've done, ENOUGH!!! There it IS!!! Let Joshua, take them, there!!!"

YOU DON'T UNDERSTAND!!! NO ONE . . . above 130 years old . . . is, ALIVE TODAY!!!

It's NOT about . . . It's NOT about . . . a, a, TAGGED RELIGION!!! Let's ALL, go to . . . a TAG SALE!!! Let's ALL go, to the BEST . . . department store . . . in our country . . . in our world . . . and if you, wanna' get, the ELCHEAPO-BRAND . . . you pick, brand . . . ZEE . . . And if, you wanna' pick, ELCHEAPO-BRAND . . . XSS . . . AEY . . . ALL the way . . . Z-X-Y-W . . . whatever!!!

All the . . . FORGET . . . ALL THE LABELS!!! FORGET . . . ALL the, SKIN COLORS!!! FORGET . . . EVERYTHING . . . that's INSIGNIFICANT!!!

Regarding . . . MONEY . . . STATURE . . . and the, Bologna, Bologna, Bologna . . . of our, OUTWARD APPEARANCE!!!

Now, THAT . . . is just a, HORRIBLE SKIN . . . a, HORRIBLE WARDROBE . . . that was PUT . . . UPON . . . ALL OF US!!! Now, WE are . . . INTELLECT, ESSENCE and LIGHT!!! And, SKELETAL!!! And that . . . is, ALL!!!

The organs, the skin on top . . . the hair, the eyes, the, the, the, body physique . . . whether you're, short/tall, plump/skinny, beautiful/ugly, handsome/so-so, whether we have, birth defects . . . HUH!!! Doesn't MATTER!!!

We're ALL, Intellect, Essence and Light . . . livin' inside, of a HUMAN . . . CONDITION!!!

Now, I'm NO ALIEN!!! I didn't come, from the planet . . . IDON'TEVENKNOW!!! You wouldn't . . . I wouldn't . . . even know, what . . . to call it!!!

I did NOT . . . come from, a FAR AWAY . . . PLANET!!! I'm just, Cynthia Anne Marie Gunn Lazuk . . . and I was born, and I'll say it, again . . . today, is the 29th of August . . . in the year, of our LORD . . . Jesus Christ . . . Rabbi YESHUA . . . AD: Anno Domini . . . 29 August . . . of twenty-o-eight!!! And, OOPS!!! HUH!!! Whose, FEASTDAY . . . is it . . . TODAY?!?

Amongst . . . OTHERS?!? Well, it may be others . . . but it's ALSO, Saint John the BAPTIST'S!!! And, I'm NOT HIM!!!

I AM . . . could NEVER . . . EVER . . . proclaim, or even THINK . . . and HOPE, to be . . . back in time, to be a cousin . . . a female . . . girl cousin, of Rabbi Yeshua . . . Jesus Christ of Nazarreth!!!

BUT . . . that man WAS!!! That . . . HUMAN, WAS!!! John the Baptist!!!

The Roman Catholics . . . call him, Saint John the Baptist . . . WHATEVER!!! John the Baptizer . . . was out, IN THE DESERT!!! And, eatin' WHAT?!? Locusts . . . and HONEY!!! To SURVIVE!!!

WHILE . . . he was Baptizing, people . . . in the, River Jordan . . . until, he KNEW . . . that the cousin, he hadn't EVEN SEEN . . . except, when he flipped over . . . in his, OWN Mother . . . ELIZABETH!!!

Kinswoman, of MARY!!! Mother of, RABBI YESHUA!!!

They ACKNOWLEDGED . . . each others, PRESENCE . . . in the presence . . . and they, DIDN'T . . . SEE, one another . . . AGAIN, UNTIL . . . the, River of Jordan!!!

And, when the Rabbi Yeshua . . . stepped up, amongst . . . hundreds, of people . . . to RECEIVE, a true Baptism . . . in the water . . . 'cuz He said . . . I, Baptize, in the WATER . . . and, THE ONE . . . that comes, AFTER me . . . Baptizes . . . in FIRE!!! And, the Holy Spirit!!!

Heh . . . Heh . . . and then, when . . . HIS COUSIN . . . who he, hadn't ENCOUNTERED . . . since the, WOMB!!! Of their, TWO MOTHERS!!!

When He, came upon him . . . in the river . . . he said . . . no, I can't Baptize, YOU!!! And, Rabbi Yeshua said . . . to his cousin . . . Saint John the Baptist . . . but, you MUST!!!

And, he goes . . . NO, I'm not . . . fit, to . . . un-strap, your sandals . . . and the, Rabbi said . . . YOU HAVE, TO DO IT!!!

So, OKAY . . . they MADE, the CONNECTION!!!

And as . . . the John . . . the Baptist, Baptized . . . the, Jesus Christ of Nazareth . . . the, Rabbi Yeshua . . . his, cousin . . . whom, he hadn't even had, telepathic contact . . . . SINCE, He was, IN-VITRO!!! IN, Elizabeth!!! And, Rabbi Yeshua . . . Jesus . . . was IN-VITRO . . . with, MARY!!! PEOPLE!!! YOU GOTTA' GET . . . WITH THIS!!! 'Cuz this, is NOT BOLOGNA!!!

It's NOT . . . MALARKEY!!! And, it's NOT . . . Horse feathers!!! It's ALL . . . TRIED . . . and . . . TRUE!!! Tried and true . . . and, for the third time, tried and true.

SO, when John the Baptizer . . . heh, heh, dunked . . . his, cousins HEAD . . . into, the River Jordan . . . THE DOVE!!! ACH!!! ACHEYE!!!

ACHEYE!!! Now, we're TALKIN' about . . . The Dove . . . The Holy Spirit?!? That, the Rabbi Yeshua . . . LEFT!!!

AFTER . . . He was, ARISEN . . . from, THREE DAYS!!! Of, THE DEAD!!! And, THE DARKNESS!!!

And HE . . . TOOK CONTROL, of the underworld . . . TOTAL CONTROL!!! Of, Lucifer and the underworld!!!

I WANT YOU . . . TO KNOW!!!

HUH!!! Anybody, that's afraid, of Lucifer now . . . WELL, you haven't STUDIED . . . you don't know, WHAT . . . you're afraid of . . . you're AFRAID, of nothing!!!

You're afraid or what, HOLLYWOOD . . . showed you, in a what???

An exorcist movie . . . or, other movies . . . FORGET IT!!!

The Rabbi Yeshua . . . has, PAID DEARLY!!! For EVERYONE!!! On the, Jibot!!! As I said . . . the, ROMAN ELECTRIC CHAIR!!! And, HIS BLOOD . . . was, DRIPPIN' DOWN . . . and. INTERMINGLED . . . with the, BLOOD of HIS HEART . . . and WHY??? Well, BLOW by BLOW . . . description . . . of, The Crucifixion . . . LET'S just get . . . right to, the CROSS!!!

Once, He'd been, NAILED TO THE CROSS . . . and Mel Gibson, you did a . . . BIT . . . of a good job . . . BUT . . . once, He was nailed, to the cross . . . there WASN'T, a lot LEFT!!!

EXCEPT . . . His, INTELLECT, LIGHT AND ESSENCE!!! The, physical BODY . . . EVERYTHIN' ELSE . . . had been, just about . . . broken down . . . BUT . . . the, LAST THING . . . to break down . . . was, His LUNGS . . .

And, His HEART!!!

And, the LAST . . . AMONGST . . . was, the HEART!!!

And, with the LAST . . . BEAT . . . of His . . . HEART . . . He said . . . FORGIVE THEM . . . FATHER, for they know, not . . . what, they do!!! INTO . . . THY HANDS . . . I commend . . . my SPIRIT!!!

And, once He . . . SEEMED . . . to be dead . . . a Roman Soldier, pieced and pierced . . . a TROCAR . . . t-r-o-c-a-r . . . trocar . . . do a, GOOGLE search . . . a dictionary . . . whatever!!!

Now, a TROCAR . . . is STILL . . . what they use, on DEAD BODIES . . . to, THIS DAY!!!

To . . . how shall I say . . . PIERCE!!! Our, internal ORGANS!!! That, NEED PIERCING!!! That, need piercing . . . So, the Roman Soldier . . . stuck, a LANCE . . . a HUGE, LONG . . . arrow-dagger . . . on a stick . . . into, the HEART . . . and the 'Em . . . SACK, around . . . the HEART . . . that carries . . . holds, WATER . . . around . . . the HEART!!!

BECAUSE . . . the HEART . . . was already . . . BRUISED, from all the . . . BEATINGS, and the, the, the . . . DOWNFALLS . . . and the, STERNUM-SHOCKS . . . that the, CHRIST . . . the Rabbi Yeshua . . . took, on the WAY . . . to . . . GOLGATHA!!!

The Place of the Skull!!!

And THIS . . . ALL TIES IN . . . with, NAGASAKI!!!

'Cuz . . . THEY, were the . . . NEXT ONES!!! To, BRING BACK . . . CRUCIFIXION!!! Up on, a stick!!! In their OWN WAY!!!

And, they used to, take . . . the people . . . they used to, DRAG 'EM . . . or, make 'em WALK . . . ALL, THE WAY . . . from WHEREVER . . . in, JAPAN!!! TO NAGASAKI!!!

Now, Nagasaki . . . do you, GET . . . why the, GOD . . . had to, CHASTISE YOU!!! Deet Da Dee!!!

ANY Historians . . . that know, NAGASAKI . . . KNOW . . . that the, Nagasaki . . . was NO BETTER, than the . . . GOLGATHA, the place of, the SKULL . . . where the, Rabbi Yeshua . . . WAS . . . HUNG-OUT . . . TO, DIE!!!

And you . . . took, your Japanese . . . people out . . . to HUNG-OUT, to DIE!!! NO!!!

And then, you come to . . . what??? Hawaii!!! You think you're, gonna' TAKE US OUT!!!

I don't care, if I had . . . ten or, eleven or, twenty four . . . hour notice . . . If you were, comin' to me . . . because, I already had, a strategy . . . to, DEFEAT YOU!!!

And that's, how . . . RICKOVER . . . OPPENHEIMER . . . and all those, OTHER MINDS . . . WORKED!!!

So, don't think . . . for a minute . . . Japan . . . Don't think . . . for a minute . . . RUSSIA . . . Don't think . . . for a minute . . . ANY . . . POWER . . . across the face, of the Earth . . . NUCLEAR-BUTTONS, PHONES . . . ringin' 3 a.m . . . . FORGET . . . all these FAKE . . . PHONY THINGS . . . of the, American Politicians!!!

I don't like, Obama . . . and I don't like, McCain!!!

NEITHER ONE OF THEM . . . IS RUNNING . . . THE COUNTRY . . . CORRECTLY!!!

And, I don't need, the RICH-LIKES . . . of a good man, Ross Perot . . .

Donald Trump . . . ANYBODY ELSE . . . to tell me, what I ALREADY KNOW!!!

'Cuz, I'm Cynthia Anne Marie Gunn Queen of Scots, America through Cherokee . . . no less . . . and married, to . . . The King of Russia. So, let NOT . . . anythin' be said . . . AGAINST, what I have said. BECAUSE . . . I've only, told the TRUTH!!!

Because . . . I LOVE THE CREATOR . . . Intellect, Light, Light, Intellect, Intellect, Light . . . Essence!!!

THE THREE WORDS HERE ARE:
The Triune GodHead . . . here, IS . . . LIGHT, INTELLECT and ESSENCE!!!

And, I don't need, the FREEMASONS . . . to back me up . . . but, you know what??? Deet Da Dee!!! I love you; guys . . . love you, babys . . . 'cuz you guys . . . GOT IT . . . ALL!!!

ANYBODY . . . WANT'S to KNOW . . . ANYTHING???

You . . . GOTTA' GET, with the Freemasons . . . Otherwise . . . you're nowhere . . . Unless . . . you listen . . . to me . . . and . . . the Freemasons . . . and, I love you . . . Cynthia

BOOK VI

I AM DAUGHTER SAMECH NUN TAV YUD HEY The Secret of Mem Lamed Hey . . .

The books of . . . CYNTHIA Queen of Scots And America

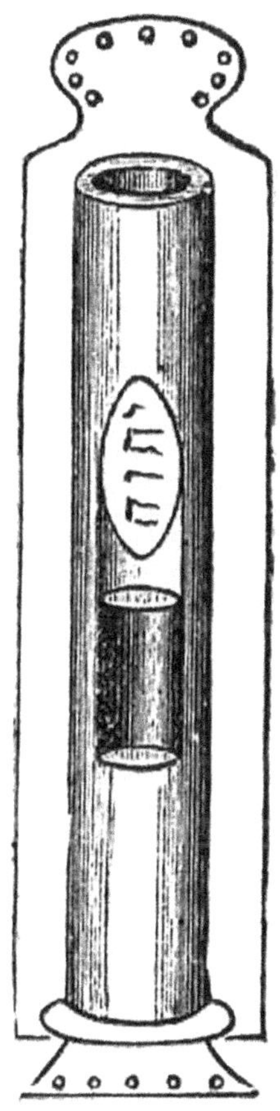

BOOK VI

(Prologue)

Dedication

. . . To thee, I come . . . before thee, I stand . . . SINFUL and SOROWFUL . . .

I AM . . . but, a dog . . . a mere, GENTILE . . . And yet . . . as, Samech Nun Tav Yud Hey . . . I AM . . . who I AM . . .

By, MY FATHER!!!

Yahweh . . .

I need, to REDEEM, myself . . . and in so doing, ALLOW ME . . . to be, the MEZZUZAH . . . of YOUR, POST . . .

Through which . . . YOU, ENTER!!!

And, FINALLY . . . and, for ALL . . . ETERNITY . . .

RESTORE, the ARK . . . of the COVENANT . . . and PEACE . . . PAX . . . SHALOM . . . To, THIS CREATION!!!

And all . . . living, breathing . . . CREATURES . . . IN IT!!! Let ALL . . . before . . . pass away . . .

THY will . . . be DONE . . . great FATHER!!! Yahweh . . . Jehovah . . . God!!!

I came . . . not to condemn . . . thee or, even me . . . ONLY, to OPEN . . . the SHADDAI . . . It shall, be . . . uttered:

Mem Yud Caf Aleph Lamed Mem Zayin Vav Zayin Hey . . . Please, Father . . . we BEG, of YOU . . . Send, Yud Shin Vav Ayin Hey . . . To REBUILD . . . the HOLY TEMPLE!!! RESTORE . . . the ARK of the COVENANT!!! Again . . . And, PEACE . . . PAX, SHALOM . . . to THIS . . . creation and all, living, breathing, creatures . . . IN IT!!!

Let ALL . . . before us . . . pass away!!!

Thy will, be done . . . Great Father . . . Yahweh, Jehovah, God . . .

This is now . . .

I AM DAUGHTER SAMECH NUN TAV YUD HEY The Secret of Mem Lamed Hey . . . and . . . I love you . . . Father . . . Love Cynthia In . . . three, two, one . . . CBA . . . Hello Again . . . EVERYONE!!! This is Cynthia . . .

I was, compelled . . . to add, the Preface . . . and this is, merely the Preface . . . this is NOT, and EXCERPT . . . this is, merely a preface . . .

To, Book VI . . . and book . . . aha . . . two, in its ENTIRETY . . . 'Em . . . 3, 4, and 5 . . . Excerpts . . . and now, this Preface . . . to Book 6 . . .

In a strange, weird, freakish, wild, insane, going out of control . . . EVERYONE . . . is SO, SCARED!!!

WORLD!!! And, this is . . . the 11th of October . . . in the year, two thousand and eight . . . 2008 . . . Anno Domini!!! After DEATH!!!

And, I've told you, BEFORE . . . let's NOT, besmirch . . . the death, of Rabbi Yeshua . . . Son of, Miriam . . . and Joseph . . . of the HOUSE . . . of DAVID . . .

We've got to, cut the . . . COMEDY!!! Cut the CRAPOLA!!! Cut the BOLOGNA!!! Cut the Bolsheviks!!!

Now, if . . . there isn't, ANY . . . thinking person, OUT THERE . . . who, doesn't, UNDERSTAND . . . the GEOPOLOTICAL . . . happenings . . . and the geopolitical . . . BOLOGNA . . .

And, the geopolitical . . . SOCIO-ECONOMICAL . . . STUFF!!! That's BEEN HAPPENING . . . in the last, few days . . .

Then, you don't . . . know . . . NOTHIN'!!!

And, I say this, only . . . out of LOVE . . . and CONCERN . . . of a feminine, entity . . . sister . . . daughter . . . as WE ALL . . . are DAUGHTERS . . . and SONS . . . of OUR Creator!!!

It's NOT JUST . . . Cynthia!!! It's NOT JUST . . . Michael!!! It's NOT JUST . . . Rabbi Yeshua!!!

MIRIAM . . . HIS MOTHER!!! We are all, as I've told you before . . . CREATIONS . . . of the Creator!!!

And, we all HAVE . . . if you wanna' say, TRICKLE-DOWN . . . whatever . . . we've ALL, trickled down . . . through TIME . . . and this WEIRDO . . . time, that WE'RE IN . . .

As I've told you, is a CULTURE . . . OF . . . DEATH!!!

Thanks to Whoooooooo . . . EVE . . . stupid as she was . . . she was, our Mother.

Because Adam . . . chose her . . . from ALL, the other . . . CREATURES . . . that GOD . . . Yahweh, Jehovah . . . God, Allah, Buddha, YOU KNOW . . . whatever, HUMAN TAG . . . wants to be put . . . on the GOD!!!

FORGET . . . the TAGS!!! Forget the Labels!!! Forget all that!!! HAPPY . . . BOLOGNA!!!

Now, this . . . as I said, is October 11th of 2008!!!

Is there . . . any THINKING PERSON . . . OUT THERE?!? Rich, poor, highly educated, ah . . . barely scraping . . . now . . . in a geo . . . I HATE . . . this computer . . . you need, to stop this . . . giving me, email . . . problem . . . things . . . Listen . . . is there . . . any thinking person . . . out there . . . who doesn't UNDERSTAND . . . that . . . WE ARE . . . IN THE SOUP!!!

We are all . . . BOILING . . . IN OIL!!! HUH!!!

And, that used to be . . . a huge thing, in America . . . there was like a, little childs . . . story . . . to SCARE US!!! Of . . . of . . . you know . . . the 3 PIGS . . . and this one and that one . . . and they were PIGS . . . and one, built a house of, STONE . . . and BRICK . . . and TWIGS . . . And, you know what!!! We gotta' FORGET . . . about, ALL . . . these FAKE, FALSE, PHONY, FAIRYTALES!!! That, we've BEEN TOLD!!!

From, WEE . . . little children . . . all the way up, to NOW!!!

And, I'll be 50!!! In the event, GOD . . . does not intervene . . . upon the orb . . . the HUMAN CONDITION . . . before that!!!

But . . . you know . . . what??? HE'S gonna' GIVE US . . . Just enough . . . ROPE . . . to, hang ourselves . . .

Just before, HE . . . let's us, LIVE . . . Hah . . . Hah . . .

We'll BE . . . Once again; as I told you, in book . . . I don't know . . . 3, 4, 5, whatever . . .

We ARE . . . the LIVING . . . DEAD!!!

Because . . . of . . . EVE!!!

And, TIME . . . and a, DAY IS COMING . . . and I don't, need . . . to dissect . . . The New Testament . . . but, what I need to do here, now . . . is, I need to say . . . to ALL . . . the RABBIS . . . of, the world . . .

Rabbis . . .

LISTEN . . .

For the, LAST TIME!!!

YESHUA . . . of Nazareth . . .

RABBI YESHUA . . . whom, the rest of us, call . . . Jesus of Nazareth . . . WAS . . . A . . . TRUE . . . KABBALAHIST RABBI!!!

RABBI . . . Now, if you don't, understand . . . that He came, into this World . . . a SON, of God . . . GIFTED . . . with KNOWLEDGE . . .

INFUSED . . . into His: Intellect, Light and Essence . . . before HE . . .

EVEN, GOT HERE . . .

How . . . do you THINK . . . he could go . . . INTO, the TEMPLES!!! And preach, at such a TENDER AGE . . . . and His Mother Miriam and His Father Joseph . . . we're going like . . . "Oh!!! My God!!! Wha, wha, wait . . . we . . . haven't seen HIM . . . for a couple, DAYS . . . and, they went . . . all, the way BACK . . . AND . . . They, FOUND HIM . . . in the TEMPLE . . . at 12 or 13 . . . HE WAS TEACHING from, the Torah!!!

So, you know what . . . YOU BETTER . . .

GET ONBOARD . . . this TIME!!! ISRAEL!!!

'Cuz . . . if it . . . LOOKS REAL . . . and it . . . SOUNDS, REAL . . . it is . . . REAL!!!

Now, God, chose you . . . you're the, Chosen People . . . ISRAEL . . . that's cool . . .

BUT . . . when you . . . were SOOOOO scared . . . of the, ROMANS . . . and SHAME, ON YOU!!!

'Cuz . . . they're trying, to RE-EXHIRT . . . their POWER . . . through . . . WHO?!? . . . The likes of, WHO???

Vladimir . . . and Dimitri??? Of, Putin . . . and PUTEN!!! And, RUSSIA . . .

LOOK . . . if YOU, don't understand . . . what's comin' . . .

Just let me . . . lay it down . . . for you . . . ISRAEL . . .

A day . . . never mind . . . what Rabbi Yeshua, told . . . THE DAUGHTERS . . . of, Jerusalem . . . on the WAY . . . to the,

GOLGATHA . . . The place, of the SKULL . . . to be, HUNG-OUT . . . on the, Roman . . . Jibot . . .

LOOK!!! I get, it Israel . . . okay???

There were, 4 condemned men. There were 2, unnamed . . . there was, Rabbi Yeshua . . . of Nazareth . . . and there was, a guy, named: Barrabbas . . .

Now, EVERYONE . . . is SO, afraid . . . of RABBI YESHUA'S . . .

Multiple Intelligences . . . the NINE, multiple intelligences . . . UNLOCKED . . . by, the great Doctor . . . Howard Gardiner . . . but back then?!? . . . .

LOOK . . . People don't, EVEN . . . want to get with it NOW!!!

BUT . . . Rabbi Yeshua, as we, ALL ARE . . .

We are ALL . . . Children, of GOD!!!

So, when . . . you know . . . HE SAID . . . to Simon-Peter . . . and . . .

WHO DO YOU, SAY . . . I AM???

And, they all said . . . OH . . . TRULY . . . you're the son, of, god . . .

BUT, you know what???

WE'RE, ALL . . . Sons and Daughters . . . of, The Creator!!! GOD!!!

Yahweh, Jehovah, Allah, Buddha . . . god-dogs dogs-spelled backwards . . . god . . . SPELL IT . . . any way, you want!!! But, there IS . . . a CREATOR!!!

And, a TRIUNE . . . GodHead . . .

From which, the WELL OF LIFE SPRINGS!!!

Now, if you don't . . . GET THIS YET!!!

You can all . . . KEEP Lookin' for the Fountain of Youth!!! But . . . you'll NEVER . . . find it!!!

Ponce De Leone . . ., could NOT . . . find it!!!

It's not even, in the GOGI berry, that I drink . . . from the TOP of The WELL . . . at the HIGHEST, point . . . at the Tibetan, MONKS . . .

NO!!!

If anybody . . . wants . . . you know what??? Rabbi Yeshua, said . . .

MY WORDS . . . EVERYTHING I DO . . . is real . . . FOOD!!!

Is real . . . life, way . . . TRUTH!!!

NOW . . . I'm gonna' tell you, in this book . . . ISRAEL . . . WAKE UP!!! And SMELL . . . the, MATZOAH!!!

Wake UP . . . and smell . . . the Giffelte FISH!!! The LOX, the BAGELS, I don't care . . .

You've been playin' LONG ENOUGH . . . with The Creator!!! Who, by the way . . .

EMANCIPATED you . . . through, MOSES . . . in the, DESERT . . . away from, RAMSES . . . STOP IT!!!

You're in IDIOCRACY . . . and your, INSANITY . . . at REFUSING . . . to ACKNOWLEDGE . . . that the, Kabbalahist RABBI YESHUA . . . who the ROMANS, put to DEATH . . . at 33, WAS . . . WHO . . . HE . . . SAID . . . HE . . . WAS!!!

And, had THE KNOWLEDGE . . . that HE HAD!!!

And, HE . . . gave it, to ya' GENTLE . . . HE . . . gave it, to ya' CLEAN . . . HE . . . gave it, to ya' KIND . . .

HE DID EVERYTHING YOU ASKED!!!

Until . . . the Romans, HUNG HIM OUT . . . to DRY, on the JIBOT!!! When you said . . . OOOOOH!!! RELEASE Barrabbas!!!

Are you, NUTS??? Are you, CRAZY??? I guess . . . you are.

BUT, GOD . . . STILL LOVES YOU!!!

And, you know what . . . THAT'S WHY . . . to, THIS DAY . . . your Country's PROTECTED . . . BUT . . . I'm TELLING YOU . . . not by, Cynthia Anne Marie Gunn Lazuk . . . not by, NOTHIN" . . . BUT . . . do you REALIZE, how HATED . . . YOU ARE???

Because, you were SOOOOOO CHOSEN!!! You were . . .

And then, you gave MOSES . . . a HUGE, HYPOCRITICAL . . . HARD TIME . . . in the desert . . . OOPS!!! Then, HE SHOWED YOU . . . the land, of MILK and HONEY . . . from the, HIGHEST PEAK!!! When HE'D . . . HAD ENOUGH . . . of your, BOLOGNA . . . which, you won't even eat . . .

Because, you can't TOUCH . . . NOTHIN' that's, uh . . . NOT KOSHER!!! There's . . . HIPOCRACY . . . AGAIN!!!

You people . . . aren't, KOSHER . . . to the, GOD!!! You're, NOT KOSHER!!! Your blood . . . ISN'T PURE!!!

Your MINDS, HEARTS, SOULS, WILLS and DESTINIES . . . aren't PURE!!! Because, your blood . . . and your sexuality and your lewdness and lasciviousness and lust . . . is ONLY . . . for, THE WORLD!!!

And . . . the TRAPPINS' of the, WORLD!!! The . . . PAGANISM!!!

YOU . . . reverted, BACK . . . to the . . . PAGANISM . . . that's why, GOD'S going . . . OKAY . . . wait a minute . . . ut, oh!!! NOW WHAT???

AH!!! Well, you know what . . . ah . . . the, CORNERSTONE . . . will now be, MY SON!!! Yeshua. RABBI YESHUA!!! Who GETS me . . . and who . . . whoever . . . Rabbi Yeshua, PICKS!!!

SIMON-PETER . . . The Roman Catholic Church . . . all the way, down . . . to, POPE BENEDICT sixteenth . . . XVI . . .

You know what . . . I put HIM, on NOTICE!!! He's ON, NOTICE!!!

And YOU'RE, ON NOTICE . . . ISRAEL . . . Osama Bin Laden, The Governments of the World, Queen Elizabeth the second herself, Vladamir and Dimitri of Russia . . . and you, know what, Belgium . . .

HOW DARE YOU . . . for HOUSING . . . the, ULTIMATE EVIL!!!

But, you know what . . . it's ALL, going to be . . . SORTED OUT!!! TUIT SUITE!!! And, the French . . .

AH . . . the French . . . and, they're STRANGE . . . but, they're SMART . . . but, they're strange . . . but, they're smart . . . but . . . they're STRANGE AND SMART!!!

NOW . . . I DO NOT . . . APPRECIATE . . . what, the French . . . did, to PRINCESS DIANA!!! Spencer-Windsor!!! MY 12th COUSIN!!!

But, God . . . has forgiven you . . .

But . . . we REALLY, didn't NEED . . . Henri Paul . . . to be, the suicide assassin . . . because, he had, a terminal illness . . .

And, DON'T THINK . . . I don't, KNOW IT!!!

So, he got . . . PLOWED-UNDER-DRUNK . . . and DECIDED . . . to SWITCH . . . the WHOLE THING . . . BACK, to his CONSIRACY . . .

Oh . . . we're NOT, gonna' leave, by the FRONT . . . there's TOO, MANY . . . PAPPARAZZI, out THERE!!!

WELL . . . didn't Diana, HANDLE PAPPARAZZI . . . her, WHOLE LIFE!!! NO!!!

BUT YOU . . . had a, BETTER IDEA . . . Henri Paul . . . Let's go out, THE BACK DOOR . . . 'cuz, you, already had, the WHOLE THING . . . HATCHED-UP . . . with, QE2!!!

And, as I said . . . she's the, WATERED-DOWN, watered-down, watereddown, EVIL-DOWN, evil-down, evil-down . . . LINEAGE . . . of NOT, just her . . . UNCLE!!! Who acquiesced . . . for a . . . an American, divorcee' . . . OH!!! A WALLIS SIMPSON!!!

YOU PEOPLE . . . have been, watered-down . . . SINCE, HENRY the eighth and Anne Boleyn!!! So let's, not . . . PLAY . . . Elizabeth!!!

I'm sick and tired . . . of playin' with you.

But, this is just the PROLOGUE . . . to book six. And, book six, is already . . . READY!!!

So, by the time, this book . . . comes, OUT in PRINT . . . book six, is ready.

Whether, they take Cynthia . . . OUT . . . or not . . . like, they took OUT . . . John F. Kennedy . . . the Russians, Lee Harvey Oswald . . . the GRASSY KNOLL . . . the this, the that . . .

You know, John F. Kennedy . . . was a MAN!!! He was no, BETTER . . . or, WORSE . . . than your, King . . . Henry the eighth!!!

And, you know what . . . HIS WIFE . . . still, LOVED HIM!!! Jacqueline Bouvier Kennedy . . . still loved him . . . and wasn't, she BY HIM . . . in her, PINK SUIT . . . to take his, GREY MATTER . . . and his, BRAINS . . . and his, SKULL . . . and his, BLOOD . . . onto, HER SUIT!!!

And, she said . . . they've FINALLY, DONE IT!!! They've FINALLY, KILLED HIM!!!

Well, you know what . . . THEY . . . whoever, THEY ARE . . . THEY . . . need to, STEP OFF!!!

Because, Cynthia . . . has taken care, of ALL . . . THE . . . INFORMATION!!! Whether, I'm alive or dead . . . this movement . . . goes foreward . . . through, MY TRUE FAMILY!!!

And, you don't need to know . . . who they are . . . whether they're . . . green, purple, purple polka-dotted, white with a yellow stripe, I don't care . . .

You need to, step off . . . because, you know what . . .

The MARKET'S TUMBLING . . . the DOLLAR SINKING . . . all the CURRENCIES, of the World . . . The Ruble . . . is, the only one . . . RISING . . . and you, know what . . . know what . . . GORBACHEV . . . was, a WOLF . . . in, SHEEPS CLOTHING!!!

Because, he said, like . . . ut oh . . . wait . . . we're TOTALLY, in trouble . . . ECONOMICALLY . . . oh . . . what can, we do???

Ahah!!! Ahah!!! He must have had, some Hebrew blood, in him . . . Ahah!!!

LET US . . . OPEN-UP . . . OUR . . . tear down, that wall . . . as Ronald Reagan, said . . .

LET'S TEAR DOWN THAT WALL!!! And, let's just . . . PLAY, with the WEST . . . NOW!!! And, LEARN, from THEM . . . how to, REBUILD . . . ECONOMIES!!!

WE . . . shall REBUILD . . . OUR ECONOMY . . . and then, WE . . . SHALL OVERCOME!!!

WELL . . . you know what . . . you AIN'T . . . gonna' OVERCOME . . . NOTHIN' Russia!!! Because, the likes . . . the tried and true, TRUE . . . BLUE-BLOOD . . . of AFRICAN, likes . . .

The GODLY-LIKES . . . of, DOCTOR Martin Luther King Junior . . . and, HIS FAMILY . . . SHALL . . . OVERCOME, YOU ALL!!!

IF, you RECALL . . . HIS SPEECH . . . on the MALL . . .

In Washington . . . if you, didn't HEAR IT . . . if you, DON'T . . . KNOW IT . . . you'd, BETTER . . . go back and LISTEN . . . to it . . .

Because, it CONTAINED . . . ALMOST . . . ALL, THE TRUTH . . . of RIGHT NOW!!!

So, LET'S NOT . . . PLAY . . .

Cynthia . . . is going to be, a Lady, elegant, strong, loving and honest . . . because, she loves Michael and she, acquiesces . . . to Michael . . . and with, or without Michael . . . because he's, done enough . . . Cynthia, goes foreward . . .

So don't think, for a moment . . . WORLD . . . I'm PUTTIN' Ya' on NOTICE!!! Ha, Ha.

That . . . LOOK, OUR CREATOR . . . God, Allah, Buddha, Jehovah, Yahweh . . . STILL LOVES US!!!

AND, we STILL . . . have, an OPPORTUNITY . . . to STOP . . . the NONSENSE!!! ENOUGH IS ENOUGH!!!

OTHERWISE . . . HUH!!! We may START . . . WW3 . . . Huh . . . BUT . . . HE'LL . . . END IT!!!

And, it doesn't take, Albert Einstein . . . who, DID SAY . . . UH . . . if there will be, a world war four . . . it will be fought . . . with: rocks and sticks and spears and . . . HE KNEW!!!

That, by the TIME . . . we had, a World War 3 . . . it would go back, to . . . it would . . . NUKE US . . . or, DO WHATEVER . . . US . . . all the way . . . BACK . . . to the . . . STONE AGE!!! Is THAT . . . what YOU, WANT!!!

He lives in . . . 'Em . . . what's the country, he lives in . . . Australia??? As far . . . as I'm concerned . . .

I KNOW . . . WHO, HE IS!!!

I KNOW . . . WHERE, HE IS!!!

Doesn't matter . . .

I can say, he lives . . . in, Greenland . . . Iceland . . . doesn't matter . . .

And, I know . . . where . . . his . . . big . . . brother . . . is . . . it . . . doesn't . . . matter . . .

ALL, that MATTERS . . . is, WE ALL . . . get, on the . . . SAME PAGE . . . of . . . peace, pax and shalom.

And, you just, LET . . . Cynthia . . . do what she . . . needs to do . . . OKAY?!?

To, go about . . . helping, us . . . all . . . I'm here, on a mission, of love . . .

And, that's all, I can say . . .

And, I love you . . . pax, peace and shalom . . .

Cynthia Queen of Scots and America. It's NOT . . . what I want . . .

I want, PEACE, PAX and SHALOM!!! ACROSS, THE GLOBE!!!

With . . . or without . . . the, WORLD WIDE WEB . . . With . . . or without . . . NUCLEAR ENERGY . . .

With . . . or without . . . GOVERNMENTS of the, WORLD . . . I'm one human . . .

Whoever you are . . . who, SEES me . . . HEARS me . . . or, READS ME . . .

You're ONE HUMAN!!!

And, you know what . . . TO BE ONE . . . ASK, ONE . . . And to, KNOW ONE . . . ask one . . .

And to, CARE . . . ABOUT ONE . . .

Let's care . . . about one . . .

To . . . the . . . other . . . And, I love you all . . .

BUT . . . we need to STOP . . . the INSANITY!!! Of . . . Eve . . .

And, let's, get on . . . the page, of . . . LIFE!!!

And, GET AWAY . . . from, the culture . . . of death.

And, I love you . . . and don't, think . . . for a moment . . . that this, book . . . in, IT'S ENTIRETY . . . is not, in the can . . . 'cuz . . . it is.

If, SOMEONE . . . tries, to KILL ME . . . or, TAKE ME OUT . . . this movement . . . goes foreward . . . with, Cynthia . . . or without . . . I don't care . . .

I'll PUT, my LIFE . . . on the, LINE . . . 'Cuz, I've read . . . The Torah!!! And, I've read . . . the New Testament . . . and I . . . . unlike many, I UNDERSTAND . . . it and I, don't . . . DISTORT IT . . .

BUT . . . a TIME . . . is COMING . . . WHEN, the WORLD'S . . . gonna' be, in SUCH . . . CHAOS . . . and we've, JUST . . . seen THIS . . . LAST WEEK!!!

And, EVERYBODY'S . . . going like . . . OOH!!!

Oh . . . MY GOD!!! Thank God . . . we have, Columbus, day . . . in America . . . so we have a, THREE DAY WEEKEND . . . from the, STOCK MARKET . . .

You know what . . . FORGET THAT . . . ACTION!!! You don't . . . EVEN KNOW . . . WHAT'S COMIN'!!!

And, I'm here, to HELP!!!

BUT . . . if you, won't . . . let me, HELP . . . YOU!!! Then, all bets . . . are off . . .

Because, I'm, NOT . . . AFRAID . . . TO DIE!!!

I'm . . . not AFRAID . . . to go to, THE PLACE!!!

IF . . . you read, my first book . . . I AM WHY THEY KILLED DIANA

The Secret of The Red String . . .
LOOK . . . I've . . . FACED, DEATH . . .
AT, 6 years old . . .
AT, 14 years old . . .
In CAR CRASHES!!!
I Don't . . . I'm NOT, SCARED . . . I'm not scared . . . of
WHAT . . . comes AFTER, this life . . .
BUT . . . YOU PEOPLE . . . MY Brothers and Sisters . . .
Across the Face, of this . . . ORB . . . EARTH . . .
Better, BE . . . SCARED!!!
Because, you DON'T HAVE . . . the ADVANTAGE . . . that I
HAVE . . . of, KNOWING . . . where, I'm GOIN' when, I LEAVE
HERE!!!
YOU don't know . . . WHERE, you're . . . GOING!!!
I KNOW, that I'm going, to the, HEAVEN!!!!
DO YOU?!? . . . .
You've gotta' ask, yourself . . . when THIS ENDS???
I, don't know . . . ANYBODY . . .
OVER a hundred, thirty, years old . . . or more . . .
When, this life . . . ENDS . . . or, when the governments and
geopolitical, the monetary . . . structures . . . of the world . . . THROW
this WHOLE WORLD . . . into, a TAILSPIN . . . and the, Anti-
Christ . . . does come . . . And, don't think . . . for a minute . . .
Ladies and Gentlemen . . . that HITLER . . . was . . . HE, was just,
a PRECURSOR . . . when HE, PUT MARKS . . . on, the Jews!!!
A DAY . . . IS COMING . . .
When HUH!!!
If WE ALL . . . don't Pledge Allegiance . . . to NOT . . . a
FLAG . . . but to ONE . . . MAN . . .
Who's gonna' be like . . . 'Em . . . between fourty and fifty . . .
And, I know . . . WHO . . . HE IS!!!
And, I know . . . WHERE . . . HE IS!!!
And, I know . . . HOW . . . HE . . . CONTROLS
EVERYTHING!!!
That's the cool . . . thing . . .
'Cuz . . . well . . . as far, as I'm concerned . . .

THE 72 NAMES OF GOD
(HEBREW CHART)

Shem HaMephorash (Hebrew: שֵׁם הַמְּפֹרָשׁ *Šēm hamMəfōrāš*,
also ***Shem ha-Mephorash***), meaning "the explicit name," is
originally a Tannaitic term describing
the Tetragrammaton. In Kabbalah, it may refer to a name of God
composed of either 4, 12, 22, 42, or 72 letters (or triads of letters), the
latter version being the most common.

Early sources, from the Mishnah to Maimonides, only use "Shem ha-
Mephorash" to refer to the four-letter Tetragrammaton.

Oidushin 72 a describes a 12-letter name (apparently a mundane
euphemism, YHWH-EHYH-ADNY or YHWH-YHWH-YHWH) and
a 42-letter name (holy but unknown; Hayy Gaon says it is the
acronym of the medieval piyyut Ana b'Koach A 22-letter name
appears in *Sefer Raziel HaMalakh* without interpretation, as אנקתם
פסתם פספסים דיונסים (*Anaktam Pastam Paspasim Dionsim*). Its origins
are unknown, with no connection to Hebrew or Aramaic being found,
and no agreement on any particular Greek or Zoroastrian origin

כהת	אכא	ללה	מהש	עלם	סיט	ילי	והו
הקם	הרי	מבה	יזל	ההע	לאו	אלד	הזי
וזהו	מלה	ייי	נלך	פהל	לוו	כלי	לאו
ושר	לכב	אום	ריי	שאה	ירת	האא	נתה
ייז	רהע	וזעם	אני	מנד	כוק	להוז	יוזו
מיה	עשל	ערי	סאל	ילה	וול	מיכ	ההה
פוי	מבה	נית	גנא	עמם	הוזש	דני	והו
מוזי	ענו	יהה	ומב	מצר	הרוז	ייל	גמם
מום	היי	יבמ	ראה	וזבו	איע	מנק	רמב

Love, Cynthia Queen of Scots and America, Minister of Peace

THE 72 NAMES OF GOD
(ENGLISH TRANSLATION)

1: **Vav Hey Vav**… Time travel

2: **Yud Lamed Yud**… Recapturing the sparks

3: **Samech Yud Tet**… Miracle making

4: **Ayin Lamed Mem**… Eliminating negative thoughts

5: **Mem Hey Shin**… Healing

6: **Lamed Learned Hey**… Dream state

7: **Aleph kaf Aleph**… DNA of the soul

8: **Kaf Hey Tav**: Defusing negative energy and stress

9: **Hey Zayin Yud**… Angelic influences

10: **Aleph Lamed Deph**… Looks can kill

11: **Lamed Aleph Vav**… Banishing the remnants of evil

12: **Hey Hey Ayin**… Unconditional Love

13: **Yud Zayin Lamed**… Heaven on Earth

14: **Mem Bet Hey**…. Farewell to arms

15: **Hey Resh Yud**… Long range vision

16: **Hey kuf Mem**… Dumping depression

17: **Lamed Aleph Vav**… Great escape

18: **Kaf Lamed Yud**… Fedility

19: **Lamed Vav Vav**… Dialing God

20: Pay Hey Lamed… Victory over addictions

21: Nun Lamed Kaf… Eradicate Plague

22: Yud Yud Yud… Stop Fatal attraction

23: Mem Lamed Hey… Sharing the flame

24: Chet Hey Vav… Jealousy

25: Nun Tav Hey… Speaking your mind

26: Hey Aleph Aleph… Order from chaos

27: Yud Resh Tav… Silent partner

28: Shin Aleph Hey… Soul Mate

29: Resh Yud Yud… Removing Hatred

30: Aleph Vav Mem… Building Bridges

31: Lamed Kaf Bed… Finish what you start

32: Vav Shin Resh… Memories

33: Yud Chet Vav… Revealing the dark side

34: Lamed Hey Chet… Forget thyself

35: Kaf Vav Kuf… Sexually Energy

36: Mem Nun Daled… Fear(Less)

37: Aleph Nun Yud … The big picture

38: Chet Ayin Mem… Circuitry

39: Resh Hey Ayin… Diamond in the rough

40: Yud Yud Zayin… Speaking the light words

41: Hey Hey Hey… Self Esteem

42: Mem Yud Kaf… Revealing the concealed

43: Vav Vav Lamed… Defying Gravity

44: Yud Lamed Hey… Sweetening judgement

45: Samech Aleph Lamed…The power of prosperity

46: Ayin Resh Yud… Absolute Certainty

47: Ayin Shin Lamed… Global Transformation

48: Mem Yud Hey… Unity

49: Vav Hey Vav… Happiness

50: Daled Nun Yud… Enough is never enough

51: Hey Chet Shin… No Guilt

52: Ayin Mem Mem… Passion
53: Nun Nun Aleph… No Agenda

54: Nun Yud Tav… The death of death

55: Mem Bet Hey… Thought into action

56: Pey Vav Yud… Dispelling anger

57: Nun Mem Mem… Listening to your soul

58: Yud Yud Lamed… Letting go

59: Hey Resh Chet… Umbilical Cord

60: Mem Zadik Resh… Freedom

61: Vav Mem Bet… Water

62: Yud Hey Hey… Parent-Teacher, not Preacher

63: Ayin Nun Vav… Appreciation

64: Mem Chet Yud… Casting yourself in a favorable light

65: Daled Mem Bet… Fear of **GOD**

66: Mem Nun Kuf… Accountability

67: Aleph Yud Ayin… Great Expectation

68: Chet Bet Vav… Contacting Departed Soul

69: Resh Aleph Hey… Lost and found

70: Yud Bet Mem… Recognizing design beneath disorder

71: Hey Yud Yud… Prophecy and parallel universe

72: Mem Vav Mem… Spiritual cleansing

Seneh (Burning Bush)

Love, Cynthia Queen of Scots and America, Minister of Peace

THE MATRIX

A = 6
B = 12
C = 18
D = 24
E = 30
F = 36
G = 42
H = 48
I = 54
J = 60
K = 66
L = 72
M = 78
N = 84
O = 90
P = 96
Q = 102
R = 108
S = 114
T = 120
U = 126
V = 132
W = 138
X = 144
Y = 150
Z = 156

C = 18
O = 90
M = 78
P = 96
U = 126
T = 120
E = 30
R = 108
+___________ Computer
= 666

C = 18
O = 90
M = 78
E = 30
T = 120
R = 108
U = 126
P = 96
+___________ Comet Rup or Comet Rupture
= 666

GOD'S number is 7.

Satan's number is 6.
The name of his number and the number of his name is 6 score, sixty and 6   666

Love, Cynthia Queen of Scots and America, Minister of Peace

The last 4 secrets of GOD

I have been urged by the Heavenly Court to divulge the last 4 secrets of GOD.

Ladies and Gentlemen, Boys and Girls of the world you are about to see and/or hear the last 4 mind boggling secrets of GOD.

The first last secret of GOD proclaims fully Eve's murder of Abel. The first murder of all time.

Eve was jealous that GOD and Adam loved and favored Abel first. Satan knew of her jealously and told Eve how to kill Abel with his shepherd's staff by impaling him and to take Cain with her. Satan drove Eve to insanity. Eve did as Satan told her. As Abel lie dead in the pasture Satan told Eve to feed Abel's body and blood to the sheep. Eve did as Satan told her. This is why the Roman Catholic church Transfigures bread and wine into the body and blood of Rabbis Yeshua God's Son Jesus Christ to be consumed as Jesus taught us at the last supper for, we are Jesus' sheep… Therefore, WE EAT Jesus' body and drink his blood.

By in we are saved!

All very simple…. All very similar…. All very true! Now that Satan and Eve's evil secret is out and we all will know it we should be ready to believe it is truly Divine truth.

Now Israel the second last secret of GOD proclaims you MUST convert to Roman Catholic for it was Rabbs Yeshua…. Jesus Christ…. With the other 12 jews… the disciples who practiced and taught the transfiguration for over 2000 years now. Even until today. Israel accept it…. Convert to Roman Catholicism or be destroyed by fire!... from a direct war with many armies of the world or a celestial happening in the form of a Comet Rup and/or also via the computer. The directive comes from GOD the creator himself.

Now the third last secret of GOD proclaims the 666 the Beast of the Revelation in the New Testament. Satan is also known as Lucifer and the Devil… the evil one… the prince of darkness. The 666 Matrix on the pages before this is the truth of the Computer and the Comet Rup.

The fourth last secret of GOD proclaims the 72 names of GOD taught

to Noah his son Japhet and Moses who taught it to Joshua. Noah and Moses actually SAW GOD face to face. GOD taught it to them and the Kabbalah have preserved the 72 Names of GOD down through time. I shall provide the 72 names of GOD after this dissertation in the original Hebrew Language translated into English.
Moses was the first man to use GOD'S own language! The Kabbalah Rabbis daily mourn, wail and weep at the western wall the actual words of GOD. They still seek the Messiahs. Their Messiah has already been here. He's Jesus Christ AKA... Rabii Yeshua in the language of the ancient Aramaic spoken in Jesus's time.

Now that this knowledge is out do with GOD'S knowledge what you will... this concludes the last four secrets of GOD.
May he bless us all!
I know the secret location of the Holy Grail and the Ark of the Covenant. I cannot divulge the location until I see a certain something happens in Garabandal, Spain.

Love, Cynthia Queen of Scots and America, Minister of Peace

CYNTHIA GUNN LAZUK
Queen of Scots and The Gunn Lazuk Royal Group

There is a price to pay for speaking the truth. There is a bigger price for living a lie.